THE LAST
BULL
MARKET

They Satisfy
Inside Wall Street
The Fallen Colossus
The Manipulators
N.Y.S.E.
Herbert Hoover at the Onset of the Great Depression
The Entrepreneurs
The Money Manias
For Want of a Nail. . . .
The Age of Giant Corporations
Conquest and Conscience: The 1840s
Machines and Morality: The 1850s
Amex
The Curbstone Brokers
Panic on Wall Street
The Great Bull Market
The Big Board
The Origins of Interventionism

THE LAST

BULL

MARKET

Wall Street in the 1960s

by Robert Sobel

W·W·NORTON & COMPANY· *NEW YORK· LONDON*

First Edition

THE TEXT of this book is composed in photocomposition Caledonia. The display type faces are hand set in Garamont and Perpetua. Manufacturing is by the Maple-Vail Book Manufacturing Group. Book design is by Marjorie J. Flock.

Library of Congress Cataloging in Publication Data

Sobel, Robert, 1931 (Feb. 19)–

    The last bull market.

    Includes bibliographical references and index.

    1. Wall Street—History.   I. Title.

    2. New York (City).   Stock Exchange—History.

HG4572.S6725   1980   332.6'42'0973   79–19281

ISBN 0–393–01309–X

1 2 3 4 5 6 7 8 9 0

To Elsie Reynolds and Joan Cooney

CONTENTS

Dow-Jones Industrial Average
1945–1969

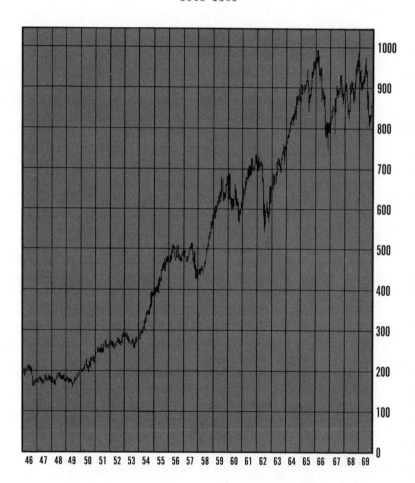

PREFACE

I N JANUARY 1966 the Dow Jones Industrials peaked at a fraction above 1,000 in interday trading. Nine months later that Index touched bottom at 736. In this period, while the market unraveled, I started to write a book about Wall Street in the 1920s, in which I analyzed the boom years and the great crash that brought them to an end. This work, entitled *The Great Bull Market*, was published by W. W. Norton in 1968, at which time stocks were on the upswing and appeared headed above the 1,000 mark, while the nation seemed on the verge of major political and social upheavals.

Despite the atmosphere in which it was written, the message of *The Great Bull Market* was generally optimistic. Most of the abuses that had led up to and caused the crash of 1929 had been rectified by the New Dealers and no longer threatened to bring down the structure. And in any case, the American economy and society of the 1960s bore little resemblance to that of 40 years earlier. There would be bear markets in the future, and even panics, I wrote, "but there will never be 'another 1929.'"

Shortly after the book's release the market started to slide, and this collapse was worse than that of 1966. Within a year and a half close to one-third of the Dow's value had melted away. According to one calculation, some $300 billion in stock values had been wiped out in the deluge. The great, long-lived post–World War II bull market had ended. There had been no crash, and no panic. Many on Wall Street hadn't realized it was all over for many months, and even then they talked of a possible upturn in the early 1970s.

Only now, a decade after that climax had been reached, can we say that the end came in the late 1960s. Still, it remains difficult to fix the actual date, or even the year, for the conclusion of the upward drive. For there would not be "another 1929" to put a cap on this bull market. Instead, it ended in a way unlike that of any previous market move in American history.

Three years ago I decided to undertake a history of this postwar market, to explore the reasons stocks took off in the 1950s and soared in the 1960s before they came down toward the end of the decade. As I saw it, this upward sweep developed in five stages, almost all of which can be isolated in earlier bull markets and may be repeated in those of the future—assuming we have them. These stages need not be listed here, for they are discussed in detail and elaborated upon in the text, but it should be noted that they are concerned more with investor psychology than with economic statistics. Both ingredients are needed, but advances in sales, earnings, and dividends by themselves cannot assure the development of a sustained bull market. These were present in the mid-1940s and again in the late 1970s, and in neither period did the markets behave as spectacularly as they had from 1949 to 1969.

Jim Mairs of Norton, who had been my editor for *The Great Bull Market,* has performed the same task for this book. He also suggested the title, an ambiguous one in keeping with the nature of the market during the past dozen years. Was the massive move of 1949–69 truly the last bull market this generation will know, or was it merely the last we had? In the last chapter of this book I try to indicate what will be needed for the foundation of the next bull move, but at this time there are few signs that such a structure is being formed.

Whatever happens, it is probable that there never again will be anything quite like this last bull market. There are many reasons for this, but the most important of them concerns the nation's position in the world, and the perception Americans have of it. The last bull market coincided with the emergence of the United States as the major world power. Its economic might, self-confidence, and ability to lead the West were almost unquestioned. The dollar was as good as gold until the very end. This changed toward the close of the decade, and the alterations helped bring the bull market to its conclusion. The American Century has ended—and it only lasted two decades, as did this bull market.

Several hundred brokers, analysts, journalists, business economists, bankers, and exchange personnel contributed toward my education on the Street during the past two decades, for which I am most grateful. To list all of their names would require many additional pages, and doubtless raise the price of the book, so they will have to be content with my verbal thanks for their help. But I have to indicate here that Chuck Storer of the N.Y.S.E. proved an irreplaceable source of knowledge and wisdom for me over much of this period, as he has for most other students of Wall Street. Yale Hirsch, one of the country's most perceptive analysts, has permitted me to bounce ideas off him and in the process sharpen and refine them. So has Jim Mairs, whose penetrating questions usually were preceded by, "I really don't know too much about this, but. . . ."

Within a few years we may collaborate on a sequel to *The Last Bull Market*, to be called *The Great Inflation*. Such a work is needed in order to appreciate what happened after the 1969 climax. The evidence is easy enough to find, and unfortunately all around us. For example, *The Great Bull Market* sold for $5 in 1968.

ROBERT SOBEL
New College of Hofstra

One

FOUNDATION

IT COULD BE ARGUED that except for the Civil War, the Great Depression of the 1930s was the most traumatic episode in American history. From it emerged the modern presidency, new and powerful social and economic dogmas, drastically altered attitudes regarding the proper role of government, and what even in the midst of the post–World War II period appeared to be a permanent residue of fear.

In the late 1940s, most of Western civilization had just started to rebuild its cities and factories. The United States was the supreme economic and military power in the world. Yet fears of a possible business turndown remained. It made little sense; the attitude was beyond reason. But throughout America, millions of sensible people who were earning more money than they had ever dreamed possible, who had growing savings accounts and secure jobs, were haunted by nightmares of breadlines, the dispossession of homes, and the loss of everything they had accumulated. Memories of the Great Depression had been etched into the national subconsciousness and would not be eradicated by even this new and glorious prosperity.

Every great movement requires a symbol, an event, or person to be used as a form of shorthand to evoke memories and emotions. The stock market collapse of late 1929 served well for the Great Depression. Even now, the relationship between the crash and the depression are not clear, and economists and historians generally agree that the sharp plunge of stock prices did not trigger the economic collapse. But the drama of that event and its timing caused many to view it as just such a symbol. In the public imagination, the Wall Street debacle and the factory and bank shutdowns of the early 1930s were closely linked. This sentiment deepened throughout the decade, as businessmen became scapegoats for the general malaise.

Wall Street was a quiet place in the 1930s, its functions atrophied and its leaders discredited. Stocks of all but the most conservative companies were deemed speculations. The new-issues market was no more. "Playing the market" and "dabbling in a few issues" were considered frivolous and downright dangerous. There were a few rallies, but most were short lived and usually credited to speculation by insiders and professionals. On one occasion, in 1936, there was what seemed to be a new bull move, but this was followed by a sudden crash. For those few new investors and speculators drawn to stocks in this period, it was known as "another 1929."

That phrase would be heard whenever stock prices advanced for more than a season. No matter how cheerful the economic news, some journalists and analysts would raise the specter of the 1929 crash. It was spoken of often during the World War II boom years, when the economy operated at full capacity, profits were high, and American capitalism seemed to have regained a measure of its predepression vitality.

Prices at the New York Stock Exchange reflected all this. In May 1942, the Dow Jones Industrial Average hit bottom at 96, and then started upward. Four years later, the Dow was at a peak of 212. But throughout this period, economists warned of a new depression that would come swiftly once the war ended, and the economy no longer would be buttressed by federal spending programs. Yet there was no new wave of unemployment and business failures in 1946. Instead, the nation was hit by its most rapid inflationary advance in history. Stock prices fell on heavy volume. By September 1946, the Dow was back to 165, and there again was much talk of "another 1929."

Stocks traded within a narrow range for the next two years, and then, in mid-1948, activity and prices picked up in anticipation of a Republican victory in the presidential election. Harry Truman, who was as unpopular on Wall Street as he was in most other parts of the country, would soon be retired, so the thinking went, and this would set the stage for a new rally. The president's unexpected reelection resulted in a selloff, but no panic. And once again the market started to drift.

The nation had come through the conversion to a peacetime economy without having had a depression. Business activity was high and demand for consumer goods increasing. In 1948 the unemployment rate was 3.8 percent, and despite grumblings from union chiefs and some anti-Truman Democrats, this was considered as close to full employment as the peacetime economy was likely to get. The Consumer Price Index rose by 2.7 percent that year, and while Republicans Thomas Dewey and Robert Taft called this "intolerable" and "unnecessary," it seemed a small price to have to pay for prosperity, especially by a generation that recalled the depression and appreciated what declining prices could mean. Those who cared about such things noted the foreign trade surplus for 1948 had been $3.3 billion. Marshall Plan and military aid programs soon would cut into this, as would investments by American firms in Europe and Asia, but the fact remained that the United States was an economic superpower. This gap between the American economy and those of other countries was a key fact of the postwar economy. By 1949, the implication of this situation had filtered down to the general population.

This status was reflected in the power of the dollar. In 1948, the United States held over 60 percent of the world's gold reserves, and foreigners preferred to own dollars rather than hoard the metal, since the currency fetched interest and in any case could easily be sold to the Treasury for gold at a price of $35 an ounce. Much of the world had gone on a dollar standard insofar as their international transactions were concerned, and there continued to be talk of a chronic dollar shortage. British Foreign Secretary Ernest Bevin said as much in several speeches and private discussions. The United States, he thought, was in much the same position as his country had been at the end of the Napoleonic Wars—the arbiter of the world.

The domestic economy appeared as secure as the dollar was strong. Not only was there a budget surplus of $8.9 billion that year—the largest in history—but it had been accomplished in the face of a tax cut.

Might there be a new depression? Some economists continued to talk of one, but the Keynesians, who had gained power and prestige within the profession, were confident that they possessed the knowledge and tools to handle it. The lessons of the 1930s and World War II indicated that increased government spending would stimulate the economy and head off any significant decline. Such a policy might result in budget deficits contributing to inflation. Still, the beliefs that higher prices, troublesome though they might be, were preferable to a new depression, and that if the tradeoff were made, there would be low unemployment and high production, were key political axioms of the 1950s and early 1960s.

By early spring, it appeared there indeed would be a depression of a sort, the first the nation would undergo after the reconversion effort, and one that would provide a major test both for economists and the economy. In May the Federal Reserve Board's Index of Industrial Production was at 179, down 16 points from where it had been on Election Day. The unemployment rate was over 6 percent; almost twice as many Americans were out of work as had been a year earlier. This bad news was balanced by signs that inflationary pressures were easing, which Truman made the most of at press conferences and public appearances. But his standings in the polls dropped, and analysts believed this was due to the economic slowdown. One survey indicated that over 40 percent of the public thought the nation was on the brink of a new depression that would be as bad as that of the 1930s.

At the same time, liberal publications warned Truman to avoid the errors that destroyed Herbert Hoover's presidency. Auto union chief Walter Reuther said, "1929 can happen again in 1949." Democrats of all political hues joined in the chorus.

As it turned out, the 1949 slowdown was relatively minor; those individuals who believed disaster was around the bend had been viewing the economy of that year through glasses manufactured in 1929. It was very different this time, and one key to the matter could be found in the area of consumer demand.

At no time did retail sales decline appreciably. Housing starts in the first half of 1949 were at an all-time high, 15 percent over that of the previous year; in 1949, for the first time in history, over one million units would be erected. Automobile sales were running over 20 percent better than they had in 1948, and more cars could have been sold had they been available. The same was true for other products, from vacuum cleaners and washing machines to nylon stockings. Over 3 million television sets were produced and sold in 1949, three times the figure for 1948, and stores had waiting lists for ten-inch units that went for over $300. Kept out of the market by a decade and a half of depression and war, and in a more liquid position than at any time in their collective lives, a generation of consumers had embarked upon a buying spree in 1946 that hadn't run its course three years later. Furthermore, the nation still was in the first stage of the postwar baby boom, which added to demands for a wide variety of goods and services.

The trouble was that many businessmen couldn't believe what their sales statistics told them. Discouraged by the election returns and having been put on notice that taxes might be increased, they anticipated a period of deflation, perhaps depression. Some actually seemed to welcome it; surely such a slowdown would dampen labor's appetite for major wage increases that year and the next, when many contracts were due to be renegotiated. So they cut back on inventories and cleared their books for the hard times they thought lay ahead. It was this, more than anything else, that resulted in the lower demands for steel and a wide variety of other basic materials, which in turn led to labor layoffs in the industries that produced them. Fabricators and manufacturers of capital goods fired marginal workers as well, as though hunkering down for a serious recession or depression.

The inflation rate did slow down, and the costs of some goods actually declined, but this came more as a result of the mistaken perception of businessmen than any economic force. For example, though demand for new cars never wavered, General Motors announced price cuts for most of its products. Companies that turned out a wide variety of consumer durables—General Electric, Electrolux, Westinghouse, Philco, and Emerson along with many others—came out with economy models as though preparing themselves for buyer resistance that never materialized.

In other words, fear of a recession actually contributed greatly to causing an economic slowdown and the kind of price behavior businessmen of that period believed was supposed to accompany a decline. The newspapers picked up on the theme shortly after the election, highlighting every piece of negative news and ignoring the real story, that of strong consumer demand. Franklin Roosevelt's admonition that the only thing we have to fear is fear itself could not have been better illustrated than by what later would be known as the "inventory recession of 1949."

This is not to suggest that this decline was unimportant, or without significant consequences. Just as a false alarm gives a community a chance to see how its fire department behaves, so the recession provided businessmen and other Americans with an important insight into the thinking of consumers in postwar society. It demonstrated that it would take more than a setback of this magnitude to cut deeply into spending for consumer goods. Apparently this generation of Americans wasn't as badly scarred by memories of the hungry 1930s as had previously been believed. Or if they had been, they wouldn't let them stand in the way of enjoying life in the 1950s. Although disposable income declined in 1949, spending on consumer durables rose sharply. This rise was made possible by recourse to savings accounts and consumer loans.

Not only were Americans in the aggregate loath to forgo such acquisitions as new television sets and automobiles, but they were willing to go into debt in order to possess them, even in the face of what newspapers, radio commentators, and their own instincts told them would be an economic decline. The first test of this new force came in the inventory recession. Others would follow in the 1950s and would sustain the growing belief that consumerism would assure economic growth and provide a safeguard against deep recession. In 1950, Americans owed banks and finance companies less than $22 billion for purchases of consumer durables. In 1960, after a war and three recessions, the figure was over $56 billion. With some hyperbole, *Business Week* wrote, "The American consumer, in the mid-20th century, has one dominant trait: He spends practically everything he makes." Furthermore, "He seems to prefer living just barely within his means. This may be profligate and shortsighted of him, in some people's eyes, but it is a powerful stimulus to the economy."

There were two implications in this of interest to Wall Streeters. For one thing, investors came to believe that the profits of selected companies that produced consumer goods were far less likely to undergo major dips than had been the case in the 1930s and earlier. Thus, consumerism would provide the economy with a major prop. While their stocks might decline on occasion, they would not do so because the companies behind them were in any trouble. In time earnings would rise, and so might dividends. The stocks too would recover—again, given time. This belief, which grew in the 1950s, made investments seem less venturesome than had been the case in the 1920s and 1930s. Also, while it was true that many would spend before they would save, the consumption-fueled economy would grow. Family incomes were bound to rise, and after a while even the hedonists would have a surplus, which would go into savings. Some of this would be in the form of stocks.

The situation, then, was one in which a large part of the population was working hard so as to be able to purchase a wide variety of goods and services, and their efforts stimulated production and employment. Such an economy was far less prone to suffer slumps than that of the 1930s—these would be dampened by consumer spending and Keynesian countermeasures instituted by government. Inflation might remain a problem, but this could be handled by a vigilant government and a prudent Federal Reserve System. Steady prices would be paid for by a lower level of economic growth, but not by a new bout of double-digit unemployment.

And how might individual Americans protect themselves against inflation? Economists suggested that investments in common stocks might be prudent, especially in those that increased their dividend payouts regularly. These would appreciate in price over the long run.

Government spending programs, in particular those involved in one way or another with national defense, provided the economy with additional support. Such expenditures at the beginning of World War II had brought the nation out of the Great Depression, and those economists who had predicted a collapse after the war did so because they believed an end to military spending would lead to unemployment and stagnation. As has been indicated, such a situation did not develop, but in the postwar period even the most pacifistic economists conceded that such a form of spending would provide stimulation for business.

Total military spending in 1944, the last full year of the war, came to over $74 billion. By 1948, the figure was $12 billion. Then, with the coming of the Korean War in 1950, spending escalated, so that by 1952 close to $39 billion went for military purposes. The figure declined somewhat after the war, but in no year of the 1950s was it below $35 billion.

The Korean War boosted the economy and showed businessmen and politicians how military procurement programs could take up the slack, should the market for civilian goods falter. This of course was the classic Keynesian prescription, but it did involve budgetary deficits, still anathema in Washington and New York.

The same kind of effect might have been obtained by spending in the civilian sector—the construction of bridges, government buildings, and the like—but both the presidents and congresses were more likely to support military budgets in a period when the nation was involved in the Cold War and patriotism was high.

Businessmen crave stability and predictability, and there is little in the way of economic activity more stable and predictable than government contracts for military and related goods. Wall Street came to realize this in 1942, when stocks rose as investors began to see that the combination of economic stimulation and long-term government spending would be translated into higher profits over several years. The financial district had the same reaction to Cold War spending. After the initial shock wore off, the Korean War too provided an upward push to stock prices. For the next decade and a half, Wall Street would greet enlarged military budgets with rallies.

This is not to say that analysts thought war was good for business. They understood that even limited fighting carried the risk of economic controls, while an all-out conflict could destroy civilization and make the matter of stock prices irrelevant. Rather, they believed that increased military spending in *peacetime* could provide them with profit opportunities. In the 1950s, stock prices would advance on rumors of an administration request for new weapons systems, but they would decline when it appeared actual war might erupt.

In 1950, when the Korean War began, the gross national product came to $285 billion. Dwight Eisenhower's last full year in the White House was 1960, and in spite of a recession—the third one of his administration—the GNP came in at $504 billion. Although this growth was impressive by prewar standards, Democratic critics argued that the Republicans had held the economy back, that greater growth was possible, and furthermore that the average American had suffered in what was a "businessman's government."

The statistics for corporate profits would appear to contradict this belief. Net profits after taxes were $25.3 billion in 1950, and in 1953, the first of the Eisenhower years, they were down to slightly under $20 billion. In 1960, they were $22.6 billion. In part this was due to the recession, but even when this is taken into consideration, the profit picture for the decade hardly is impressive. The peak year for the 1950s was 1955, when net corporate profits were only $26 billion. These are aggregate figures, of course, so that while some corporations experienced declines and others stagnated, a large number reported rising profits and some of them did quite well. Still, on the basis of profits alone, there was no reason to think a major bull market would develop. Nor was it true that the advance resulted from a spectacular increase in dividend payouts, though these did advance. Yet in this decade, when the earnings and dividends reported by the Dow stocks were mediocre, prices more than tripled, the yield on them was cut by more than half, and the price/earnings (P/E) ratio went from 7.7 to 19.8. Investors were willing to pay more money for smaller earnings and dividends in 1959 than they had in 1950.

Why?

One important reason was that Americans simply had more disposable income in the 1950s than at any previous time in their lives. In 1950, the labor force was 63.8 million, and it rose to 72.1 million by 1960, for an increase of 8.3 million, or 13 percent. Over the same span, wages and salaries went from $146.8 billion to $270.8 billion, an increase of $124 billion, or 84 percent. The unemployment rates for both years were approximately the same (5.3 percent and 5.5 percent), and, after 1951, inflation was not an important factor. The message of these figures is clear enough: labor received a far greater share of the benefits of a growing economy

The Market and the Economy in the 1950s

YEAR	CLOSING DOW	EARNINGS	PRICE/EARN- INGS RATIO	DIVIDENDS	YIELD
1949	200	—	—	$12.79	6.4
1950	235	$30.70	7.7	16.13	6.9
1951	269	26.59	10.1	16.34	6.1
1952	291	24.78	11.8	15.43	5.3
1953	280	27.23	10.3	16.11	5.7
1954	404	28.18	14.4	17.47	4.3
1955	488	35.78	13.7	21.58	4.4
1956	499	33.34	15.0	22.99	4.6
1957	435	36.06	12.1	21.61	5.0
1958	583	27.94	20.9	20.00	3.4
1959	679	34.31	19.8	20.74	3.0

SOURCE: Adapted from Yale Hirsch, *The 1979 Stock Trader's Almanac* (Old Tappan, 1979), p.27 and *Barron's*.

than did the corporations, or, to put it differently, wages rose more rapidly than profits. It was a portion of this newly affluent wage-earner group that entered the stock market in the 1950s and helped bid up prices of shares even though the profit picture in the aggregate was unimpressive.

But the economy was strong, resilient, and possessed far more stamina than had been imagined earlier. Toward the end of the decade, some analysts argued that prices had been artificially depressed in the late 1940s due to fears of a new depression, dismay regarding the Truman electoral victory, and uncertainties about the Cold War. The Dow bottomed out at 160 in 1949, below where it had been thirteen years earlier, in large part due to these factors. According to these analysts, in the 1950s Americans came to believe that prosperity was here to stay and that the political leadership in Washington was fully capable of handling international relations so as to assure peace, while at the same time keeping the economy on a course of moderate growth without inflation. They stressed the statistics, but in themselves these would not have justified the better than threefold advance in the Dow. Implicit in their argument, however, was another factor, more psychological and sociological in nature than economic, without which no major bull market can begin and develop. In the early 1950s many Americans felt more confident about their future than at any time since before the Great Crash of 1929. This confidence prepared them for the messages put out by a new generation of Wall Streeters with the right kind of sales pitch for the times. Finally, in this period several new groups of stocks made their appearance on the trading lists, and these provided the market as a whole with a touch of glamour and excitement, which also was a necessary ingredient for any sustained and spectacular upward move. All of these appeared and developed in the 1950s, and taken together they provided the market with a strong foundation for the blazing actions and wild activities of the next decade.

No person better symbolized the new confidence of the 1950s than did Dwight Eisenhower. National morale was at a low point in 1951, when it appeared Harry Truman would not run for another term or that, if he did, he would be badly defeated. Some Democrats doubted he could win the nomination. The reasons were obvious and would be iterated and reiterated many times by Republicans during the presidential campaign: Communism, Corruption, and Korea.

Senator Joe McCarthy and other Republicans accused the administration of being "soft on Communism," and McCarthy often referred to "twenty years of treason." The White House handled matters badly, angering both the McCarthyites and their opponents. At the same time there were scandals within the administration itself, with most of the trouble at the Bureau of Internal Revenue and the Reconstruction Finance Corporation. There were clear indications that members of the White House staff had accepted bribes from businessmen. Senator Estes Kefauver, a Tennessee Democrat who had announced his intention of challenging Truman for the nomination, uncovered corruption in several of the nation's largest cities, all of which were controlled by Democrats. Finally, the Korean War peace talks dragged on, with the president apparently incapable of concluding them satisfactorily. Public opinion polls indicated that Truman's popularity was at an all-time low. Trust in political institutions had eroded badly. Not since 1932 had the time seemed so ripe for a "savior."

Commentators in both parties cast Eisenhower in that role. The *New Republic* called him "one of the country's precious national assets." Democratic Senator Paul Douglas suggested that the general be given the nomination of both parties in 1952. There is evidence that Truman offered to support Eisenhower on several occasions. Clearly Eisenhower was the most popular person in the nation, and after he won the Republican nomination, his victory was never really in doubt.

Wall Street felt it had special reasons to celebrate the Eisenhower nomination and then the election. Not only was the new president a Republican, as were most of the financial district's leaders, but his rhetoric was the kind they liked to hear. They believed Eisenhower would revive the nation spiritually, end the unpopular war, and prevent a new round of inflation. During the campaign he had promised to eliminate economic controls, modify irritating New Deal reforms, and cut federal spending. All of this was supposed to be good for business, or so the district believed in 1952.

There was a general feeling on Wall Street that stock prices had been held down by distrust of Truman. Although the Dow had risen steadily in late 1949 and continued onward into 1952, having gained more than one hundred points in three years, the move was credited to a bounceback from the inventory recession and Korean War–related spending programs and, toward the end, a belief that a Republican would preside over the White House in 1953. Some analysts held that Truman had cost the Dow at least another hundred points. Now the average not only would make this up but also would add a few dozen more in celebration of the Eisenhower victory.

The district craved confidence in Washington. Everything else was in place. The economy was strong, stock prices were not overly high, and the Street's salesmen were prepared to make a big push for new clients. Eisenhower would provide the missing ingredient for the bull market: stability and security. He would not disappoint his admirers in lower Manhattan.

There would be an Eisenhower boom, greater in scope than any the most sanguine bull of 1952 expected it to be. But the raw material for the bonanza existed during the Truman years. While it was true that the Eisenhower market would be based upon the growing feeling of security, salesmanship, and glamour, much of the drive and momentum would be provided by the release of pent-up investment energies kept in check by distrust and dislike of Harry Truman. Once Eisenhower brought the Korean War to a conclusion and led the economy into a "soft landing" through the 1953 recession, the way was clear for a major market advance.

No strong move could be possible without the presence of a new generation of investors, people who knew about the 1929 crash but were too young to have experienced it. Some of them filtered into the brokerages after the 1949 inventory recession, attracted to stocks by high yields and a belief that they might provide a good defense against inflation. But the investment business hardly was booming. The vast majority of Americans would have nothing to do with Wall Street, and in fact were generally ignorant of what went on there—except that in some way its operations had helped cause the Great Depression. A survey taken of middle-class families in the Los Angeles area in 1949 showed that of 375 respondents, 328 did not know what a stock broker did, and of the 47 who had some idea of his function, only seven were able to mention the name of a single brokerage house. A similar study in New Haven indicated that almost all of those asked could not properly define a bond. *Collier's* magazine reported that when 5,000 Americans were asked what was traded at stock exchanges, 64 percent replied, "Livestock." Of course, only a few people had active brokerage accounts in this period, or even had seen the inside of an investment office of any kind. Above all, most people did not trust stock brokers.

This was a poor time to be in the selling end of the business. Trading volume was low and income meager. Whatever status remained for Wall Street accrued to the investment bankers and trust officers, and they, too, held brokers in low esteem. The brokers understood this. In June 1949, one of them told a *Wall Street Journal* reporter that without a successful new selling effort he could not survive. According to the reporter, "He's about concluded that he must either sell to the little man or look for another job."

A few leading investment houses mounted imaginative advertising and educational campaigns in the late 1940s and early 1950s in an attempt to alter the view toward investments. They set up exhibits at flower and furniture shows, where free literature was distributed and brokers were present to answer questions. Several brokerages offered free courses in investments "for women only" and reported better attendance than had been expected; one San Francisco branch office had expected 50 or so enrollees and received over a thousand applications. "Some stock and bond merchants think one of their biggest problems is education," wrote the *Journal* in 1949. "The wartime and post-war inflation has put money into the hands of many folk unaccustomed to buying securities. At the same time, lofty income taxes have prevented lots of stock-minded people in the $10,000-a-year and up income group from buying stocks." It seemed clear that such individuals wanted to know more about securities than they already did but had no clear idea of how to initiate the process and weren't sure they could trust those slick young men who handed out pamphlets, the urgent voice on the telephone, or the executives who spoke to them at free classes. In sum, most investment firms were unable to take advantage of those forces that were impelling middle-class Americans to reconsider their ideas regarding investment in common stock.

Charles Merrill, the head of the investment firm of Merrill Lynch, Pierce, Fenner & Beane, understood the problem and even had a solution. In the late 1940s and early 1950s he not only remade his own commission house but managed to convince others in the industry to follow his example. In so doing, he accomplished for the selling end of the industry what J. P. Morgan had done for syndication a half century earlier: Merrill showed the way, became a spokesman, and was one of the few Wall Streeters to achieve celebrity status among the general population.

Merrill was no newcomer to the district. He was 62 years old in 1952 and had been in Wall Street, on and off, for more than forty years. But after all this time he still was considered an outsider by many financial leaders. They resented his brash and cocky style, his genius at self-advertisement, and his general unwillingness to genuflect before the old Wall Street Establishment. Merrill was not stuffy; he loved parties and good-looking women and preferred the company of artists and writers to that of bankers and brokers. Had he been born a couple of generations later and in different circumstances, he might have become a member of the jet set of the 1960s. As it was, he was the head of America's largest brokerage and in the midst of revolutionizing the industry at the dawn of the Age of Eisenhower.

In the 1920s Merrill had been a specialist in underwriting shares of companies in the retail business, and at the same time he took pride in the way his brokers cultivated small investors. Thus, he had a long-standing interest in merchandising. Merrill got out of the market just before the Crash of 1929 and lived well during the depression. He returned to the business in 1939, and after the war planned his campaign to interest middle-class investors in stocks. Merrill thought this could be done, given an expanding economy and an altered public image of brokerage.

He started by remodeling his brokers. Merrill organized the most ambitious training program in the industry, at a time when most firms offered little in the way of orientation, deeming it wasteful and in any case unnecessary, since brokers could pick up what information they needed while on the job. In this program Merrill Lynch not only taught the essentials of investment, but informed trainees they were not to pressure clients into making purchases or try in other ways to maximize commissions. In fact, they were to be paid straight salaries, though they also would participate in a company-wide profit-sharing plan. The Merrill Lynch broker was at his desk and telephone to provide potential and established clients with services and not to tout them on stocks. Merrill even changed their designation: his people were to be referred to as "account executives"—not "brokers" or "customer's men."

These freshly minted account executives would be provided with the largest and according to some the best-trained research staff in the field. The company churned out reports and newsletters, which were distributed freely to interested investors and not reserved for established clients, as was then customary in the business. Most of the recommendations were on the conservative side, since Merrill still believed this was the best way for his middle-class investors to start out. "We must draw the new capital required for industrial might and growth *not* from among a few large investors but from the savings of thousands of people of moderate incomes," he said in 1946. Other commission houses behaved as though they were the Tiffany or Cartier's of the industry, while marginal firms functioned like mom-and-pop delicatessens. Merrill's model was Safeway, Kresge's, and Penney's—the securities of which he had helped bring to Wall Street in the 1920s.

It worked. Merrill Lynch grew rapidly in the late 1940s, and by 1950 had over 150,000 accounts, far more than any other firm in the business. Other commission houses studied its operations and imitated some of its programs. While retaining the commission system for account executives (they even adopted this designation), the Street's leading firms instituted training programs and cautioned newcomers against hard-sell tactics. They produced market letters and research reports for open distribution, and in other ways attempted to professionalize operations and eliminate features that might frighten newcomers away.

Merrill had a clear idea of just who it was he wanted to attract to Wall Street. It was the middle-income veteran with a wife, kids, car, and home in suburbia. Such a person might do well to place a portion of his savings in "sound common stocks" like Standard Oil of New Jersey, General Motors, and General Electric. This "nest egg" would grow as the economy expanded and provide dividends that would be used for home improvements, education, and, eventually, retirement. It was a picture that suited the mood of the early 1950s.

Yet Charles Merrill was not destined to become the most prominent human symbol of this new investment atmosphere. For one thing, he wasn't that interested in such a role, and for another, he preferred playing at work and working at play too much to fit himself into such a mold. But George Keith Funston, who became president of the New York Stock Exchange in 1951, not only was the right man for the task, but had been given the job with this role in mind.

Funston, who was only forty years old in 1951, had been a businessman, navy officer, and college president prior to arriving at the N.Y.S.E. He was a handsome, all-American type, and articulate—the perfect person to sell Americans on the idea of stock ownership. But he knew very little about the securities markets, and old-timers at the Exchange were appalled at his ignorance of financial affairs. In time Funston absorbed all the knowledge he would need for his internal tasks at the N.Y.S.E., but in any case he was there not to advise members on how to run their operations but rather to serve as their front man and super-salesman.

Funston's first official act as president was to open trading on the morning of September 10. The Dow rose by a point and a half that session and volume was close to 2.2 million shares, considered hectic for that period. These were good omens for floor personnel, who took such matters seriously.

Then he went to Washington to meet with Truman, Treasury Secretary John Snyder, and other leading government officials. Nothing of substance was said or accomplished; this was conventional public relations. Funston was demonstrating that although a novice at Wall and Broad, he knew his way around the capital and had access to important figures there.

Later that month Funston reworked one of his speeches into an article that appeared in *The Exchange*, a magazine published by the N.Y.S.E. The title told it all—"Should You Buy Shares of America?" In it Funston urged young people, especially veterans, to consider stock ownership as a form of savings and insurance. This article was reprinted in *Reader's Digest* the following month, and with it, Funston was well on his way to becoming a national figure.

During the next few years Funston emerged as the first Wall Street leader of his generation to achieve widespread recognition beyond the limits of the financial world. His face appeared on the covers of *Time* and *Newsweek;* he was a guest on radio and television talk shows; he was mentioned as a potential candidate for the Senate or the Connecticut state house, and even for the presidency. In the process, he created a new image for Wall Street and sold it effectively to people who might otherwise not have considered the purchase of securities. Merrill remade the brokerages; Funston helped lure a new generation of Americans to their doors.

On arriving at the N.Y.S.E. Funston was surprised to learn that no one there had any clear idea of what kind of people owned stock, or for that matter, the actual number of shareholders. How could he begin a selling effort without a firm notion of the market for his product? Thus, he commissioned the Brookings Institution to undertake the first shareholder census. Funston did tell reporters he had a good idea of what it would demonstrate. "I suspect that the survey will produce evidence that Main Street—not Wall Street—owns the nation's industries."

No such demonstration was made, but the project did serve Funston's purposes. Brookings reported that there were some 6.5 million shareholders and that 1.3 million of them had purchased their first stocks during the previous three years. Clearly, interest in securities was increasing. The census also indicated that the median age of the American shareholder was fifty-one, and his/her income came to $7,100. There emerged from this a picture of a middle-class, middle-aged couple, living in a small town or a new suburban development, putting away part of their savings in common stock. Funston hailed the report and its findings but noted that tens of millions of Americans held no stocks at all. These would become the targets of a large-scale public relations campaign.

Funston often talked of the "lost man," who to him was akin to Franklin D. Roosevelt's "forgotten man," who obeyed the laws, lived a quiet life, worked hard, and saved as much as he could. "Agriculture, labor, and manufacturing—the producers are organized; the consumer is protected by competition or, in its absence, by government regulation. It is the saver who has to take what is left." Common stocks would be his haven. Funston said that his lost man should purchase life insurance, have equity in a home, and put something aside in savings bonds. Then he should consider the purchase of good-quality common stocks.

Seizing upon the national mood in the early 1950s, Funston suggested that stock ownership not only made sense financially but also was a sign of patriotism, of faith in the American system. "Capitalism will rise or fall in direct ratio to the support it gets from the public," he said in an address kicking off "Invest in America Week" in 1952. "That support will be fully forthcoming only when all the people share in capitalism. The goal of the securities industry is to create a nation of shareholding capitalists; to make every man and woman a shareholder in our great corporations."

This was soon changed into a variety of "soft-core Mc-Carthyism." "A nation of shareholders is our strongest defense against the foreign 'isms' that would sap our vitality and eventually turn us over to the evil enemy we know as communism." In Funston's lexicon, the N.Y.S.E. became the bulwark of the American Way. "There is no stock exchange in Moscow, nor is ownership in promising enterprises in Russia available to the public." To him, those who attacked profits were "lukewarm friends at home"—a phrase that in the context of the anticommunist crusade covered a wide spectrum of belief, from old-fashioned conservatism to New Deal–Fair Deal liberalism.

Funston believed in what came to be known as "People's Capitalism," which to him meant a system based upon widespread ownership of stocks. "The way to fight communism is through American prosperity, which has proven it can accomplish more for more people than any other system in the world," he told a Philadelphia audience in mid-1952. In an interview with a *New Yorker* writer, Funston said, "We're the epitome of free enterprise. Once that's lost, we're gone." And one of the ways the average American could fight communism would be to buy stocks. "We're trying to broaden the base of stock ownership and thus strengthen the basis of democracy." *Forbes* wrote that Funston had become the "chief booster" for Wall Street. The Old Guard there thought of stocks as a way to make a living. "To Funston, and the Young Turks, they are a means to a way of life."

Funston did whip up enthusiasm for stocks, but in the nature of things he addressed large gatherings, not individuals. An exchange president can act as a leader of and spokesman for a community, but the daily work of winning converts had to be undertaken by an army of missionaries, and he lacked such a force.

Charles Merrill's new breed of account executives might have performed that function, but most of them were content to wait for clients to walk through their doors. Some brokerages did purchase lists of potential clients, who were telephoned in the evenings by brokers who tried to sell them on the merits of one stock or another, but the larger houses frowned on such practices. But another army did exist, and this one did not flinch at using hard-sell tactics. These were the mutual fund salesmen, led by a cadre of managers, each working for a fund or group of them.

Mutual funds in their modern incarnation had been in existence since 1924, but during the great bull market of the 1920s they were overshadowed by glamour stocks touted by hot brokers and analysts. Mutual funds were and are portfolios of securities managed professionally for a fee. Their shares are offered on a continual basis by sales organizations, most of which charge commissions in the neighborhood of 8 percent. Owners of fund shares might redeem them, usually at net asset value without additional charge, simply by contacting the company and making their desires known.

By itself the growing interest in common stocks might have swollen the sales of mutual funds. "Sales" was the key word, for these funds were peddled by representatives of the offering organization, almost all of whom worked on a commission basis. By the mid-1950s some of the larger funds had forces of several hundred representatives, most of whom were part-timers, with few having more than a passing knowledge of securities. They were not brokers. Many of them were full-time salesmen of such consumer goods as used cars and vacuum cleaners. Elementary and high school teachers would try to sell fund plans to parents of students, and clergymen would do the same for members of their congregations. The more plans were sold, the higher would be the commissions.

High-pressure tactics were the rule. Lists of potential purchasers could be obtained from insurance companies, hospitals, and other organizations that sold them for a fee. Then the representative would arrive at the client's door, often without an appointment so as to catch him or her off guard. And the pitch would begin. Occasionally the initial contact would be made by telephone. Some representatives offered free gifts, such as ballpoint pens or address books, as a lure for a presentation opportunity.

Due to the high commission structure, purchasers might not break even until their share quotations rose considerably. Still, many people who made purchases in the 1950s did fairly well and were able to boast of profits after a few years or even months. Without really understanding what they had done, these newcomers had stumbled into the market at its low point and then rode it up to new highs.

The rising quotations for mutual fund shares interested additional people in this form of investment, and of course each new investor spoke of it to friends and associates and so acted as an unpaid publicist for the funds. In 1950 there were fewer than 100 mutual funds in existence, with a total of 939,000 accounts and assets of $2.5 billion. Five years later there were 125 funds, over 2 million accounts, with assets of $7.8 billion. By 1960 the number of funds had swollen to 161, accounts to 4.9 million, and assets to over $17 billion.

The increased popularity of these funds helped swell the demand for common stock in two ways: the mutuals invested most of their new money on Wall Street, and ownership of fund shares introduced many newcomers to the ways of investment. Apparently most of those who purchased funds in the early 1950s knew little about common stocks; the mutual fund commission was their entrance fee to the Street. After a while these people learned something about investments, if only by pouring over reports sent out quarterly by the funds, and then they would try to buy and sell on their own. In time they might place all new money into stocks, and either sell the fund shares or keep what they had as a cushion, a managed portfolio selected by experts. Thus, the part-time salesman often functioned as a means whereby middle-class Americans were led to one of Charles Merrill's account executives.

Finally, millions of Americans who continued to think stocks were chancy, who resisted mutual fund salesmen and had never seen the inside of a brokerage, became involved in the market through the medium of pension funds, one of the most striking elements in the investment picture, and one that many Wall Streeters considered a major support for the market.

Only a handful of companies provided their employees with pension plans at the turn of the century, and despite their growing popularity in the 1920s, fewer than 2.7 million Americans had such coverage in 1930. One-third of all plans were unfunded, which is to say that payments were made out of general revenues, with no sinking fund at all. The total assets of the other plans were estimated to be $500 million, and none of this was in the form of common stock. Instead, the plans placed assets in government and high-grade corporate bonds as well as mortgages. To do otherwise would be to invite charges of gambling or worse. The same was true for assets of insurance companies; these too were placed in debts instruments of various kinds. This was the case for a large variety of special accounts, from college and university endowments to trust funds administered by court-appointed officers for widows and orphans.

This situation remained essentially unchanged through the first part of the 1930s. By the end of the decade, however, some pension funds had already started buying and holding small amounts of blue-chip common and preferred stock. In 1945, these funds had $2.3 billion in assets, of which $212 million was in stocks and $663 million in bonds. Five years later the pension funds had $5.6 billion in assets, and the amount in common shares stood at $774 million and bonds at over $2 billion. Stock ownership was increasing, but not at a much faster pace than ownership of the funds themselves.

In 1950, during negotiations for a new labor contract, General Motors President Charles Wilson proposed the establishment of a pension fund that was to contain a large amount of common stock. The union wasn't particularly pleased with the idea but in the end went along with it. The GM pension fund, which quickly became one of the largest in the nation, was to be heavily invested in common shares. Perhaps Wilson thought this would give the workers a stake in the company's future, in which case they would work harder and be less eager to strike. But whatever the reason, the investments were made at a time when the market was starting its great advance.

Given its good results, other plans followed the GM model. By 1955 the nation's pension plans had $16.1 billion in assets, of which $2.5 billion was in bonds and over $5.3 billion in stocks. In five years these funds had added more than $4.5 billion worth of shares to their portfolios. Increasingly, pension payouts to workers were tied to prices at the N.Y.S.E. According to some, the prices would be buoyed by large and constant pension plan purchases. It seemed a simple and foolproof guarantee of ever higher quotations for blue-chip shares.

In 1951, several life insurance companies in New York petitioned for the right to invest up to 2 percent of their assets in common stock, and the state legislature granted this request. Other states followed suit. By 1955, the life companies owned over $3.6

billion in common stock. The property and casualty companies, which always had that right, owned another $5.4 billion of them, having nearly doubled their holdings in less than a decade.

This institutional support for stock prices helped reinforce the growing confidence in securities. Those economists who continued to warn of another 1929 had to concede that there had been nothing like this in the 1920s. Comparatively few Americans owned shares in that decade. Many more had savings accounts, of course, and so were indirect participants in the bull market, as the banks invested funds in securities or loans based upon securities. Thus, the market's collapse weakened the banks; and many innocents, who never would have dreamed of owning shares, saw their savings melt when the banks came down with a crash in 1931 and 1932. The situation was quite different and far more complex in the 1950s. An ever increasing number of Americans owned stocks by then and may also have had shares in mutual funds. Individuals with trust accounts knew part of their assets were in common stock. But millions of other people—including those who considered themselves too poor even to have a checking account—had an important stake in the movement of securities prices. Union pension funds, reserve funds of insurance companies, and other large financial aggregates depended upon the fortunes of leading stock issues for income with which to pay out benefits. The so-called little guy was in the market whether or not he wanted to be there. The institutions were the backbone of Keith Funston's People's Capitalism, though this would not become evident until later on.

Still, the Funston-Merrill approach had its victories too, and one of them was signaled in 1956, when the N.Y.S.E. completed its second shareholder census, the results of which Funston released with considerable pride. The study indicated that there were more than 8.6 million shareholders, for an increase of 2.1 million since 1952. One out of every sixteen adults in America had owned shares that year; the figure for 1956 was one out of twelve. As had been anticipated, the median age for shareholders had declined, going from 51 to 48. The Exchange had projected a slight decline for median income of shareholders as well, but no one there was prepared for the finding. In 1952 the median income had been $7,100, and in 1956, $6,200. Funston had gone further with his ideas of People's Capitalism than even he had realized.

By then the Wall Street nexus had become an integral part of a new stage in the nation's development, and the economic importance of securities-based capitalism hardly could be denied. The markets were stronger and more secure than they had been in the 1920s; as yet there had been no major outbreak of speculation; the wild men and esoteric stocks had just begun to make their migration to the financial district. No one could seriously question that this was a bull market of major proportions, but at the same time every Wall Street veteran knew that prices could not rise indefinitely. At one point or another there would be a break, and then the nation would learn whether "another 1929" was possible. But with each decline came a new rebound, while at the same time fears evaporated and confidence grew.

And then, when the critical point of unbounded euphoria appeared, the most dynamic stages of the last bull market would begin.

Two

SETTING THE STAGE

IN mid-1949, stocks broke out of their two-and-a-half-year trading range and headed upward. Over the next decade, in three massive leaps punctuated by periods of consolidation and regrouping, the Dow Industrials would rise from a low of 161 to a peak of 685. Millions of people made money on Wall Street in the 1950s, confidence in investment grew, speculation appeared, and all the while fears of a new crash faded. Yet later on, in discussions and analysis of the postwar bull market, attention was focused on the events of the 1960s, while those of the 1950s were slighted.

The reason for this is not difficult to find. Some bull markets capture the national imagination by their boldness, innovation, and cast of characters, while others seem to lack all three. Americans know of the great bull market of the 1920s, for example, when the Dow went from 88 to 381, from 1924 to 1929. Who but a financial historian has much to say about the bull move that opened in 1933 with the Dow at 50 and came to an end in 1937, when the Index stood at 194? The two advances were of approximately the same magnitude and duration, and each was followed by a collapse. The first has become one of the centerpieces of American history; the second is ignored.

The market of the 1950s cannot be slighted in the same way, not if one is to appreciate what happened on Wall Street the following decade. It set the stage for the more colorful and spectacular advance of the 1960s and was important and interesting in its own right. But it did lack a certain flair and spice. Financial historian John Brooks indicated as much in the titles of two of his books. One, which covered part of the 1950s, he called *The Seven Fat Years*, while another, in which he dealt with the 1960s, was titled *The Go-Go Years*.

Spectacular crashes often climax major bull markets, but there are no signals given at their beginnings. None was observed in 1924, when the great upward sweep was about to start, and there was no indication in 1949 that a postwar bull market was getting underway. Trading volume at the N.Y.S.E. that year came to 272 million shares, which was 30 million fewer than had changed hands the previous year. Of the ten most active stocks, five ended up at below 10. Most were speculative in nature, a sure sign that investors were out of the market. The nation's leading exchange was more a playground for traders in 1949 than anything else.

Major bull markets cannot be started or sustained by such individuals dealing in these kinds of stocks. Rather, investors—those who will buy and hold the blue chips—have provided the foundation for all important advances, while bullish speculators lead the way to new highs. Prior to their arrival the scene is dominated by traders who do not expect broad moves in either direction to last for long. They are skittish, moving in and out of the market rapidly, and are quick to take profits when they occur. Thus, their activities cause prices to decline after they undergo slight advances, and sudden bursts of activity are followed by long stretches during which little seems to be happening.

This condition is altered considerably once the investors arrive. Their purchases usually are regular, and they retain stocks during advances, even adding new shares to their portfolios. Trading volume becomes steady, giving the market a continuity it lacked during the trader phase. Then, attracted by higher prices, the specula-

N.Y.S.E. Most Active Stocks, 1949

STOCK	CLOSE	NET CHANGE	DIVIDEND	EARNINGS PER SHARE
Commonwealth & Southern	5½	+ 2½	nil	0.51
United Corporation	5	+ 2¾	stock	0.19
Radio Corporation	12½	− 1⅛	0.50	1.58
U.S. Steel	26⅛	− ½	2.25	5.39
General Motors	71⅝	+12⅞	8.00	14.64
Benguet Consolidated	1⅝	0	0.02	nil
Socony Vacuum	16⅝	− ¼	1.00	4.18
Columbia Gas	18⅞	− 1¾	0.75	0.84
Pepsi Cola	8½	+ ½	0.20	0.37
American Airlines	9⅞	+ 2⅜	nil	0.79

SOURCE: *New York Times,* January 3, 1950, p.51.

tors arrive, adding glamour to the scene, and this is a major factor in any major bull market. But without the small investor, their activities may count for little.

Just as it is difficult to convince investors that the purchase and retention of stocks is both sensible and prudent, so it is with great reluctance they abandon their hopes of capital gains once they have had their taste of them. Small investors are the first to arrive at the feast and the last to leave. Very often they manage to get in on the ground floor of bull markets, but they remain too long and may be forced to leap from the roof in the end.

There is no satisfactory method of determining why large numbers of Americans decided to purchase common stocks toward the end of the 1949 inventory recession, but on the basis of odd-lot figures, it can be seen that the change in attitude began around this time. Small investors wanting to purchase shares in General Motors during the spring of that year would have learned that the stock was going for around 53, so that a round lot would have cost $5,300 plus commission. This was a large sum of money at that time. A wealthy investor might purchase a round lot of GM, while a speculator would use margin for the buy. The small investor would have to settle for an odd lot of less than 100 shares.

The purchase and sales of odd lots in 1949 totaled $58.1 million, a six-year low. During the following year, however, odd-lot dealings came to $97.2 million, the second highest total in a dozen years. Furthermore, the balance of purchases over sales in 1950 was $7.4 million, also second for all years since 1937. Clearly the odd-lotters were out in force by then.

Other statistics support the view that there was a pickup of new investment during the post-recession period. After 1946 the amount of new money coming into the market declined steadily, going from $1.76 billion in 1947 to $1.5 billion in 1949. Then, in 1950, the amount rose to $2.14 billion, the highest since 1929, and in 1951 some $2.56 billion flowed into common shares.

Of course, much of this came from large private and institutional investors, but increased traffic at the commission houses indicated that by 1951 at the very latest the so-called little guy had begun his trek back to Wall Street, where he hadn't been seen in any great numbers for two decades.

What caused this increased interest in investment? Some

thought it resulted from a growing sentiment that there would be no major postwar depression. Others noted that blue-chip common stocks with secure dividends offered investors higher yields than could be had from savings accounts. Had they been lured back to the Street by excellent corporate earnings and safe dividends that were three or four times as much as bank rates? This would seem to be the case, and some articles on the subject of good opportunities in the market appeared in the autumn and early winter of 1949.

The desire for high dividends lured investors to Wall Street, and their purchases caused prices to advance. Thus, a stock selling for 20 with a $2 dividend carried a yield of 10 percent, which was four times the interest offered by insured savings bank deposits. Some investors might buy it at that price, but, should their actions cause the stock to rise to 25, the return would be cut to 8 percent and would be less attractive to conservative investors. An advance beyond the 25 level in this case would be difficult—unless and until the dividend was increased.

Few thought the market would rise much beyond the stage where yields on blue-chip securities were around 5 or 6 percent and those for more speculative issues were 8 percent or so. Additional upward movement would require an alteration in investor demands—from dividends to capital gains, from a craving for security to one for profits. By the early 1950s dividends on the blue-chip issues appeared secure. They would arrive every three months and were seen as rewards that came out of the economy—from work, profits, sales, and earnings. Capital gains, in contrast, were chancy, for stocks could decline as well as advance. Profits such as these resulted from supply and demand forces on Wall Street, which could not be predicted with any degree of accuracy. To many this was akin to gambling and, as such, to be avoided. Furthermore, capital gains were produced by market actions and were not the creation of new goods and services, and investors in this period still distrusted the market mechanism.

Bull markets begin with an appreciation of economic fundamentals, but they will stagnate unless investors start looking into the future as well and have dreams of capital gains. Wall Street hadn't known such a market since the late 1920s. Few thought one was developing in the postwar period.

Prudent investors in the early 1950s sought stocks of large, secure companies that paid respectable dividends that were in little danger of being cut. At first they concentrated upon the major electric utilities and old favorites like American Telephone & Telegraph, but even then, Merrill Lynch thought some venturesome investors might explore a handful of growth stocks. Some of these paid high dividends because they were considered a trifle risky—General Motors, which with its year-end extra payout offered a return of 13 percent was one of these. Others, like Coca-Cola, fetched 5 percent, low for the time, but Merrill Lynch thought the stock would advance faster than would the general market, and so was worth having. Also in the list was Libby-Owens-Ford with a 9 percent yield and Minnesota Mining & Manufacturing with a 5 percent return. Such was the nature of informed speculation in the late 1940s and early 1950s.

Prices were moving upward in the aftermath of the inventory recession, but there was little in the way of glamour in the advance. The best performing stock groups for 1949 were leathers, utilities, papers, and soaps, and the most popular stocks were in these areas—the kinds of issues that paid good dividends and had stable earnings.

This was the kind of market one expected from an economy that was mature and stagnant, not one with growth potential that offered premiums to innovation. The American economy was expanding and on the verge of a technological boom that would alter the fabric of national life. The 1950s and 1960s would be exciting decades for American business and one of the best times in history for new companies with novel products and technologies to get their starts. Little of this could be found in the 1949 advance. Had this continued—had investors maintained their interest in dividends to the exclusion of capital gains and avoided risks entirely—there would have been no bull market, but instead an important rally that might have come to an end after a few months.

The first signs of glamour appeared in 1950, when there was a flurry in the stocks of companies that produced television sets. Sales of sets had advanced even during the recession, and the industry reported record backlogs and excellent earnings. For example, in the first quarter of the year Motorola had sales of $35.5 million and profits of $3.50 per share; the 1949 figures were $15.2 million and $1.14. The stock paid a $1.50 dividend, and some Wall Street houses thought earnings for the year could be more than $15. Yet the stock sold at 23 in January, or less than twice anticipated earnings while yielding more than 6 percent.

Such a situation could not be maintained for long; even the most cautious investor could not ignore such a record, and it was certain to attract interest from speculators. Motorola advanced early in the year and the stock soared when the first quarter's results were made public. Within four months the stock doubled, and so did those of Zenith, Admiral, and Emerson. Radio Corporation of America, the best-quality issue in the group, rose by 80 percent in this period.

Still, many analysts hesitated when it came to recommending such issues. Perhaps they feared so great an upward move could not be sustained. Some considered the possibility of a shakeout in the industry, with several manufacturers squeezed out by the survivors. Brokers urged conservative clients to seek other investments, while speculators were told to take profits and invest in other areas. One analyst who had recommended television set manufacturers in 1947 thought his followers should sell them. These stocks had been good risks when yields were over 10 percent but were no longer so after having been sliced to 3 and 4 percent, especially when safe electric utility issues yielded 7 percent. *Business Week* joined in the chorus, warning investors not to anticipate rapid or sizable dividend increases. "When you are growing as fast as TV, you have to conserve cash to take care of expansion costs and needs for new working capital. It's doubtful if the industry will be able to pay out in dividends more than a small part of earnings for a long time." In 1950, this kind of rapid and profitable growth was considered a bearish omen.

The television set manufacturers understood this situation and investment philosophy. Hoping to boost the prices of their stocks, they did increase dividends. But the shares rose more rapidly, and the dividend yields declined. Paradoxically, the stocks could not escape being labeled as speculative vehicles, despite all that was done to prevent this from happening. It was the kind of market in which investors almost feared price advances and were wary of capital gains that came too rapidly.

This same psychology and approach penalized young companies in exciting new areas that were trying to raise capital through the sales of stock. Such firms hadn't much hope of attracting investors, and there weren't enough speculators in the market to take their shares. Thus they were left with unhappy alternatives: they might remain small, try to expand on retained earnings, attempt to borrow money (at a time when banks frowned on such loans), seek some larger company that might be willing to buy them out, or die.

Eckert-Mauchly Computer Corp. was one such company. Not only was it the leading manufacturer of computers in America, it was the only one. Computers weren't esoteric dreams in this period. Rather, businessmen appreciated their potential, the government had ordered several, and clearly the market for data-processing equipment would grow over the years. In the 1920s and 1960s, a firm like Eckert-Mauchly would have had no difficulty raising funds through the sale of common shares, but the situation was different in the postwar period. Due to a lack of capital, E-M was unable to fund research or even fill orders. Because of large start-up charges, there were no earnings and certainly no dividend or even the hope of one. The company could not borrow money either, and the sale of stock was out of the question—who would purchase shares in such an enterprise at that time? In the end, Eckert-Mauchly sought a corporate partner with the capital needed for expansion. In March 1950, it merged into Remington Rand, where it became the Univac operation. This was the conventional way to do things at the time.

In this first stage of the bull market, the Dow went from 162 in June 1949 to 294 in January 1953. Except for a sharp selloff at the outbreak of the Korean War in June 1950, the rise was steady. Leadership rested with the secure, familiar issues, and these were purchased by investors willing to sacrifice a small amount of safety for a larger yield. A Federal Reserve study completed in 1952 bore this out. In 1949 almost four out of every five family units with incomes of more than $3,000 preferred fixed-income investments, such as savings accounts and bonds, to stocks and market instruments. By 1952 this proportion had dropped to two out of three, and preference for common stocks rose from 2 percent to 8 percent. These new investors were buying high-yielding shares and in the process had caused their prices to advance much faster than did their dividends. In fact, due to wartime pressures, the growth in dividends slowed down. That year the yield on the Dow Jones Industrials fell to 5.3 percent, the lowest in seven years, leading some analysts to conclude the time had come for a correction. This sentiment was reinforced by the postwar recession of 1953, and, taken together, they brought a conclusion to the advance.

The Dow fell to 255 in September before it bottomed out. As yet there was no sign of panic, but some expected this to transpire the following year. New York University economist Jules Backman, for example, issued a baleful prediction for 1954. There would be "an inventory recession, an automobile recession, a housing recession," he said in December 1953. "To me that adds up to a sharper setback than in 1949. . . . I think it will continue through 1954." British economist Colin Clark, who had an international reputation and a good record at forecasting, was even more pessimistic. By midyear, he said, the American economy would sink to the level reached in 1949, but no recovery would follow. Instead there would be a collapse and possibly a panic rivaling that of 1937, if not of 1929. The gross national product would be slashed by 15 percent, and the unemployment rate would be well over 12 percent.

As it had in 1949, Wall Street girded itself for a major depression that never came, and this apprehension, more than the economic facts, caused the first stage of the bull market to end. The statistics for the first half of 1954 were poor, but far from disastrous. Profits did decline, but they picked up somewhat in the second half. For 1954 as a whole, net corporate profits came to $19.8 billion, only $100 million less than they had been in the previous year, and dividends actually increased to $11.8 billion from $11.5 billion. But the biggest surprise came from the market itself. In the face of the economic slowdown in the first part of the year, prices actually rose, going above Dow 300 in March and topping 350 in early August.

This spectacular advance in the face of dire predictions resulted from better-than-anticipated earnings reports and dividend hikes and, most important, confidence that Eisenhower would not permit a serious economic crisis to develop. In the process the bull market entered a new, second stage, one in which greater stress would be placed on growth than on dividends.

Investors were more secure in mid-1954 than they had been in more than a generation, and this confidence permitted them to look ahead as well as at the existing record of companies and industries. At first they did so timidly, making investments in such stocks as International Business Machines (IBM), Corning Glass, and Eastman

Kodak, hardly new, untested companies and securities. These combined stability with growth and had done so for many years. Given a strong economy—moderate increases in gross national product and low inflation rates—investors were prepared to look ahead a few years and were not as concerned about economic and political dislocations as they had been in the Truman years.

The *Wall Street Journal* explained the basic theory of growth stocks to its readers in mid-1954:

> The good growth company, experience shows, may pay out only a small part of its earnings in cash dividends, using the rest for research, development of new products and expansion. . . . In the growth company, the plowed-back earnings should bring larger earning power—and in the long run bigger dividends—always assuming that the company's products or services are well accepted, and that its management is alert and forward-looking. And, when the dividends increase, the yield on the original stock investment goes up with them.

Thus, the *Journal* stressed yield but showed that growth stocks might do better in this department than the old blue chips. Investors might do well to purchase growth shares yielding 5 percent today in the expectation that in a few years the return on the original investment could be twice that, as a result of dividend increases. Significantly, the newspaper did not mention capital gains on this occasion, but clearly these would come, too.

Other newspapers, magazines, and advisory services picked up on the growth theme. *Financial World* started a regular section on growth stocks in 1954. The *New York Times* took note of the phenomenon early in the year, observing that the prices of some growth issues were rising more rapidly than was the general list. In late May, *Moody's* issued a report on the advances posted by several growth stocks. Since January 1, 1953, the Dow had risen by 12 percent, it noted, and in this same period IBM's increase had been 25 percent, Scott Paper rose by 56 percent, Minnesota Mining & Manufacturing (3M) by 44 percent, and Minneapolis-Honeywell Regulator's advance was over 40 percent. This publication thought the rally overdone and recommended switches to the less adventuresome issues that offered higher dividends.

Moody's position was typical of those of most old-line advisory services in early 1954, but it had little effect on the market. Instead of going back into the income stocks, some investors were putting their money into more speculative issues that offered the promise of capital gains. In July *Barron's* noted a divergence between the action of the Dow Industrials and the daily figures for advances and declines; some days the blue-chip index would slip, while many more issues rose than fell. This could only be due to a new interest in speculative stocks, thought that publication. "The month is only half gone," wrote *Business Week* on August 14, "yet there are more erratic daily fluctuations than the Street has seen in years." Such secondary stocks as Avco, International Telephone & Telegraph (ITT), General Dynamics, and Martin showed monthly advances in the double digits, while the Dow had fallen by a handful of points.

Some in the district started calling these and similar stocks "light blue chips," implying the hue might darken over the next few years. Several of the stocks did make the grade, but most did not. What was more important, however, was that for the first time since World War II, large numbers of investors were willing to take some risks. The investment atmosphere in the autumn of 1954 was quite different from what it had been during the Truman bull market. Values had started to change. *Business Week*'s last editorial for the year—entitled "1954: Turning Point in History?"—did not refer to the rally but in one sentence summed up what was perhaps the major reason for the advance and the key factor behind the initiation of the bull market's second stage. "Certainly 1954 will go down as the year when we conquered the depression phobia."

That year Wall Street looked less to the past—to a possible new 1929—and more to the future—to the promise of an expanding economy. Gradually investors became concerned less with dividends and more with capital gains. In other words, a spirit of speculation was being nourished in the district that year, and a new breed of speculators appeared in the brokerages, along with a variety of tipsters and touts.

These people are important ingredients in any sustained bull market. Their task is to stir things up and create an atmosphere of excitement and tension, along with fabricating a patina of glamour for securities dealings. Such individuals provide good copy for newspapers and magazines. Articles regarding their exploits attract thousands of amateurs and lesser fry, who dabble in stocks, hoping to make quick profits. Their purchases cause the prices of chancy issues to rise, and this too receives featured coverage in the press.

For a while the two markets—that of the investors and this new one dominated by speculators—coexist. Then, as the participants in the first come to appreciate the capital gains realized in the second, they start to migrate there. This movement from investment to speculation often is dramatic, though it may require months, even years, before becoming evident. In time, however, the speculative impulse becomes as great or greater than that for investments.

Speculators usually are scorned and castigated just prior to this switch in interest, and they become the scapegoats after everything falls apart in the major decline that brings the bull market to its conclusion. During the long bearish interludes between bull markets they are ignored or viewed as relics; most degenerate into petty traders or leave the scene entirely. But while prices are soaring and everyone seems to be making money, these speculators and tipsters are heroes and seers, praised for their abilities to foretell the future, and they attract cadres of acolytes. They appear to have the passkey to the future.

What little speculation existed in securities during the immediate postwar period was more akin to gambling than anything else. Marginal brokers who spent their evenings making blind telephone calls from purchased "sucker lists" considered themselves fortunate if able to sell a few hundred shares in a small gold mining company or, later on, new prospects in uranium or some other aspect of atomic energy. Low-priced stocks of marginal mines had lured speculators since the gold rush of the late 1840s, so this kind of dealing was not unusual. By 1948, however, it had overflowed into a new area.

That year several leading national magazines featured stories about the economic potential of Canada—"the colossus to our north" was the way one of them put it. "What Americans accomplished in the late nineteenth century, Canada will do in the second half of this century," said another. A third compared post–World War II Canada with the United States trans-Mississippi West in the aftermath of the Civil War—"an open area ripe for development." "Canada should have no trouble in achieving a growth rate higher than that of the United States," wrote a fourth, and so it went.

Many of these articles stressed Canada's mineral wealth, its oil fields and uranium deposits in particular. As a result, several low-priced petroleum stocks listed on the Toronto Stock Exchange

(TSE) boomed in 1948, and the uraniums soon followed suit. Some of the money that pushed these stocks upward came from Americans. By 1950 news of Canadian bonanzas appeared regularly in the nation's financial press. The American markets were doing well by then, but those of Canada fairly glowed with bullishness.

This rise continued with minor corrections for the next two years, and then, in early 1953, there occurred a buyers' panic at the TSE, when news of a major uranium find in the Athabasca region came to the floor. Other mineral strikes were reported in New Brunswick, followed by news that American steel companies were investing in Canadian ore fields. By March the Toronto market had attracted thousands of Americans, most of whom were interested in "penny stocks" that were touted by small advisory services as "sure to double" in a short period. In writing of this mood, C. Norman Stabler of the *New York Herald-Tribune* said, "Most of it [speculation] is based on sound consideration of the Dominion's unquestioned wealth in natural resources, but there is evidence that part of it stems from the gambling spirit usually associated with horse races." But a good deal of money was being made there. In one month, for example, New Larder Uranium went from 12.5¢ to $2.76, and similar moves were made by Gunnar Gold Mines, Chimo Gold Mines, and others. Compared to this, investment in AT&T or General Motors appeared rather tame. So the Canadian markets enjoyed a bonanza, made possible in part by the participation of American speculators. In March a TSE seat sold for $90,000. That month one at the N.Y.S.E. could be had for half that price, while membership at the Curb Exchange changed hands at $12,000.

For many years the Curb had listed Canadian stocks, and in fact members liked to boast that their exchange had more of an international flavor than any other market in the United States. Curb President Edward McCormick, a gregarious man who was as much a supersalesman as Keith Funston, went north seeking new listings. Why shouldn't American speculators be afforded the opportunity to buy and sell Canadian stocks in New York as well as in Toronto and Montreal, he asked? In 1951 the Curb had 75 Canadian listings. At the end of 1953 that market—now renamed the American Stock Exchange, or Amex for short—had 93, and McCormick was shuttling back and forth across the border seeking new listings.

As the 1954 bull market opened, some American speculators switched their interest from Canadian issues to low-priced American ones, and helping make this switch was newspaper and radio personality Walter Winchell. The most influential journalist in New York during the 1940s, Winchell's reach had declined badly in the next decade. At one time over 500 newspapers had carried his syndicated column; by 1953 it was appearing in fewer than 170. His once feared and respected radio show was slipping in the ratings, and he had trouble attracting sponsors, but Winchell retained a core of followers, and show business and political personalities still paid him court.

In 1954 Winchell started touting stocks on his radio program, probably to boost his ratings. After each broadcast some of his listeners would act on his advice, and the prices of these stocks would rise. He would take note of this the following week and make new recommendations. Additional buyers would appear, and the process would be repeated. This snowballed over time, so that Winchell's popularity among stock traders rose. Perhaps without meaning to do so, he served as a pied piper luring small-time speculators to the Street.

At first Winchell concentrated on familiar stocks that sold for low prices. He spoke highly of Eastern Air Lines, Bell Aircraft, 20th Century Fox, and Western Union, among others, and all rose after his recommendations—before drifting back to their old level. Then he shifted to less familiar issues. Winchell said that shares in Amurex Oil Development, a small producer, would soon advance— the company was about to report "the biggest oil strike in North American history." This stock had been selling at 14⅞; in one session it rose 5 points. Missouri Pacific, a railroad with little in the way of glamour, advanced 5½ points when Winchell told his listeners it would "make market news." Amurex never did find that oil, and the management of Missouri Pacific was genuinely puzzled about talk of anything newsworthy there. Undaunted, Winchell touted Webb & Knapp, American Bosch, Universal Consolidated, and similar marginal issues. All advanced smartly, only to fall back later on.

Critics charged Winchell with fabricating these stories, and they warned that anyone acting on his tips should be on guard that they were baseless. This was so, but still the speculators followed their leader. In January 1955, Winchell claimed that had an investor purchased a round lot of each of the 40 or so stocks he had touted the previous year, he would have had a paper profit of around a quarter of million dollars. This wasn't true either, but if anyone bothered to check it out, he was unable to get the story before the public.

A few weeks later Winchell spoke glowingly about Pantapec Oil, a little-known issue listed on the American Stock Exchange. There was a buyers' panic on the floor the following day, and talk of investigations and possible legislative action to curb speculation.

The activities of Walter Winchell, the Canadian boom, and increased interest in low-priced stocks—all were signs of a new speculative fever on Wall Street. But there was no evidence of high-powered manipulations, price riggings, or for that matter even the dawning of the kind of stock mania that had thrilled the district in the late 1920s. Both the Winchell and Canadian phenomena faded within a year, but speculation in low-priced issues continued and even accelerated. Speculator enthusiasm had been ignited and would continue strong for the next decade and a half, providing spice for the bull market. Still, the second stage was led by the glamour/growth contingent, which was comprised of well-established stocks with "clearly defined growth patterns." This was a good time to have owned IBM, National Cash Register, Corning Glass, Procter & Gamble, Reynolds Metals, and dozens of other stocks in this category.

The second stage is generally considered to have begun in September 1953 and ended in April 1956. In this two-and-a-half-year period, the Dow went from 255 to 521, more than doubling. But the glamour/growth stocks did even better—few of these were Dow stocks—while the speculative sector outperformed them all.

By mid-1956 there were signs that the economic recovery had run its course. *Forbes* thought "a mood of uncertainty" pervaded the financial district, while *Business Week* predicted that historians would call 1956 "The Year of the Slowdown." During the election campaign that year, President Eisenhower promised to keep inflation in check and try to balance the budget, while Democratic candidate Adlai Stevenson warned that administration policies were leading the nation into a new recession. Eisenhower won in November, and on Wall Street his victory was taken as a sign that the slowdown would continue.

In January, as the president pledged himself to spending cuts and a policy of fiscal conservatism, leading firms in such key industries as steel, copper, and rubber reported that demand for products was easing. *Moody's* predicted a "moderate sag in industrial production in the second half of the year, perhaps beginning before then." Several leading Keynesian economists, led by Paul Samuelson, called for vigorous countermeasures to prevent the decline. But there were no Keynesians in the White House. Instead, Eisenhower served notice that he would engage in a struggle against inflation and continue on even if this meant a slowdown in economic growth. Somewhat innocently, Treasury Secretary George Humphrey said, "I would deplore the day that we thought we couldn't even reduce expenditures of this terrific amount, and the terrific tax we are taking out of the country. If we don't over a long period of time, I will predict a depression that will curl your hair." The statement was reported in a distorted manner, and many believed Humphrey had flatly predicted an all-out economic collapse. Former President Herbert Hoover didn't help matters when he followed this up with a comment to the effect that "Mine has already been curled once, and I think I can detect the signs."

The stock market had behaved erratically throughout the second half of 1956. Now prices declined sharply, so that by the end of January, the Dow was below 480. Analysts talked of a resistance level at 460–65, but if there was one, it was broken in early February. In mid-month, the Index slipped to 455 before leveling off.

By then it had become clear that the nation was on the edge of the second Eisenhower recession. Yet there was no panic on Wall Street, not even strong selling pressure. Whereas some of the highly speculative stocks did fall sharply, the glamour/growth contingent suffered relatively small losses, while the Dow Industrials actually rose, going above 500 in May and remaining there for three months before sliding once again. In late September the Dow was under 460 again and apparently had entered a pattern of drift and gradual decline. But mutual fund sales remained high, and on several occasions large-scale fund purchases were credited with having prevented price collapses on the part of leading blue chips. No one was quite certain how long this would continue. If, as anticipated, bond yields rose significantly, the funds might be tempted to switch into debt instruments, and such a move might trigger a selling panic.

The Street was pondering this possibility when, on Friday, October 4, the Soviet Union launched its first space satellite. That weekend the story was featured on television and in the newspapers. For years Americans had simply assumed they were scientifically superior to the Russians; now it appeared the United States was laggard in at least one important aspect of technology. Some commentators found it difficult to believe the Soviets had done it all on their own. They supposed the "sputnik" had been perfected by captured German scientists or made possible by secrets stolen from the United States. All agreed that the satellite posed a threat to America in several areas, and that responses would be required.

Wall Street agreed, and its answer took the form of a major selloff on high volume. The Dow fell by more than 20 points the following week, with brokers blaming the decline on selling by Europeans and margin calls as well as fears that America was on its way to becoming a second-class power. Some analysts thought sputnik was only the catalyst for a new bear market—one would have developed anyway, given the recession—but that because of this dramatic turn of events, the slide would be precipitous. Sputnik, as *New York Times* financial writer Albert Kraus put it, "has cast a long shadow on the United States money market," and he saw a "testing period" ahead. If so, the market appeared to have failed, for the decline continued, with the Dow going below 420 on October 22. "The market has passed into the domain of the psychological, where sober analysis is at a discount," wrote the brokerage house newsletter of A. M. Kidder & Co., while Josephthal thought that Washington held "the key to a change in speculative psychology." (Whenever analysts talk of the importance of psychology, it is a good indication that they are confused and haven't much of an idea where prices are headed.)

The market rebounded on October 23, and then stocks traded in a narrow range for the rest of the year, as the Street's wise men tried to sort out information and foretell the future. Clearly sputnik had altered investor and speculator sentiment, and its reverberations were being felt in Washington and throughout the nation. The second stage was over, and what might follow wasn't evident yet.

The 1953–57 bull market had been based upon several factors, chief among which were the beliefs that the economy would continue to expand, that inflation could be held down, and that there would be no more limited, indecisive wars like the Korean conflict.

In this stage investors and the institutions had paid far more attention to the stocks of old, established companies than to those of the newer firms that had emerged in the postwar period. Also, investors seemed to prefer stocks of companies that produced consumer goods or at least familiar items such as television sets, office equipment, drugs, cosmetics, and cameras. Several novel, esoteric technologies had been developed in the past generation, and some of the young companies had exploited them successfully. Their products, many of which involved electronics in one way or another, were unfamiliar to most consumers, for they were sold primarily to the government or to capital goods manufacturers. Engineers and military officers knew of these companies; housewives did not.

The sputnik challenge focused attention on these companies and their stocks. Investors seemed to have concluded that the Soviet satellite somehow discredited consumerism and that a new period of sacrifice would be required if the Soviets were to be bested. Presidential aide Sherman Adams tried to play down sputnik, calling it an "outer-space basketball game," while Defense Secretary Charles Wilson had called it little more than a "nice technological trick." But across the country millions of Americans noted that Ford Motors had introduced its new automobile, the ill-fated Edsel, at around the same time the satellite was put into orbit. This country spent its time and energies in turning out such cars, while the Russians had been engaged in more important pursuits. Referring to the Edsel, Senate majority leader Lyndon Johnson took note of an administration promise to put an American satellite into space the following year. "Perhaps it will even have chrome trim," he said, "and automatic windshield wipers." What was needed, he said, was a major national effort in space combined with a military buildup.

The implication was that Americans would have to learn to consume less and spend more in public areas. Wall Street took this as meaning that there could be a new bull market, one led by the stocks of companies that sold weapons and electronic gear to the government, postwar technology stocks, many of which weren't known to the average investor.

The administration gave evidence that it was moving to meet this new challenge. In his January budget message, Eisenhower asked for a supplement of $965 million for defense spending for the second half of the 1957/58 fiscal year. Pressures had developed for higher educational expenditures on the theory that they were needed to bring American schools up to the Soviet level; Eisenhower requested $100 million toward this end. The president wanted additional funds for international relations, and there would be a boost in federal spending for space research and technology.

Eisenhower got all he had asked for, and in addition Congress appropriated larger-than-anticipated sums for housing and highways. Meanwhile the Federal Reserve increased the money supply and lowered the discount rate. Both actions indicated to Wall Streeters that the Fed believed economic expansion was in order and would do all in its power to end the recession. The financial district was further cheered by record offerings by the Treasury, which contributed to depressing the bond market and making fixed income securities less attractive. All this pointed to higher levels for the stock market.

Meanwhile the electronics and defense-oriented stocks staged a rally of their own, as fund managers and investors started to add their shares to portfolios. Particularly popular were Douglas Aircraft, General Dynamics, and United Aircraft. E. F. Hutton put together a "missile stock index" and observed that it had outperformed the Dow by a wide margin in late 1957. The financial press, which earlier had featured stories on such stocks as Eastman Kodak, Sears Roebuck, and Motorola, now turned its attention to Aerojet General, Reaction Motors, and Marquardt. Raytheon soared in late 1957, the result of new defense contracts. In February *Moody's* noted that Sprague Electric and Texas Instruments had received major research and development contracts from the Defense Department, and both stocks had outperformed the market. Reynolds & Co. said that such developments were changing the focus of Wall Street. In the mid-1950s, investors were interested in stocks of companies that dealt primarily with the civilian market. The new stars were stocks of firms seeking government contracts. The award of a major contract might mean billions of dollars in sales over many years, and this was far less chancy than hoping to sell television sets to fickle consumers.

Stock prices remained firm in the first quarter of 1958, when the Dow Industrials even managed to post a gain of 12 points. This was considered quite remarkable, since a majority of analysts were gloomy and most economic indicators continued to point downward. By March it had become clear that hopes for a bright future outweighed fears for the immediate present in the minds of a large number of investors. Then, too, government spending and Federal Reserve policies were counted upon to slow the decline. In late April, the National Bureau of Economic Research announced that several key lead indicators were pointing upward. The Dow Industrials added another 9 points that month, and the Rail and Utility indices did even better. This showing was cheering, given not only the bearish forecasts but also a steady stream of disappointing earnings and dividend reports.

Business Week reported that "many Street conservatives" thought the advance "illogical." The projections in May and June weren't good, and there were additional dividend cuts. In late May Joseph Granville of E. F. Hutton said the Dow would fall to 410 in June, and Anthony Gaubis thought the Index would decline to 390 "plus or minus 2% later in the year." The following month *Forbes* reported that a large majority of analysts "remain on the bear side of the market." The *Wall Street Journal* noted that many on the Street were warning of a major collapse, for the rise was senseless and prices were badly inflated. But the Dow crossed the 470 level on June 12 and was at 480 on July 2.

The next stage in the bull market had begun, unheralded and unnoticed. Not until mid-July did sentiment start to shift to the bull side, and even then the reasons behind the advance were not understood. The Wiesenburger investment service came over at this time but also quoted "an astute Scottish investment trust manager" to the effect that "your New York market reminds us of the old Indian rope trick—it stays up with no visible means of support." Other Wall Street veterans said as much, and they watched with amazement as the Dow crossed over the 490 mark on July 21 and five days later was above 500. A minor correction followed, but that September the Index crossed over 530, as scores of experts warned that the speculative bubble soon would burst.

These people had been aware of speculation earlier in the decade, but this was of the kind that featured Winchell's tips and penny stocks on the Canadian exchanges, as well as a handful of issues listed at the Amex. Now, however, the fever had struck the N.Y.S.E. stocks. Even such ailing railroads as the New York Central, the Pennsylvania, and the Erie-Lackawanna shot up by close to 100 percent in 1958. Not only did it seem that investors and speculators were ignoring the old rules regarding price/earnings ratios and yields, but they were buying shares in firms with dubious prospects. Underwood, which had lost almost $11 a share in 1956 and over $2 the following year, had sold for 12 in early 1958; by December the stock was over 18 on talk that Olivetti, which had purchased an interest in the firm, might manage to turn it around.

How long could this advance continue? In mid-November the Dow went over 560, after which stocks fell back and regrouped for a year-end rally. What lay ahead? asked the analysts, and as though to answer their own question, most talked of the need for a correction. "Many of today's stocks are so high that they can't possibly be discounting any expected near-term improvement in earnings," said the writer of one newsletter. "Instead, buyers must be primarily discounting earnings they expect some time in the 'fabulous mid-1960s.' "

Such indeed was the case—this was a market of hope and dreams, not reality, and the phenomenon escaped most analysts. Such individuals tend to view the market as a conglomeration of buy and sell impulses, each separate from the others, and all translated into trades by brokers, specialists, and other Wall Street figures. There are no forests, they say, but only trees and clusters of trees. Technicians attempt to uncover patterns in stock trading, while fundamentalists assume that good or bad news sooner or later will be reflected in the way prices behave. Almost all act on the assumption that the market somehow performs automatically, or at least mechanically, and that future actions may be anticipated or predicted by recourse to their theories and data.

Those who work at the exchanges and the over-the-counter (OTC) houses take cognizance of these ideologies, but along with sensitive investors and speculators they understand that on occasion the market takes on a life of its own; it seems to become animated and fairly pleads for excuses either to rise or fall, grasping at the slightest morsel of good or bad news and then going on to make major moves in one direction or the other. Analysts were seeking reasons for a decline in 1958. Prices had risen too much and too rapidly, and there was a generalized feeling of exhaustion in the district. On several occasions during the year, they had predicted that the long-awaited correction had at last begun and each time were wrong. But the market wanted to go up, and so confounded the brokers and analysts. These people would send out bearish advisories, and their readers would buy stocks anyway. The experts went one way, the public the other, and as usually is the case on such occasions, the public was right. After all, they made the purchases.

Major rallies seek symbols just as armies must have banners, and the symbol of the great 1958 rally that ushered in the third stage of the bull market was the dividend action at American Telephone & Telegraph. Throughout the depression the company had retained its $9 payout, even though it had not been earned in some years, and by 1958 it had taken on the appearance of permanence. AT&T was a fine holding, especially for those who sought steady income with little excitement. More than a million Americans owned the stock, and most belonged to that contingent who remembered the Great Crash and the depression. In time all might be swept away, they seemed to be saying, but AT&T will hold firm, its dividend intact. Speculators disdained the issue; prudent middle-class conservatives swore by it. Clearly this was not a growth stock. Other issues might participate in the 1958 boom, but AT&T would go its own way.

The stock had traded within a narrow range ever since the end of World War II—around 150 on the downside and 185 at its top—with moves caused more by changes in the interest rates than by corporate developments. But the stock was stirring in late 1958, when almost all industry groups joined in the celebration. Telephone went over 200 at that time, with analysts saying that this was a case of the incoming tide causing all of the boats to rise. But a few wrote of a rumor that AT&T was about to increase its dividend. So it did. In early December the company's directors not only raised the payout to $9.90 but announced a three-for-one split.

At the time the stock was trading at 202. A flood of orders hit the N.Y.S.E. floor, and so dealings in the stock were suspended. After several hours Telephone opened at 225, and now the entire list joined in yet another unanticipated and exhilarating rally. Brokers now said that even Telephone had become a growth issue. Some analysts spoke of the electronics capabilities of Bell Laboratories and Western Electric, and others noted that many old-line firms might undergo rejuvenations—at least insofar as their stocks were concerned. More important than any of this, however, was the fact that those many AT&T stockholders had their first important taste of capital gains that result from glamour. Hundreds of thousands of them became converts to the new dispensation, and they ventured into the arena, purchasing shares in stocks they would have considered far too speculative for people like themselves.

N.Y.S.E. *Most Active Stocks, 1958*

STOCK	CLOSE	NET CHANGE	DIVIDEND	EARNINGS PER SHARE
American Motors	39⅜	+31⅜	nil	4.50
Studebaker Packard	14¼	+11¾	nil	(2.08)
General Motors	49½	+16	2.00	2.22
Royal Dutch	47⅞	+ 9⅛	1.32	4.11
Bethlehem Steel	53⅜	+16	2.40	2.91
Standard Oil (N.J.)	57⅝	+ 7¾	2.25	2.62
U.S. Steel	96¼	+44⅞	3.00	5.13
Avco Mfg.	11⅝	+ 6	0.40	1.02
Lorillard	79¼	+46½	2.20	4.20
Aluminium Ltd.	33	+ 4⅜	0.75	0.74

SOURCE: *New York Times*, January 12, 1959, p.49.

With the AT&T dividend action, one of the last bastions for those who remembered 1929 and feared a repetition of the collapse fell. Speculators now purchased AT&T, and old-time owners of that stock became speculators.

The Dow crossed into the 570s on December 18 and ended the year at 584, an all-time record. The Index had risen 148 points in 1958, another record. During the heated sessions in October, more than 118 million shares had been traded, the best showing for one month since 1933. Annual volume came to 747 million shares, and this was a post-1930 record.

It had been a very good year.

"To some Wall Street veterans," wrote *Business Week* in its year-end issue, "the cult of equities has some ugly parallels to the New Era of the late 1920s. They are worried by the fact that stock yields have dipped below the yields available on high-grade bonds. And they feel that the abandonment of historical price-earnings ratios means the future is being discounted too far. If the economy does not have an inflationary binge, they warn, many of today's

Three

THE FURTHBURNER
SYNDROME

I
N 1959 the N.Y.S.E. released a report on its third shareholder
census. This study revealed that some 12.5 million Americans
owned common stocks, or 6 million more than in 1952, when
the second stage of the bull market was about to begin. The median
age of the shareholder had increased by one year; now he or she was
49.

These figures had important implications. Allowing for deaths
and related factors, it would appear that a clear majority of shareholders had undergone their first investment experience during the
second stage. They hadn't been at the brokerages before, during, or
immediately after World War II; nor had they purchased stocks during the first stage of the advance from 1949 to 1953. A 49-year-old of
1959 would have been 19 in October 1929, the time of the Great
Crash. His family and friends might have suffered losses, but
chances were his own traumas would have been minor.

Every weekday additional young people made their first stock
purchases, while older investors left the scene for one reason or
another. If time didn't heal wounds caused by panics and depressions, it did serve to remove those investors with severe scars. Increasingly the "typical" investor was becoming a person with no
direct relationship to the pains inflicted by major corrections. The
new investors and speculators appeared bold when compared with
those of the late 1940s and early 1950s. Some analysts thought they
were of a new breed, "the confident American" who had emerged
from the war. Others—usually the older men—said they acted as
they did because of inexperience. An Exchange survey showed that

two out of every five investors could not define the term "common stock," while a quarter of the group thought the most important reason for purchasing shares was the "opportunity for quick profit." Each wary veteran who had withdrawn from the market was being replaced by two unsuspecting young people looking for action. Or at least so it seemed.

Wall Streeters debated the nature of the new investors and concluded they bore more than a surface resemblance to the amateur speculators of the 1920s.

Whatever the reasons for and the nature of the newcomers, the calendar and the market itself combined to strengthen the bull contingent. Ever higher levels truly seemed possible; the newcomers appeared to believe that pauses and corrections were unnecessary—that what went up need not come down. The decline of 1953 had been followed by a steady upward climb that lasted two-and-a-half years; the sharp break of late 1957 had been succeeded by the phenomenal move of 1958 and early 1959. Meanwhile the passage of time continued to remove skeptics from the scene, and warnings of a possible crash started to sound alarmist and even a trifle addle-pated.

The market's rise in the face of poor economic news had caught most analysts by surprise. These people had anticipated price movements in terms of values acquired during the first and second stages of the advance, which is to say they tended to evaluate earnings and dividends, cash flows and balance sheets and judged a firm's merits by its positions within familiar, established industries. Most analysts knew of the young companies whose shares were listed at the Amex or traded on the OTC market, and a few of them recommended purchases to their more adventuresome clients. They understood that novel technologies and products were being developed at these companies, especially at firms headed by scientist-businessmen. Almost to a person, however, they believed these would be fully exploited by the existing giants. A glance at a list of the top hundred firms in America in terms of sales or assets indicated that big business was dominated by aged firms; entry to the club might come by means of a major war or a new round of major innovation, and few anticipated either would be seen in the near future.

On learning that Polaroid had developed instant photography, for example, a majority of analysts thought it only a matter of time before Eastman Kodak came out with a competitive product that would steal the play from the newcomer. One analyst described Polaroid as "an interesting toy company, but no more than that," while another wrote that its new camera was "bulky, overpriced, unattractive, and certainly nothing that should worry the men at Kodak." Polaroid had sales of $34.5 million in 1957 and Eastman Kodak, $798 million. How could the result of any contest between these two be in doubt?

Syntex was incorporated that year, and the Street's drug analysts had read of its researches into birth control drugs. The betting was that if and when a pill to control pregnancy appeared, it would emerge from Merck, Upjohn, Pfizer, or another familiar, old-line firm.

Control Data was a young company still trying to develop a major product; its sales were less than $2 million. The district knew about transistors, which had been developed at Bell Telephone Laboratories in 1948. Nine years later the two leading firms in the field were Texas Instruments (TI), with $67 million in sales, and Transitron, with $16 million; the former company had been a minor factor in petroleum exploration before entering the electronics field, while Transitron, which had manufacturing facilities in shabby former shoe factories on the outskirts of Boston was in shaky financial condition. Haloid Xerox had sales of less than $26 million in 1957 and, like Polaroid, was looked upon by some of the Street's analysts as a producer of interesting toys.

Could any of these companies survive? IBM posted sales of more than $1 billion in 1957. Rumor had it that the company was developing a dry copier than would undercut the Xerox models. It was a leader in computers, the only firm to turn a profit on them. Other computer manufacturers were such old-line business machine companies as Burroughs, National Cash Register, and Sperry Rand, and there was talk that General Electric, RCA, Bendix, Philco, and a handful of other major firms would present their models sometime in the next few years. How could Control Data survive in this kind of environment? TI's leading customer was IBM, which was expected to enter the field on its own. Not only would this eliminate a large portion of the young company's business, but IBM might become a direct competitor. Furthermore, GE, RCA, Raytheon, and Sylvania all were entering the business or already had started manufacturing the small electronic devices. In time their superior reputations, marketing forces, and financial strength would dictate a victory over TI, Transitron, and other small firms, which either would disband or sell out to one or another of the leaders.

A relative handful of the new firms managed to survive, and several went on to become major corporations. In 1957 and 1958 the selection of winners involved a good deal of guesswork and no little faith. For example, TI became a giant firm, Syntex prospered, though not to the point where it became a dominant force in the drug industry, and Transitron went broke. The stocks of these and other new companies dealing in what to the 1950s seemed exotica provided the market with the kind of glamour it hadn't known since the 1920s. These issues and those of second-stage companies able to enter the new technology areas provided part of the foundation for the third stage of the bull market.

At first Litton Industries seemed another one of these new electronics companies, but it was more than that. The firm had been founded in 1953, and four years later it posted sales of $28.1 million. That year *Moody's* called it "a relatively young, but spectacularly growing factor in the electronics field." In early 1959, *Financial World* wrote this about its business:

Manufactures electronic equipment and components and office machines, notably radar equipment, aircraft and missile guidance, and control systems, communication and navigation equipment, power tubes, computers, transformers, delay lines, precision potentiometers, and microwave components. Has a portable computer of typewriter size. Acquired Airtron, Inc. (electronic components) in 1958.

The developing mania for new electronics issues helped make Litton a glamour stock, but even more important a factor was an aspect of the firm not mentioned in *Moody's* or *Financial World*. Litton did acquire Airtron in 1958, and in previous years it had added West Coast Electronics, Automatic Sereograph, Ahrent Instruments, and other small entities, most of which were involved in new technologies. Other mergers would follow, and while most were for electronics or electronics-related companies, others were not. Business writers, government lawyers, and academic scholars already had provided a name for firms engaged in this kind of growth: the rapidly expanding companies were known as conglomerates.

The conglomerates eluded simple definition, and in fact many analysts weren't happy with the word; they substituted terms like "multi-industry," "congeneric," and "free-form," among others. Wall Streeters knew a conglomerate when they saw one but could not say how they differed specifically from other firms that possessed some of their attributes. For example, conglomerates were in a variety of nonrelated businesses at the same time, but so were older firms like General Electric and American Home Products, and these were not considered members of that group. Leaders of conglomerates talked about their new management techniques, but most could be traced back to those utilized by railroaders in the late nineteenth century. Conglomerates came into being by means of acquisitions—and that is how William C. Durant put together General Motors, which was not considered a conglomerate but which in addition to autos manufactured refrigerators and locomotives.

Like the electronics industry, the conglomerate movement was a product of postwar America. Some believe it originated with Royal Little, who turned a drab, unpromising textile firm into Textron, a company that engaged in a wide variety of enterprises. Little would buy out companies with product or financial difficulties and then try to invigorate them. Writing in 1956, when conglomerates were still somewhat novel, he said: "It has been our policy to buy only well-managed businesses and to give the old management complete autonomy except for financial control. Many of these former owners feel that under our plan they can have their cake and eat it too; in many cases they can convert ordinary income into capital gains and still have the fun of running their own businesses."

The tax code played a role in the creation of Textron, and what was termed "full utilization" of laws, together with "creative accounting," would be important in the development of other conglomerates. Tex Thornton and Roy Ash, who put together Litton, used ballyhoo, bookkeeping devices, and inflated stock to take over companies with little in the way of reputation and low price/earnings ratios. The exchange of Litton paper for the assets and earnings of small companies usually would result in higher per-share earnings for the mother firm. The stock would rise again, and Thornton and Ash would repeat the process.

Their successes encouraged others to try their hand at conglomerate building, and several Litton vice-presidents (called "Lidos") went off on their own to spread the gospel to other companies that they came to head. Later on, a third wave of conglomerate building would be typified by Charles Bluhdorn of Gulf + Western, James Ling of Ling-Temco-Vought, and Harold Geneen of International Telephone & Telegraph. Where Ash and Thornton usually sought acquisitions from among the ranks of small and medium-sized firms, Bluhdorn, Geneen, and Ling gobbled up companies with several hundreds of millions of dollars in revenues and assets—each man would have one year in the 1960s during which he absorbed firms with more than a billion dollars in sales—and did so with financial finesse that astounded and confused many analysts while rewarding investors.

Most of these conglomerates acquired subsidiaries in the electronics fields, and so they combined the two glamour hallmarks of the late 1950s and early 1960s, one in products, the other in corporate form. Additionally, these firms went after government contracts, for this was the last part of the triad upon which the third stage of the bull market rested.

President Eisenhower had tried to keep defense and related spending down after the Korean War. This part of the budget had accounted for $50.4 billion in 1953 and $44.4 billion in 1958. In this period expenditures for space went from $79 million to $89 million, a minute part of the total budget. Five years later, on the eve of the Vietnam War in 1963, defense spending stood at $52.2 billion and space programs took another $2.6 billion. By 1968, at the height of the war, defense took $80.5 billion and space, $4.7 billion.

An increasing share of these budgets went for research and development and the procurement of complex electronic gear, much of which was produced by subsidiaries of conglomerates and other large firms whose sales and earnings advanced smartly in this period. These were able to apply the expertise obtained in the military market to the production of consumer goods, and so they had a double return on their investments.

In his Farewell Address, Eisenhower would warn the nation against the power of the "military-industrial complex." Many investors had an inkling of this power several years earlier, for its arrival helped boost stocks to new highs in 1958.

That Wall Street's wise men failed to comprehend the nature of these new forces should not be surprising. Nor did this lapse demean their abilities. For one thing, the shape of these emerging market forces remained somewhat nebulous in the late 1950s. At the time electronics seemed a minor appendage of the familiar electrical supply industry; the conglomerate mania was in its infancy; no one knew just how far the government would go in its procurement program. Certainly no analyst who hoped to be taken seriously would say that sometime in the next few years stocks in these fields would dominate trading.

In 1959 mutual funds made heavy commitments to Ford and IBM. General Telephone & Electronics became a favorite, as did North American Aviation. Few funds owned Polaroid, Texas Instruments, Litton, and other such stocks. The drift of Wall Street thinking could be seen in the way two highly promoted new mutual funds of late 1958 made their initial investments. Lazard Fund, out of the respected investment house of Lazard Frères, made a major commitment to AT&T just prior to the dividend hike and stock split. Lehman Brothers' new fund, One William Street, favored IBM but put most of its assets into government bonds and other paper and kept them there for almost a full quarter before investing heavily in a wide variety of old-line blue chips that had performed so well during the first and second stages of the bull market. Each fund was billed as being "aggressive," but neither did more than dabble lightly in the new-technology issues or the conglomerates. The same situation prevailed at the investment clubs being organized throughout the nation in the late 1950s. These groups brought together novices and other small investors who pooled knowledge and money and then entered the market. The National Association of Investment Clubs reported that the most popular holdings were Sperry Rand, Monsanto, General Dynamics, Olin Mathieson, and General Motors. Of these only General Dynamics might be considered one of the new glamours, but even here the firm did have pre–World War II components, and it hardly was a small firm—GD posted sales of $1.5 billion in 1958.

The economic recovery continued into 1959, and so did the bull market. In February the Consumer Price Index rose at an annualized rate of 1.5 percent and was declining. Unemployment had fallen to 5.9 percent, another notch in the continuing improvement from the 7.5 percent rate of mid-1958. "Steady as she goes would be the best course for the Administration and the Federal Reserve to follow" was the advice of the *New York Herald-Tribune*, while *Time* complimented the country on having achieved strong growth and steady prices simultaneously. On Wall Street bond traders were convinced that money rates would remain about where they had been for the past several months, ever since the Fed had increased the discount rate to 2½ percent in November 1958.

The Dow's move over 600 in late February seemed to trigger some kind of mechanism at the central bank. On March 6, after the market closed with the Index just over 609, the Fed increased the discount rate to 3 percent. Yet prices continued to advance; the Dow went over 618 during interday trading on the 18th, on expanding volume. "Completely uncalled for" was the verdict of the *New York Times* in writing of the central bank's action, and the *Wall Street Journal* called the move "unnecessary." *Business Week* noted that the "nation's productive capacity is still not fully utilized. Unemployment is still high. Demand for credit is slack. According to many economists, the threat of inflation has been overdramatized." Why, then, had the central bank taken this move? "In making this decision, we strongly suspect, the Fed has been influenced too much by what has been going on in the stock market and not enough by what has been going on in business as a whole." Perhaps there was some justification in this, however. "It is true that the stock market's behavior in the past month or so raises the question of whether Wall Street has cut loose from sanity."

Clearly a speculative mania that had begun in late 1958 provided a glow for the stock market in early 1959. The district was learning a new vocabulary in order to keep up with some of the new-technology stocks that were on the rise; analysts who a year earlier had been engrossed with point-and-figure charts now spoke meaningfully of klystron tubes and micro-circuits. Similarly, fundamentalists who for years had concentrated on the N.Y.S.E. issues now turned their attention to stocks of new, small firms, most of which were traded over-the-counter or at the Amex.

In mid-1958 trading at the Amex had been brisk but orderly, with volume less than a million shares most of the time, and occasionally dropping below the half million mark. That summer an Amex seat changed hands at $18,000, the lowest price in almost three years. Then the bull market revived at the N.Y.S.E., and by late autumn the action had spread to the junior exchange. In December, 2-million-share days were commonplace, and these brought the daily average for 1958 to 953,000, a new high. Meanwhile the price of an Amex seat skyrocketed, with one going for $42,000 in December.

By March 1959, 3-million-share days were regular occurrences, and President McCormick admitted that his clearing house had fallen behind in its work; the Amex had to call upon the N.Y.S.E. for assistance in settling trades. "It's reaching crisis proportions," complained one harried broker. "Some trades are taking two weeks to clear." This heavy trading resulted in the creation of new committees at both exchanges to study the paperwork problem and come up with new ways to deal with it.

Meanwhile such new glamour issues as General Transistor, Kaweki Chemical, Belock Instruments, and Cenco Instruments led the way to new price and volume levels. Almost all of these small firms had little in the way of sales or earnings, but this didn't seem to bother investors, who rushed into them so as to be on the ground floor of "the next IBM." The floor contingent at the Amex was weary but were making more money than seemed possible only a year earlier. Membership at the exchange was profitable; a seat sold or $52,000 in March.

Trading was even more hectic at the OTC market, where several glamour stocks doubled and redoubled in a matter of months. Collins Radio, Cutter Laboratories, Gyrodyne, Haloid Xerox, Ling Electronics, were star performers. Tracerlab tripled in price in less than a month. Aerovox, Hewlett-Packard, and Varian Associates had major moves, though none of them had earned a cent. By spring 1959, investors started lining up to buy shares of newly formed companies involved in their first offerings. FXR, a small firm in the microwave industry, went public in late March at $12 a share and two months later sold for $22. Loral Electronics, a manufacturer of military equipment, made its first stock offering in early May at $12, and within a week the price was up to $20. Coil Winders, a minor factor in the electronics industry with assets of $133,000, was sold to the public at $2 a share, and the following day the stock was at 4¼—giving the total offering a market value of $1.8 million.

Advances such as this helped create and reinforce a pattern of investment and speculation. Individuals who first had entered the market in the early and middle 1950s with purchases of old-line industrials such as General Motors, U.S. Steel, and Standard Oil of

New Jersey would have done fairly well, but their stocks had been outperformed by established companies in glamour technologies—IBM, RCA, and GE, for example. They switched into these issues later on and, in mid-1958, had gone into newer stocks listed at the Amex—Cenco, Belock, and Kaweki, among others—whose performances were even better. From there they went into QTC glamours, and then on to the new issues in early 1959.

"Electronics is the magic word in today's bull market for stocks," wrote *Business Week* in the spring of 1959, as those stocks soared wildly. That this was so appeared obvious, but a case could be made that the magic word was not electronics, but "performance," at least insofar as investors were concerned. At each turn of the wheel, the investor cared less about dividend records and earnings, profit margins, assets and liabilities, and even the basic business of the firm.

People who owned Ford or General Motors thought about such things. Some might see a factory owned by "their company," all lived near dealers, and of course they saw the cars on the roads. These were tangible companies, whose stocks paid dividends every three months and had billions of dollars in assets. A few years later this same person might have sold his Ford or GM stock in order to purchase shares in FXR, not knowing its business or even what the initials stood for. All that mattered was performance. And FXR was a good performer. The investor was pleased, but not nearly as much as he might have been had he purchased shares at the initial offering. So he would sell FXR and use his money to get in on the ground floor when the next new offering was made.

On Wall Street in 1959 this was known as investing on the "other-idiot principle." One would buy a stock not because it was a sound company with good prospects, earnings, and dividends, but because some other idiot would buy it from you at a higher price tomorrow. After a while the new investors came to realize that they were some other idiot's other idiot, but this did not trouble them. Everyone seemed to be making money, and there was a festive mood at the market for young, untried companies.

No one profited from this mania more than did those individuals who underwrote the new issues. Few of them were handled by the large, old, familiar houses like Merrill Lynch or Bache or Reynolds. Rather, they were marketed by small, new firms, that concentrated on this end of the business.

Myron A. Lomasney & Co. was a typical new-issues underwriting establishment. In early 1959 Lomasney's office consisted of him and two employees; a year and a half later the office had 29 employees and Lomasney was a multi-millionaire—on paper, at least. All of this was accomplished by new issues. It was a simple matter. For example, Lomasney underwrote a 100,000-share issue for BBM Photocopy at $3 a share. As part of his contract, he was granted 20,000 warrants, each to buy one share of stock for the price of a penny apiece. Lomasney & Co. had no trouble selling out the issue, and for the effort received a commission, and this meant that BBM received approximately $250,000 in cash for its stock, which proved to be a "hot issue." The operations of the other-idiot principle took over, and BBM eventually went to $40, which gave the warrants a market value of $800,000. Thus, Lomasney received around $850,000 on paper for his work, while BBM's treasury was richer by a fraction of that amount. And in the process, Lomasney's fortunate customers had huge profits.

Lomasney repeated the operation many times during the next two years, and while none of his other offerings performed as well as had BBM, almost all shot up immediately on coming to market. For example, in May 1960 Lomasney underwrote Aero Industries at $3.30, and in four months the stock had doubled. Lomasney received his usual fee plus 20,000 warrants to buy the stock at a few pennies a share. This deal netted the company over $100,000, and of course the clients once again did much better for themselves.

By this time Lomasney & Co. was known as "the deal-of-the-month club," and would-be clients were lining up at the door, hoping to be accepted for the next underwriting. The new-issues underwriters would accept them on certain spoken and unspoken conditions. For example, the client understood that he or she would not sell until "the word" was given. Also, the client agreed to take shares in the next new issue out of the firm, often without knowing what it would be. Thus, the underwriter knew in advance that the entire issue would be sold and that his buyers would hold on until they were told they might dispose of their shares. In practice, this meant that the underwriter might offer, say, 100,000 shares of stock in a small company at $3, and the price would be reported in the newspapers. He controlled the supply and also could help create a demand. Orders to purchase a few thousand shares might cause the price to go to $4 or so in a thin market. This advance would lure "other idiots" to the stock, which then would rise to above $5. At this point the original purchasers would start to sell, placing the proceeds in the next new issue, after which the process would be repeated.

Lomasney by no means was the only operator in this part of the industry, the members of which knew one another and engaged in a mild form of friendly competition—mild because there was no shortage of small firms needing capital and there was certainly an oversupply of willing clients. S. D. Fuller & Co., one of the largest in the field, was headed by Stephen Fuller, who had gone to college with Myron Lomasney. Donald Marron of Marron, Sloss & Co., who was only 27 years old in 1959, spoke openly of his ambition to create an underwriting establishment capable of working with the largest houses on the Street. Michael Kletz, the head of his own firm, ran a small operation—"just me and 11 girls"—and challenged Lomasney in the number of underwritings. Each of these men had devoted followers. Speculators who were able to get on the new-issues lists at several houses and who plunged into the shares in 1958 and 1959 often became millionaires. Their stories and those of the new-issues underwriters were reported in newspapers and magazines. Each person who made a killing in the new-issues market seemed to have scores of relatives and friends eager to press their money on underwriters, who in this period appeared to have a patent on a miraculous money machine.

This approach to speculation troubled some old-timers, who saw in it another parallel to what had transpired in the late 1920s, prior to the crash. They were only partially correct. The atmosphere on Wall Street and in the brokerages at the close of the 1950s did resemble that of 30 years earlier, but the approaches to, vehicles for, and results of the speculation were quite different.

Higher stock prices and the new-issues mania meant that untried companies had a relatively easy time of it when they needed additional capital. That some of these firms were boondoggles certainly was the case, and for every outright fraud there were scores of other firms that lacked the patents and techniques, management, market, and good fortune required for success. Eventually most of the new companies that sold shares to the public in the late 1950s and early 1960s either went out of business or were absorbed by larger firms. Only a handful survived as independent entities. As has been indicated, some of these went on to become major corporations and leaders in their fields, making contributions of products and processes that were of major importance. Thus, the new-issues market of this period performed an economic function apart from that of redistributing wealth from one speculator group to another.

There had been a new-issue market toward the end of the 1920s, and some new firms organized in this period had been able to sell shares to the public. For the most part, however, speculative interest in this period was centered on holding companies, most of which were highly leveraged—distant relatives of the mutual funds of the 1950s. These firms had been organized to purchase previously issued shares and bonds of other companies, not to turn out products or services other than those relating to underwriting. The 1920s counterpart of the new-issues merchandiser of the late 1950s was the bond salesman, who attempted to talk investors and speculators into purchasing debt instruments of many companies and government units, and the large majority of the former paper was for established firms. In that period it was customary for the founder-owners of new companies to retain most of their shares until the enterprise was on firm ground, and only then go to the market to sell stocks that offered some safety and usually a dividend. In contrast, the entrepreneurs of the 1950s often attempted to sell shares even before their business went into operation.

If the new-issues markets of the 1920s and 1950s differed from one another in several important respects, the manipulators bred by these and other bull markets bore greater resemblances. In the 1920s the key speculative figure had been the pool manager—the individual who organized a temporary or permanent group whose money was used to push up or pull down the price of a well-known issue. Although there were some surface resemblances between them and men like Lomasney and Fuller, the differences were far more important. The underwriters of the late 1950s were small fry, operating in a glamorous but peripheral part of the market. In the first half of 1960, Fuller & Co. managed underwritings of $5.5 million; in the same period First Boston, the leader in the field, handled deals totaling $738 million. Also, Fuller, Kletz, and others of their breed were interested in the aftermarket only insofar as it could be used to promote their major business, that of underwriting.

In contrast, the great plungers of the 1920s had made their

killings by manipulating the stocks of several well-known firms, Radio Corporation being a particular favorite. News that one of them was behind a stock or had engaged in a duel over its price would draw in hundreds of amateurs and lesser fry, who purchased and sold shares as though placing wagers on one side or another. Such a contest would have winners and losers, of course, but no product other than brokers' commissions would result from their efforts. The underwriters of the late 1950s and early 1960s were providing funds for small businesses even while enriching themselves and their clients. The pool managers of the 1920s, in contrast, operated as though the exchanges were racetracks or gaming rooms. Still, they did make the big time; when they entered the market all eyes were upon them. They held center stage.

A somewhat closer counterpart to the economically sterile pool managers of the 1920s appeared on Wall Street during the first stage of the bull market, and at that time their impacts were felt by only a small number of speculators. In time their circles of followers expanded, but they remained second-class members of the investment community. These men manipulated minor companies and their securities and stayed away from the big stocks for several reasons. For one thing, much of their work was illegal. Also, the big stocks were far more heavily capitalized in the late 1950s than they had been during the 1920s, and in addition margin requirements were higher and call money was more difficult to obtain. In the 1920s, Arthur Cutten had been able to depress General Electric by using a pool of around $1.5 million. At the time that he was engaged in pushing RCA to record highs Jesse Livermore had no more than a million dollars in capital, and much of that was in the form of pledges, not actual cash in hand. That kind of money in the late 1950s and early 1960s would have made almost no impact upon such leading issues at the N.Y.S.E. Finally, the kinds of people who in the 1920s became pool managers found they could make far more money in the late 1950s and early 1960s by entering other aspects of the indstry, such as new-issues underwriting, brokerage, and fund management and sales.

Walter Tellier was fairly typical of these new manipulators. His firm, Tellier & Co., underwrote dozens of stock issues, usually for companies organized primarily to sell shares to foolish plungers. There were television set manufacturers with no products or even plans for them, antenna producers consisting of two executives and one secretary, and most important, uranium mines that turned out to be abandoned copper, lead, or silver operations. Tellier & Co. employed hard-sell brokers, some of whom were recycled used-car salesmen. Tellier provided them with telephones and sucker lists, and they set to work unloading the shares on the public. These "boiler rooms" were widely imitated; by the late 1950s every major city had several of them. As for Tellier himself, he was convicted of violating the fraud section of the Securities Act in 1957 and was given a jail sentence and a fine.

Lowell Birrell, another manipulator, had formed his first Wall Street firm in 1935 and for a while specialized in reorganizing depression-struck corporations and then offering new shares to the public. The market for such issues was small in the late 1930s, but Birrell managed to earn a living while learning a craft. After the war, he bought out, reorganized, and then sold several firms, among them United Dye & Chemical, a N.Y.S.E.-listed company. In 1954 he took hold of Swan-Finch Oil, a small operation whose shares were traded at the Amex. Birrell sold additional shares to the public and used the money to purchase several oil and gas companies, a grain storage warehouuse, and several other properties, all the while touting the stock to potential buyers. In 1956 he used unregistered Swan-Finch shares to purchase Doeskin Products and then neglected to turn over the shares to the new owners. Thus, Birrell committed embezzlement and fraud simultaneously. Now he entered into a collaboration with Jerry Re, who was the Swan-Finch specialist at the Amex, and several other figures to manipulate the stock's price and volume and to pocket large profits. The Amex decided to investigate the situation in 1956 but did nothing initially to halt the operation. Then the Securities and Exchange Commission (SEC) looked into the matter, and it too moved slowly. Meanwhile Birrell, Re, and their collaborators manipulated other Amex stocks, all of which rose and fell according to their wishes.

Arthur Cutten at one time had been the master of RCA and Chrysler stocks; Jerry Re and Lowell Birrell considered Swan-Finch the keystone for their operation. In itself this is the best comparison of the manipulations of the 1920s and the 1950s.

In late 1959 the Amex exonerated Re of any wrongdoing, and at this point the SEC moved more swiftly in its investigations. A few months later Re was charged with multiple violations of regulations, specifically that during the past six years he and his associates had illegally sold over a million shares of stock in nine corporations worth approximately $10 million.

The Re case unmasked Birrell as well and in the process demonstrated that several Amex officials—including President McCormick—were guilty of irregularities. McCormick had used questionable means to obtain and then distribute stock listings and had been personally involved in speculations. In the end McCormick was forced to resign, and, with the help of the SEC, the Amex reorganized and expelled wrongdoers. Birrell escaped punishment, however. In 1958 he had fled the country and relocated in Brazil.

In 1954, when he needed funds for the Swan-Finch takeover, Birrell had sold his United Dye holdings to Alexander Guterma, a mystery man of sorts who had entered the United States in 1950 claiming to be the son of a Czarist general. A short while later he organized Western Financial Corporation, an entity with little in the way of assets, whose unregistered shares he sold to the public. With the money he obtained from this deal, Guterma organized Shawano Development, a land company supposed to have oil reserves and a new fabric, ramie. Somehow eluding the SEC, Guterma sold close to 18 million unregistered shares to 150,000 investors, and emerged a millionaire. After he took over United Dye from Birrell, Guterma looted that company and next purchased two other N.Y.S.E.-listed companies, Bon Ami and F. L. Jacobs, where he repeated the operation.

The SEC finally caught up with Guterma in 1959, when he was arrested on charges of stock fraud; he was found guilty the following year. Appeals followed, in the course of which Guterma disclosed that he had paid some of Amex President McCormick's gambling debts. Later on he followed Birrell to Brazil, which fast was becoming a haven for failed stock manipulators.

Birrell, Tellier, and Guterma were typical of the manipulators of the late 1950s. They possessed the flash of sleazy hustlers and the cunning of ferrets, but none made much of an impact on the general market, or for that matter on any speculators except those they swindled. They made the headlines only when taken into custody, and then for their notoriety, not their real financial or economic importance. Later on another manipulator, Edward Gilbert, would use his control over an Amex company, E. L. Bruce, to attempt a takeover of Celotex, a much larger firm whose stock traded on the N.Y.S.E. Gilbert failed and in the process violated securities laws. In 1962 he fled to Brazil, where he joined Birrell, Guterma, Texas embezzler BenJack Cage, and Earle Belle, who had sold millions of dollars of stock in a worthless company, Cornucopia Gold Mines, to the unsuspecting citizens of Saltsburg, Pennsylvania. None of these men possessed the class and power demonstrated by their predecessors in earlier bull markets.

Perhaps it wasn't their fault; they simply had been born at the wrong time. In the past the manipulators and wheeler-dealers had been able to do their work in markets frequented by a relatively small number of investors and speculators. They were out of place in the huge arena of the late 1950s. Whatever else it was and would become, the markets of the period were not manipulated by small bands of men. Close to a century earlier it had been said of Daniel Drew, a leading manipulator of his day, that "Uncle Dan'l says go up, it goes up. Uncle Dan'l says down, it goes down. Uncle Dan'l says wiggle-waggle, it goes wiggle-waggle." It had been that way with Drew, Cornelius Vanderbilt, and Jay Gould in their time, later on with Bernard Baruch and Thomas Lawson, with Livermore and Joseph Kennedy. Their counterparts of this bull market lacked their power. They couldn't send stocks up or down. They couldn't make them go wiggle-waggle.

Instead, stock prices in the aggregate rose and fell due to groundswells of public sentiment that developed throughout the nation and carried quickly to Wall Street. This truly was a mass movement, and not simply the actions of many speculators acting on hunches, tips, and the like. That there were speculators in the market in 1959 cannot be doubted, but at no time did they dominate trading. Nor could they multiply their power through the use of borrowed funds. The plungers of 1929 might purchase shares with as little as 10 percent margin, borrowing the rest from their brokers; in contrast, 1959's speculators had to put up 90 percent of the purchase prices.

The American middle class—the people who had helped fight the war, had gone to school under the G.I. Bill, had moved to suburbia and become professionals or now ran their own business—provided the backbone for this major move in stock prices. Nothing less than so large and powerful a constituency could have caused this vast market to move as rapidly as it did. And it was immense. In 1959 there were 6 billion shares listed for trading at the N.Y.S.E. alone; in contrast, less than a billion shares had been listed in 1929. Pool managers and touts had been able to make large waves in that relatively small market; only massive buying and selling by large numbers of individuals and major financial institutions could perform this task in the late 1950s.

Such people and organizations had to be united by the same or similar dreams or at the very least had to share several common beliefs if there were to be cohesion and movement in the market. These did exist on Wall Street during the tail end of the Eisenhower years, and at that time they coalesced.

Most Americans believed the Cold War could continue indefinitely and that because of it there would be increases in military procurement budgets. To this was added a conviction that the United States would have to respond vigorously to the Soviet challenge in space, and large amounts of money would be required for the effort. Consumerism clearly would continue to be a strong force in national life; Americans wanted butter along with their guns and rockets. Productivity would have to be increased in order to keep standards of living high and the inflation rate low for this to happen.

Even before Eisenhower spoke of the military-industrial complex, Wall Street discerned that it would require a major change in technology and business structure and that electronics could be the key to it all. The industry would grow rapidly and soon become a central factor in the economy. New companies would show the way, though revamped older ones might join in. They would report good profits; their stocks would be good speculations.

"The price of admission to the computer industry, as it has developed, runs in the order of $50 million," said a Minneapolis-Honeywell Regulator vice president in early 1959. "There aren't many of us who can afford it, but I'm sure that those of us who have committed ourselves to this investment are confident of our potential returns." As a producer of automatic controls serving the housing and manufacturing industries, Honeywell had become a profitable company, rewarding its stockholders with regular dividend increases and steady capital gains. As late as 1956, the stock might be purchased for less than 20 times earnings. Then Honeywell "went electronic" and in particular announced its entry into the computer market. The stock doubled in 1958–59 and in March 1959 was selling for 40 times the previous year's earnings. This was not an unusual move; other electronics stocks performed even better and were selling for higher P/E ratios.

When the Dow moved over the 600 level during the last week in February, it did so slowly and with some hesitation. This was not a reflection of the general market, where prices were booming on heavy volume. The Dow was heavily weighted with old-line stocks, giant firms whose shares had led the way during the first and second stages of the advance, such as Eastman Kodak, RCA, General Electric, and General Motors. Other, non-Dow stocks, rose more rapidly in this period. Some did so because of splits—White Motors, Interchemical, Motor Products, and Purex had multi-point gains that week due to such decisions by their boards of directors. Zenith closed at 213 after a 21-point advance for the week. The company reported higher sales and profits, and rumor had it a split would be declared within a few months. But the best percentage moves were made by missile and electronics issues. Thiokol advanced 21 points, on top of a 10½-point move the previous week; the stock now was above 150 and sold for 70 times earnings. Litton, Aerojet, and Texas Instruments also had major advances. "Equities like these, of course, have been in the vanguard of the vast price upheaval of the past 15 months," wrote *Barron's.* "Indeed, the discovery of 'Instruments,' 'Controls,' and the like in a company's title frequently has served to touch off a burst of speculative interest in its shares. Moreover, the more abstruse the activities of a company, the higher a price-earnings ratio the speculative community has been willing to pay."

The magazine was troubled by this phenomenon and warned that "even a company of the highest scientific proficiency can prove unequal to the critical task of translating laboratory progress into profits." Warren Hayes of Thompson-Ramo-Wooldridge, itself one of the newer space-electronics firms, which in a previous incarnation had been involved with heavy equipment and auto supplies, agreed. "The market's appraisal of future growth potential," he warned, "is not a reliable indicator. The market too often succumbs to technical fads and to superficial appraisals." But the boom continued, and Jack Dreyfus of Dreyfus & Co. summed up the matter best on taking note of the many new electronics and space issues coming to market at high prices.

Take a nice little company that's been making shoelaces for 40 years and sells at a respectable six times earnings. Change the name from Shoelaces, Inc. to Electronics and Silicon Furth-Burners. In today's market, the words "electronics" and "silicon" are worth 15 times earnings. However the real play comes from the word "furth-burners," which no one understands. A word that no one understands entitles you to double your entire score. Therefore, we have six times earnings for the shoelace business and 15 times earnings for the electronics and silicon, or a total of 21 times earnings. Multiply this by two for furth-burners and we now have a score of 42 times earnings for the new company.

The Furthburner Market had arrived, and almost everyone on the Street and nearly every investor seemed pleased with it.

Four

WALL STREET'S
NEW FRONTIER

G EORGE SCHAEFER of Indianapolis, the somewhat eccentric
publisher of the *Dow Theory Trader*, had a large following
among market theoreticians in the late 1950s. In October
1959, Schaefer wrote that he expected a strong rise for the next six
to ten months, and that this would be followed by a "long term 'primary' bear market." In early December he purchased five pages in
Barron's in which he presented his views. The centerpiece of the
advertisement was a chart comparing the bull markets of the
1920s and the 1950s. Both had developed in three phases, and in the
Schaefer projection the analogue of October 1929 would come in the
summer of 1960. "I think it is extremely important that every investor realize that—as the Industrial Average pushes up into new
high territory next year—history is most likely to repeat."

The Dow had risen steadily in the first half of 1959, but there
was a sell-off in the fall, after which the market recovered to close at
a new all-time high of 697. But there were indications that a new
recession was developing, as President Eisenhower swore to balance the budget and strike one more blow at inflationary pressures
prior to leaving the White House. Schaefer had this in mind when
he wrote. More than three decades had passed since the Great
Crash, but its specter still haunted Wall Street whenever the economy gave indications of a downturn or the market sold off.

Schaefer was a showman of sorts and wasn't known for his
moderation or prudence. But analyst Garfield Drew was, and in
early Janauary he all but endorsed the views of Schaefer and others
who predicted a major correction. Drew thought stocks would rise

through most of 1960 but that there would be "difficulties" late in the year and that these would persist through 1961.

Stocks declined sharply in January, recovered somewhat, and then plunged again, not stopping before cracking below the 600 level in early March. Richard Russell, a leading technician, wrote that the long-awaited collapse was imminent. But Schaefer disagreed; he remained convinced that one last upward spurt was needed before the house came tumbling down. Hamilton Bolton, a proponent of the Elliott Wave Theory, told subscribers that "we are well-entranced in the fifth and final upward wave—the last in the bull market," and so seemed to agree with Schaefer.

There was a mood of Armageddon on Wall Street in 1960. Although stocks see-sawed for the next half year, the Eisenhower bull market clearly had ended.

The recession deepened. The automobile companies closed down assembly lines and the housing industry was dormant. In September the unemployment rate was 5.5 percent. Corporate profits came under severe pressure, as the quarterly reports issued in October indicated. Net after-tax profits for the year as a whole would come to $22.6 billion, down from $25.1 billion in 1959. By this indicator, the third Eisenhower recession was the most crippling of all.

By then the economy was close to its bottom, and a sluggish recovery would commence in October and November, though this was not realized at the time, of course. The turnabout came too late and was too faint to help the fading presidential candidacy of Richard Nixon. "In October, usually a month of rising employment, the jobless rolls increased by 452,000," Nixon would write in his memoirs. "All the speeches, television broadcasts, and precinct work in the world could not counteract that one hard fact."

Eisenhower had achieved his yearned-for budget surplus, though it came to only $300 million. In the process he had wrung almost all the inflationary expectations out of the economy. The Consumer Price Index rose by 1.5 percent in 1960 and, the following year, a scant 0.7 percent.

Had it been worth the price? Workers and machines had been underutilized, and in December the unemployment rate came to 6.6 percent, more than twice what it had been when Eisenhower came to office. Economists and politicians debated the issue with no clear resolution. Eisenhower was aware of this. "Critics overlooked the inflationary psychology which prevailed during the mid-fifties and which I thought it necessary to defeat," he wrote later on. Conservative economist Milton Friedman concurred, noting that this was the last period during which the White House made a serious effort at keeping inflation in check. Middle-of-the-road Keynesian Paul Samuelson disagreed, and he called the wringing-out process "an investment in sadism," which, however, had left his successor with a clear field in which to operate. Discussing the issue in 1967, Samuelson said that Eisenhower had "created conditions which were helpful to the long expansion which we have had in the 1960s and which perhaps we still are having."

Eisenhower's successor, John Kennedy, had based a good deal of his campaign upon the need to "get the country moving again," and he spoke of his willingness to "seek new directions." Kennedy had criticized Eisenhower for allowing "the missile gap" to develop, and he promised increases in military procurement and the space program, as well as new social welfare initiatives. As for the economy, he said the Democratic Party believed it "can and must grow at an average rate of 5 percent annually, almost twice as fast as our average rate since 1953. We pledge ourselves to policies that will achieve this goal without inflation." How he would manage this, however, was not indicated.

"The future, everywhere indeed, seemed bright with hope," wrote historian Arthur Schlesinger Jr., recalling his perception of the national mood in March 1961, at which time he had just returned from a fact-finding trip through Latin America. "The capital city, somnolent in the Eisenhower years, had come suddenly alive. The air had been stale and oppressive: now fresh winds were blowing."

Schlesinger, of course, was a partisan, a member of the new government, and he wrote these lines in 1964, while still deeply affected by Kennedy's unexpected death. Also, Schlesinger's focus was Washington, and not New York's financial district. Wall Street certainly had been a lively place during the Eisenhower presidency, but even there a feeling of weariness existed in 1960.

The district's leaders did not fear the New Frontier, which by March they correctly had assessed contained more rhetoric and bombast than substance. They knew Kennedy had not been the first choice of the Democratic left wing, and as the election campaign wore on his statements regarding the economy had become more conventional. The Street applauded Kennedy's selection of Douglas Dillon as Secretary of the Treasury; Dillon had been in the State Department under Eisenhower and before that had been an investment banker and a member of the N.Y.S.E. They liked Kennedy's pledges to stimulate business and enlarge profit margins and in particular applauded his support of investment tax credits.

By March there were signs that liberals of various persuasions had become disillusioned with Kennedy. The unemployment rate was close to 7 percent, yet the president refused to ask for new spending programs. Labor leaders George Meany and Walter Reuther complained that Kennedy was doing little for working people, and by and large they were correct. While on the campaign trail in 1960, Kennedy had tried to appear a liberal in the Roosevelt-Truman tradition. In office, he seemed more like Eisenhower than any Democratic president of recent memory. Candidate Kennedy's inner circle included economists John Galbraith, Walter Heller, and Paul Samuelson, all of whom Wall Street simplistically perceived as being "spenders" and even "radical." By March of 1961 Galbraith was far away, having been named ambassador to India, Samuelson was back at M.I.T., and Heller wasn't very close to the president, even though he had been named chairman of the Council of Economic Advisors. Rather, Kennedy seemed to rely upon old friends like Ted Sorensen and his brother Robert, both of whom were political animals without much in the way of economic baggage, and Treasury Secretary Dillon and Commerce Secretary Luther Hodges, two moderates. The president had gone out of his way to establish a friendly relationship with Federal Reserve Board Chairman William McChesney Martin, which Wall Street noted with approval. Finally, there were unmistakable signs in March that the recession was ending, and although Kennedy had done nothing to make this possible, he enjoyed the political benefits therefrom.

The combination of fresh, attractive leadership and the kind of moderation in practice the American people appeared to prefer at the time helped boost Kennedy's popularity. In late March a Gallup poll indicated that 73 percent of the public approved of the way the new president was handling his job. After his second month in office, Eisenhower's popularity rating had been only 59 percent.

By then the investment community thought the new president would do all within his power to create a favorable environment for stocks. The Dow closed at 632 on January 19, the day prior to the Inauguration. Then, with the electronics issues leading the way, prices moved up, to end the month slightly below 650. After some consolidation, stocks pushed ahead and went over the 660 level in late February. March was another good month. The president offered his revised budget for fiscal 1961/62, and it showed increased spending for defense, education, and housing. Stocks in these groups participated in bull markets of their own, with the rest of the list joining in. On April 10, the Dow closed at a new all-time high of 692. In slightly less than three months the Dow had advanced by close to 10 percent.

Analysts attributed this action to growing confidence in Kennedy and a belief that the White House and the Fed would unite to ease monetary conditions, while the Kennedy budget would provide fiscal stimulus as well. These in turn would end the recession and establish a foundation for a major economic thrust. In fact the discount rate was not lowered in this period, but through open market operations the Fed did act to increase the money supply at a more rapid rate than previously had been the case.

Kennedy continued to genuflect in the direction of a budget surplus, but Samuelson and Heller spoke of a concept that to most Wall Streeters was new and intriguing: a full-employment budget. In effect, they were saying the administration really was thinking of presenting a budget that would be balanced, assuming full employment, but that this could mean a sizable deficit. The district took this as doubletalk, but if put into practice it would imply a higher level of economic activity, larger profits, and probably higher stock prices. So it accepted the concept as a coverup for major spending programs and sought out stocks that would benefit from them. For a while the housing, steel, copper, and other cyclicals did well. The glamour issues, which by then seemed to have unstoppable momentum, joined in, and these were followed by the old-line blue chips.

Analysts were on the lookout for "Kennedy stocks." Whenever the president talked about the need for new programs, stocks that might be affected by them rose. Kennedy asked for $5.6 billion in educational assistance, and this helped American Seating and several major publishing issues. There was talk of subsidies for American flag lines, and U.S. Lines hit a new high. The space-related stocks outperformed the market consistently, as it became evident the new administration meant to make a major effort in this area.

The new-issues market came alive in late February. "Large or small, well-known or not, any new offering connected with the electronics, photography, or publishing business promptly commands an astonishing premium," wrote *Barron's*, and the revived mania spread to most other low-priced stocks, a sure sign of renewed speculation. Comedian Lou Holtz, a guest on the Jack Paar television show, told his host of killings he had made in the market, and then said he knew of a stock that would go from 10 to 1,000 within a decade. Before a commercial break Holtz whispered the name in Paar's ear, and the camera lingered on him long enough for viewers to try to read his lips. The following day a wide variety of $10 stocks moved upward on heavy volume. A SEC investigation followed, during which the name of the stock was revealed: it was Canadian Javelin, a highly speculative issue whose president was then under indictment. Now that stock shot ahead, reaching 16 in a week. But other low-priced issues also rose—perhaps Holtz would recommend them the next time he appeared on the Paar Show.

For a week or so there was talk of a "Holtz Market," which replaced enthusiasm for the Kennedy Market. In essential respects, they were similar. The president would speak of the need for better housing, and the housing stocks would rise; Holtz would suggest

Value of New Issues of Common Stock, 1949–61

YEAR	VALUE (MILLIONS OF DOLLARS)
1949	736
1950	811
1951	1,212
1952	1,369
1953	1,326
1954	1,213
1955	2,185
1956	2,301
1957	2,516
1958	1,334
1959	2,027
1960	1,664
1961	3,294

SOURCE: *Historical Statistics of the United States, Colonial Times to 1970*, vol. 2, p.1005.

that an "undervalued situation" would rise, and it would soar, accompanied by a flock of other issues. Investors and speculators alike were coming to believe in gurus. Some were in Washington, others were old vaudevilleans. Nicholas Darvas, a professional nightclub dancer, had a huge following; he had written books and had been the subject of articles about speculative techniques. At the time, New York State Attorney General Louis Lefkowitz investigated Darvas and pronounced him a charlatan. But Darvas's audience grew, and his books continued to sell well.

This factor led some analysts to conclude that a new bull market had been hatched. Garfield Drew felt this way, and he became the herald of the new dispensation. It was different, he said, from the Eisenhower Market, though the Kennedy Boom possessed the same verve and excitement that had existed when that move was young. A few weeks later Drew pointed to the cracking of the old high as a further indication that the interpretation was fair and valid.

Rarely do major bull or bear moves begin or end simply because a new president takes office, however. The market's sharp advance in early 1960 was quite similar to that of 1958–59—in fact the same kinds of stocks advanced both times and for pretty much the same reasons. Whatever differences existed were of degree, not kind, and of levels of enthusiasm and rationality. The business press considered this significant and groped for a way to describe the situation. *Forbes* observed that the market no longer was a simple recorder of impressions and sentiment; rather, it was composed of several complex groups—electronics, retailing, publishing, autos, steels, and so on—some of which moved against the market. For example, the blue-chip electronics had been far stronger than most other stocks in 1959–60, the military-industrial issues reacted to news from Washington and not the economy, and the new issues defied rational explanation. Perhaps in the future there no longer would be bear markets. Rather, some groups would pause, while others would surge ahead, and then the roles would be reversed. Rotating leadership might replace bull and bear moves in the 1960s. *Business Week* added the notion that in the past stocks moved up on good news and down on bad. Increasingly there was a tendency to anticipate news, especially information relating to sales and earnings, and this the magazine took as an indication of heightened speculation.

The market, then, was reacting to rising expectations. Speculators in 1961 spoke of stocks that were selling for 40 times *anticipated* 1963 or 1964 earnings but which were going then for 400 or 500 times *reported* 1960 earnings. Who could tell what the nation, the economy, or the industry might look like in three or four years? An investment guru, such as Holtz, might offer projected figures, and speculators would purchase shares, thinking them low in terms of future statistics, some of which were concocted from thin air by a union of analyst and computer, while others were simply fabricated by imaginative amateurs.

The *Wall Street Journal* remarked that analysts were talking and writing more about cash flow and less about earnings than they had during the mid-1950s. In fact, a few years earlier some of them hadn't even known the meaning of the term. The concept was simple enough and known to all first-year accounting students. Cash flow is earnings plus depreciation. A firm with large depreciation accounts might report per-share earnings of $1, but the cash flow could come to $2 or more. Firms with heavy start-up costs might report profits but large negative cash flows. Conversely, established firms with accumulated depreciation could have cash flows many times that of earnings. Analysts picked up on this. They might hesitate to recommend stocks selling for 100 times earnings but would speak highly of issues going for 30 or so times cash flows. Clients looked at numbers, not concepts, and purchased the shares.

The *New York Times* noted that some new, small companies had no visible earnings and negative cash flows to boot. How could analysts calculate P/E ratios for these issues? Should it be done on a negative basis, and if so, what constituted a "prudent man's stock" in such an investment universe? Daring analysts with imagination projected statistics a few years out and came up with remarkably optimistic sets of numbers. They claimed the truly prudent man would look to the future and not become ensnarled in the past, which in any case had little or no bearing on the ever changing present. Many people believed this. A new cosmology had invaded the Street, and it won many converts.

Without meaning to do so, Kennedy had set the tone. Now it was youth, excitement, and originality that commanded attention. Older men—those 40 or above—were considered incapable of appreciating the market. A youth cult had developed on the Street. It could be seen on the new-issues frontier and even more so on the new men who appeared at the brokerages.

Barron's appreciated the change, and in fact was among the first to understand it. One of the magazine's veteran columnists, H. J. Nelson, brought a measure of perspective to the phenomenon. "Since the market is divorced from the earnings factor—stocks are bought on the imminence of good earnings or bad, the one denoting the presence of the fundamental upward curve, and the other the presumed climax to what statistically can be demonstrated as a mild business recession—the guidelines of the past are of small help to the present-day investor." As Nelson saw it, "Pressure to invest is relentless. The speculative urge is nationwide."

Reason, logic, and tradition were selling at discounts on Wall Street, and so was experience. Emotion and blind hope were in charge. In Nelson's view, the future belonged to Darvas, Holtz, Winchell, and other assorted tipsters. Stock prices in early 1961 did not make sense when seen through conventional eyes, and so a new reference point would be needed.

Talk of full employment budgets, negative P/E ratios, cash-flow ratios, and other rationalizations distressed many on the Street. After years of urging the public to buy and hold stocks, even Keith Funston showed signs of being troubled by this kind of market and its rationale. Somewhat cautiously, he told reporters, "There is disquieting evidence that some people have not yet discovered that it is impossible to get something for nothing," by which he meant that speculators were wheeling and dealing in shares of companies "whose names they can't identify, whose products are unknown to them, and whose prospects are, at best, highly uncertain." Funston was troubled by the market's rapid advance on heavy volume in early April, and he urged "moderation."*

In so acting Funston categorized himself as a man of the second and third stages of the bull market. Now the fourth stage was about to begin, and this one would be characterized by fantasy, dreams, and a divorce from conventional yardsticks by which stocks had been measured in the past. Such elements had existed in the third stage but always were in the background. One might argue, for example, that such third-stage companies as Texas Instruments, Xerox, and Polaroid had excellent patent protection, good market penetration, and adequate finances, and that these were true

---

* Cynics might have noted that most of these stocks were traded over-the-counter or at the Amex, and Funston really was arguing that investors should stick to N.Y.S.E. issues.

The New-Issues Market in January 1961

COMPANY	OFFERING PRICE	PRICE ON MAY 15, 1961
Click Chemical	3	2
National Trust Life Insurance	3	3¼
National Research Associates	1½	8
Pathe Equipment	5	8
Cold Lake Pipe Line	3½	⅝
Pocket Books	26	39
Brothers Chemical	3	11½
Holden-Day	1	3
Edlund Engineering	3	3¾
Designatronics	2¼	5
Long Island Plastics	1	4
Chemtronic	2	3¼
Cyclomatics	1	1⅝
Garsite Products	3	10
Marine View Electronics	3	6¼
Peerless Tube	4	7½
Automatic Concessions	4	10¾
Cove Vitamin & Pharmaceutical	3⅛	55½
Geotechnics & Resources	2	4⅛
Reser's Fine Foods	7	24
School Pictures	9⅞	24¼
Plated Wires & Electronics	4	8¼
Pneumodynamics	9	19½
Restaurant Associates	11	15
Varifab	2	12½
Heinicke Instruments	7½	41
Reynolds & Reynolds	15	29
Colwell Co.	10	22
Glassco Instruments	5	45
Medco Inc.	5	28
Madigan Electronics	4½	8
Henry Engineering	2½	2¼
Measurement Systems	1	5
Great American Industries	2⅛	2
Universal Electronics Labs.	4	11½
Vacuum Electronics	15	30½
Avery Adhesive Products	17	28¾
United Automotive Inds.	3	2½
J-F Machine, Diesel & Electronics	3	2¾
Speedee Mart	6	15
Vim Laboratories	3¾	3⅝

SOURCE: *Barron's*, May 15, 1961, p.5.

growth companies of the future. As for BBM Photocopy and Ny-
tronics, they were interesting speculations and their underwriters
curious and even fascinating figures, but none could hope to operate
in the main arena on Wall Street.

Now they seemed to be coming to the fore, and "new old-
timers" like Funston found it difficult to adjust to the situation. It
was not true, for example, that speculators couldn't get something
for nothing as the N.Y.S.E. leader had claimed. Many of them had
done so consistently. and by dealing in stocks whose names and
businesses they didn't know. "People are trading pieces of paper,
and not stocks," said one broker, critical of the market and clearly a
young old-timer himself. This doubtless was true for increasing
numbers of small investors and plungers, and all involved appeared to be doing well at the game. An anonymous wit put it this
way: "The market isn't only discounting the future—it's discounting
the hereafter as well."

But he really missed the essential point. During the dawning
fourth stage the present was all that mattered. Rosy dreams were
fabricated of a future few really believed in or cared to explore in
any great detail, while the past wasn't merely or even prologue—it
was irrelevant. Long before it appeared in the rest of the country,
the "Now Generation" arrived on Wall Street.

It did not arrive at once, and this fourth stage would not be
long-lived but rather would turn out to be a long transition to another level, one in which fantasies did become true, and little was
beyond imagination. From its beginnings in 1949, this bull market
had moved progressively from the conventional to the bizarre, from
the ordinary to the shocking, and the fourth stage was one more step
along the way.

The January–April 1961 advance had been based upon percep-
tions regarding the economy as well as dreams and fantasies.
Foreign affairs were important too, but only insofar as they affected
the arms budget and related matters. For all of his talk about the
need for a new look and direction at and in foreign policy, Kennedy's approaches in this area appeared essentially the same as
those of Eisenhower. The new president moved deliberately, refus-
ing to take a role in the Congo War, for example, and for the time
being he treaded water on the Vietnam issue and in Laos. During
his first weeks in the White House, Kennedy developed plans to

increase the nation's armed strength and dispatched emmissaries overseas who later helped develop the Peace Corps. In mid-April there was some talk of a $12.5 billion outlay to assist underdeveloped countries, which the newspapers promptly dubbed "a new Marshall Plan" and the *New York Times* thought might become the keystone of the Kennedy foreign policy. There was little thought of war, either large or small. Defense procurement spending would increase, however, but the president told Congress in April that only "the most urgent and obvious recommendations" of the Joint Chiefs of Staff would be acted upon.

In his Inaugural Kennedy had spoken of the need for both sides in the Cold War to "begin anew the quest for peace," while warning that America would "pay any price, bear any burden, meet any hardship, support any friend, oppose any foe, in order to assure the survival and success of liberty." Which was the real Kennedy? Any heating up of the Cold War would mean accelerated defense spending programs, and these in turn would be translated into higher corporate profits and stock prices on Wall Street. In early 1961 the conventional wisdom held that there could be a major recession "should peace break out," and this would result in a major decline at the securities markets.

Such was the situation on Friday, April 14, when the Dow closed at 694 on heavy volume. Led by office equipment issues, electric utilities, and electronics, the market continued to press forward. The defense and military-industrial issues lagged. "The drab market for guided missile stocks requires no elaboration," wrote *Barron's*. The new issues continued to dominate speculative action, and even the underwriters were troubled by the wide price movements. "The job of the underwriter now is to protect the public against itself," said Donald Marron, who continued to thrive in this segment of the industry, but the others said little, as though hoping to cash in as quickly as possible before the SEC arrived on the scene. The outlook was bright; analysts seemed certain the 700 level would be cracked the following week.

The following day the American-backed invasion of Cuba at the Bay of Pigs commenced, and on Wall Street stocks of companies with holdings on the island advanced smartly. Then, as it became evident that the invasion had failed, stocks declined. The Kennedy administration had been involved in a major blunder, and the president looked reckless and inept. At no point did it seem America would become involved in a war with Cuba, but the administration was tarnished; the honeymoon was over. On Wall Street stock prices declined, and the Dow ended the month below 680.

While the attempted Cuban invasion was bad news in the political and even global sense, by late April Wall Street had concluded it meant that Kennedy would be more adventuresome militarily than had been Eisenhower. Further confrontations might be expected, and for these the president would require much larger amounts of military hardware. Having digested this thought—and realizing that the recession clearly was ending—investors and speculators moved back into the market. The Dow once again crossed the 700 level on May 21, exactly one month after the Bay of Pigs fiasco.

Soviet Premier Nikita Khrushchev continued making bellicose speeches that spring and in particular threatened to sign a separate peace treaty with East Germany. Kennedy responded by preparing a revised military budget, which he presented to Congress in late July. There would be $1.7 billion for limited war weapons, $751 million for additional military personnel, $543 million for missiles and navy fighter planes and a like amount for the army, and so on down the line. In all, he asked for $3.2 billion more than Eisenhower had believed necessary. *Business Week* observed that these new spending programs would have a major impact on the prospects of dozens of companies, among them General Dynamics, FMC Corporation, North American Aviation, Lockheed, Grumman, and Fruehauf Trailer. The nation's shipyards could expect larger contracts than they had known since World War II. Kennedy wanted appropriations for fallout shelters, and this would help create additional companies, jobs, and stocks to be floated on Wall Street. "The new buildup will also have an important impact on communities near military bases, shipyards, and depots." On top of all this would be major increases in spending for the space program and more foreign aid—over $500 million for Southeast Asia in 1961 alone. In effect the nation was to have a wartime economy without suffering the actual torment of fighting. Kennedy was to be a true Cold War president after all.

The Street now understood that the president was willing to accept unbalanced budgets in order to carry through on international commitments of various kinds. Prior to the Cuban episode the district had wondered whether he would prove a fiscal liberal or conservative. His rhetoric had been that of an old-fashioned New Deal Democrat, but until that disquieting spring and summer only a few of his actions had indicated that Kennedy would be much more of a spender than, say, Nixon might have been had he won the November election. Now these doubts were dispelled. Just as the advent of World War II and the military buildup it required had helped take America out of the Great Depression of the 1930s, so the Kennedy Cold War budgets reinforced the developing recovery from the last Eisenhower recession. These, at least as much as Walter Heller's economic programs, were responsible for the economic boom of the early 1960s. And to Wall Street, it all meant higher stock prices.

The Kennedy defense programs helped Heller achieve greater prominence than before. The CEA chief continued to advocate a major tax cut and increased fiscal and monetary stimulation. In effect, he had told the president that he could have guns and butter without worries regarding unemployment and inflation, and a troubled Kennedy welcomed such news. At the same time the Federal Reserve, through open market operations, was gently pushing interest rates downward. The revived Cold War and the Heller brand of economics appeared to go together, and this too was observed by Wall Streeters.

Many investors went to the sidelines in June, as though awaiting a sign that these factors were falling into place. A new glamour category had appeared—real estate investment trusts—but outside of this group most moves were minor. The Dow drifted lower on reduced trading volume and ended the month below 684. The bulls were gathering strength, however, and made their move in early July. The Dow crossed 690 on the 2nd, pulled back, and then went over 700 on the 27th, with volume and excitement increasing along the way. The military-industrial stocks took the lead, followed by housing-related issues benefiting from the economic upturn, while the electronics and office equipment issues kept rolling ahead as before.

The Heller program was in full swing, thought *Barron's*, with Treasury officials stating that economic recovery "would so stimulate revenues as to balance the 1963 budget."* Wall Street's bulls

---

* In fact the Kennedy administration never accomplished this feat. The 1961 deficit would be $3.4 billion, and those for the next two fiscal years were $7.1 billion and $4.8 billion.

might purchase shares with the knowledge that Washington was prodding business recovery, while their conservative consciences would be assuaged by faith and hope that the Heller programs would lead to a surplus.

The digestive and assimilative processes appeared to have been completed by the end of July. Stocks now moved ahead on good volume, closing over 720 on August 8. "Pres. Kennedy's decision to step up defense spending brought buyers into the stock market with a rush," wrote *Business Week*. "The vital news of the week was the prompt unanimous passage by the House of the $959 million weapons procurement authorization requested by the President," wrote *Barron's*. The magazine noted that the Senate had just approved a military spending bill that would cost $4 billion more than one passed by the House in the last weeks of the Eisenhower administration. "It is now crystal clear that the Government is planning an extraordinary expansion of spending." The *New York Times* and the *Wall Street Journal* ran stories about companies that had benefitted from the new programs and the way they were cutting into unemployment. Several brokerages put out special advisories on military-industrial stocks.

On August 13 the East Germans erected the Berlin Wall, and this act both confirmed and completed the crisis mentality. Now investors and speculators awoke to the dangers and opportunities involved in military confrontation. Spending money on arms would be bullish; fears of a possible atomic confrontation switched many to the bear ranks. Stocks sold off, as the Street and the rest of the country awaited further developments in central Europe.

There were none. The wall remained in place. There would be no war.

"Buy on the rumor, sell on the news," is one of the district's oldest clichés. Another is that investors dislike uncertainty. Perhaps it was for these reasons that stocks churned aimlessly for the next three months. Everyone knew that economic recovery was proceeding and that the Kennedy programs would assist the defense-related stocks, and this news had taken the Dow over 700. By August these developments had been factored into the market and no longer could provide sustenance for the bulls. Now bearish news and rumors became the vogue. The White House was planning a new investigation of the district, and in Congress there was talk the president might ask for wage and price controls. The Justice Department had initiated several antitrust suits, and on the Street there were rumors that additional ones would be brought against American Telephone, General Motors, and IBM. Kennedy had sent a letter to the steel companies asking them to keep prices down, and there were implications in this that strong government action would be forthcoming unless his request was heeded. In late September *Business Week* took note of a spreading "wary" attitude among many investors, due to the reappearance of a chronic fear. "Much of the rise since last October was stimulated by the belief that Washington's desire to promote economic growth would also lead to a further dose of inflation. Now, investors and speculators are worried that the Administration will resort to controls over prices, wages, and profits if the boom appears to be getting out of hand."

In the mid-1950s one anonymous observer of the Wall Street scene referred to the "bicycle market." "These glamour stocks remind me of a person riding a bicycle," he said. "All goes very well while you're moving ahead, but if you try to stop, the bicycle falls over." In other words, when the glamours stopped moving ahead, for whatever reason, they started to fall behind. This happened in the autumn of 1961. Rumors of controls, fear of war, and a nagging thought that stocks in untested companies should not sell for 100 times earnings resulted in sell-offs. Such electronics issues as Transitron, General Instrument, International Rectifier, and Standard Kollsman were down by more than 50 percent from their all-time highs, and leading vending and publishing issues lost many of their followers. Despite this, few analysts thought the market was in any danger of a substantial correction. The old-line blue chips were doing well, as was the economy. In October U.S. Steel Chairman Roger Blough predicted excellent earnings for his company and the industry, due in large part to substantial demand from the automobile and housing markets.

But trust in the blue chips was eroding. One sign of the times was a cartoon in the *New Yorker* that portrayed several businessmen discussing the market while on a commuter train. "I had the weirdest dream about my mother last night," said one. "She said I should sell all my AT&T when it hits 132." In November *Barron's* reported that many mutual funds were selling stock and going to short-term Treasury notes. *Forbes* noted that the Street was adopting a "hunkering down" posture. The Dow rose to 734 on the 15th, but it declined for the rest of November, and matters were little better in December. There would be no year-end rally in 1961. On the last trading day, the Index closed at 731.

Business Week asked "top investment men" their views of the future. "The almost unanimous opinion" was that "the bull market in stocks, which has pushed the averages to an all-time peak this year, will continue into 1962." William Kurtz of Paine, Webber, Jackson & Curtis thought the Dow would top 850 "and keep on rising." Sidney Lurie of Josephthal said that "the business outlook is better than people believe and the market will perform better." Bradbury Thurlow of Winslow, Cohu & Stetson agreed, but he was troubled about the possibility of "irrational speculation." Edmund Tabell told the magazine that he felt confident the Dow would go to 825, but there would be a decline in the second half of the year. "We are looking for common stocks to turn in quite a good performance in the coming year," wrote Heintz & Co., while Fahnestock & Co. believed "a backlog of reserve purchasing power" would result in new highs along the line. About 45 percent of mutual fund managers expected the Dow Industrials to reach a new high early in 1962, and only 10 percent thought there would be a decline by the end of the year. The magazine agreed, and noted that "there seems

Declines of Selected Glamour Stocks, 1961

	Trading Range		
STOCK	HIGH	LOW	CLOSE
ABC Vending	27¾	17¾	21⅜
American Photocopy	46⅜	29⅜	30⅛
Ampex	27¾	17⅛	20½
Bell & Howell	69⁷/₉	46¼	48⅝
Circuit Foil	57¾	24	26½
Crowell-Collier	50⅞	24	39
Fairchild Camera	88¼	62¼	62½
Hewlett Packard	53	26	37
International Rectifier	35⅞	16½	17¼
Itek	61	25½	25¾
Minnesota Mining	87⅝	66⅜	67⅛
Pocket Books	43¼	21¾	22¼
Perkin-Elmer	83½	43⅝	58
Transitron	42⅜	16¾	18
Varian Associates	77⅜	38⅛	44⅞

SOURCE: *New York Times*, January 8, 1962.

little chance of any sharp decline, for many institutions are ready to buy in the event of a drop."

The business news in early January was mixed. The steel mills were operating at close to full capacity—but this was seen as an attempt to build inventories in anticipation of a strike later in the year. The SEC announced an investigation of charges of manipulation in the new-issues market—and the Justice Department denied it would seek antitrust divestitures for GM, IBM, and American Telephone. In his State of the Union Message President Kennedy reiterated his pledge that America would beat the Soviets to the moon, while Senator John Williams of Delaware warned that the unbalanced budget that increased space and defense spending had created would cause "grave difficulties" and "shake confidence in the dollar," and Senator Harry Byrd of Virginia announced the Finance Committee would conduct an "intensive" hearing before voting to approve a hike in the debt ceiling.

On Wall Street a large number of dividend increases failed to move stocks higher. The Dow opened the year with a 7-point drop on the first trading session, and prices continued to slide, hardly stopping to pause along the way. The Index fell below 700 on January 17 before some lackluster buying appeared. Fourth-quarter earnings, released in February, proved excellent, and some stocks moved on the news, but with little display of investor enthusiasm. Days in which glamour stocks added 10 and more points appeared over; fractional changes became the rule. Clearly Wall Street was troubled.

The reason was fear of inflation, that key phenomenon that had crippled bull moves since the end of World War II. The Kennedy budget had been superimposed upon an already reviving economy, and now there was fear of overheating. In his Budget Message the president had said "the Federal Government is expected to operate in 1963 with some surplus," but the proposed deficit for the current fiscal year was to be $7 billion. Furthermore, Kennedy asked for standby authority to cut taxes should a recession threaten—a clear support of the Heller approach that still troubled Wall Street. Finally, in its annual report the Council of Economic Advisors came out in favor of new spending programs.

The combination of a large deficit and a tax cut frightened many conventional legislators, and at his February 21 press conference the president tried to calm them down by saying that "for the present time there is not a chance of a tax reduction." Still, his talks and actions appeared inflationary and caused stocks to dip to lower levels.

In early 1962 the president made several appeals to both business and labor to keep price and wage increases and demands at low levels; specifically, he wanted them to be tied to increases in productivity. This was a general recognition that inflation was becoming an important concern but also was meant as a clear signal to the steel industry and the Steelworkers Union, then engaged in preliminary contract negotiations.

On January 23 Kennedy met secretly with union chief David McDonald and U.S. Steel President Roger Blough and urged each side to accept the guidelines. Both men fought the idea, but in the end McDonald agreed to take a 10-cent wage package on the understanding that the steel companies would hold the line on prices. Kennedy was delighted. Not only would the nation avoid a crippling strike, but the steel wage-price settlement could be used as a model for other industries. The contract was signed on March 31, at which time the Dow was 707.

Most business leaders had been caught off guard by the quick settlement, which they were almost unanimous in praising. A General Motors spokesman thought it would be salutory for the economy, "materially offsetting the effect that stockpiling would otherwise have had." His counterpart at Ford said "the settlement was psychologically helpful." But there was no similar outpouring of congratulations from Wall Street. The correction that had begun in early January rolled on, with the glamours especially hard hit. The Dow fell below 700 once again in early April, with IBM losing 22 points, General Tire 17, Litton 11, and Texas Instruments 5½ in the first week of the month.

Barron's offered this explanation for the decline: Wall Street had been anticipating a large-scale buildup prior to a strike; "by forestalling a strike, the agreement puts a quietus upon any scramble for inventory and thus acts as a temporary restraint upon business activity." In fact some businesses already had started building up inventories in anticipation of a steel strike, which would be followed by a costly, inflationary settlement. With this threat out of the way, several major users left the marketplace, and so demand declined considerably.

On April 10, even though its plants were operating at below full capacity and despite its agreement with the union and the White House, U.S. Steel decided to raise its prices by $6 a ton on the average. Roger Blough flew to Washington to inform the president of the decision, while most of the other companies fell into line and boosted their prices as well. Kennedy clearly was angered by what he considered a gross betrayal, and he knew that other businessmen would interpret the steel move as a sign that another round of price increases could commence. Just as Khrushchev had tested him the previous summer over Berlin, so big business appeared to have thrown down the gauntlet. At least, that's how it seemed in the Oval Office. Fuming and bitter, Kennedy said to his associates, "My father always told me that all businessmen were sons of bitches, but I never believed it until now."

The president mounted an all-out campaign against the companies. Secretary of Defense Robert McNamara announced that steps would be taken to purchase foreign steel for defense purposes. The IRS would investigate steel company tax returns—and those of leading executives. "The simultaneous and identical actions . . . constitute a wholly unjustifiable and irresponsible defiance of the public interest," said Kennedy in a television broadcast. He praised Inland and Kaiser Steel, which had not gone along with the price boosts and implied further actions would be taken against the other companies.

The companies were surprised by the force of the reaction. Such an onslaught could not be withstood. Bethlehem Steel rescinded the increase, and shortly thereafter the other companies backed down as well. Kennedy had won his battle.

The public reaction was mixed. The *Wall Street Journal* wrote, "We never saw anything like it. One of the country's companies announced it was trying to get more money for its product and promptly all hell busted loose." The Senate Republican Leadership Committee demanded an investigation, asking, "Should a President of the United States use the enormous powers of the Federal Government to blackjack any segment of our free society into line with his personal judgment without regard to law?" Conservative economists and some liberals too said the action was unnecessary; market pressures would have forced U.S. Steel to lower its prices even had the president not intervened. On the other hand, the unions applauded Kennedy, and even those who thought he acted recklessly agreed he had shown firmness and determination. "We do respect decisiveness in an executive and so do the people," wrote the *New York Herald-Tribune*. "We can only wish it had been displayed in a better cause." A Gallup poll released soon after showed the president's actions in office had earned him a 79 percent approval rating.

Kennedy now attempted to assure businessmen that he was no opponent of the free enterprise system. Sanctions against and investigations of the steel companies and their executives were dropped. The episode was finished, but wounds remained at U.S. Steel, Bethlehem, Republic, and other producers.

And on Wall Street. Just as Kennedy's swift actions after the Bay of Pigs had convinced analysts and investors that he was a spender who would accept unbalanced budgets, so the steel crisis led them to conclude that this would be the most anti-business administration since the New Deal.

In early April the SEC prepared to begin its investigation of Wall Street. Rumors persisted that Attorney General Robert Kennedy (believed more opposed to big business than his brother) was set to spring an antitrust action against the steel firms. Inflationary pressures were rising and profit margins shrinking; Wall Streeters thought many companies would not raise prices in fear of government retribution, and with a heavy hand at that. The *Journal* called this situation "troublesome" and "vexing," and *Business Week* wrote, "In the spring of 1962, business finds itself in the midst of one of the most paradoxical upswings in the annals of the U.S. economy," one in which "economic expansion continued but unemployment persisted [at 5.6 percent in April] and profits declined." Within a few months the government was supposed to unveil a program permitting corporations to depreciate assets more rapidly and so increase their cash flows; would Kennedy permit this accelerated depreciation allowance to go into effect?

There was no indication he had changed his mind on the subject, but the mood on the Street was such that the question was asked anyway. *Barron's* put it this way: "If the Federal Government fights attempts to relieve a profits squeeze, thereby confiscating reinvestable corporate profits requisite for business expansion, what then is to be the Government attitude toward faster depreciation of property values—the program several times pledged by the Treasury Department and promised in final form by June 30?"

The market had been weak and indecisive in early 1962, due to fears regarding inflation, the unknowns associated with the Heller tax strategy, and varied problems regarding economic recovery. Little the president had done during his first year in office had convinced Wall Streeters he was a competent chief executive; they missed Eisenhower. The steel confrontation did not create a bearish mood in the brokerages, but it helped crystallize one. And it added a strong dose of paranoia as well.

It was "cold sweat" time on Wall Street, something that occurs occasionally during all bull markets, and always at the end. Each upward sweep has its corrections, and seasoned investors and speculators learn to recognize them. Stock prices may fall 10 percent or more, there may be dire rumors and forecasts, but in their hearts the veterans know that prices are declining on unreal fears. They retire to the sidelines and prepare to pick up bargains at the bottom—a stock that sold at 90 a week ago had fallen to 75, and the veteran awaits a selloff to 60, at which time he will consider purchases. On other, rarer occasions, these same people start to believe rumors of disaster, and let their imaginations conquer their reason. Why buy the stock at 60, when it could go down to—how far?—to 40, 30, or even 10. On such occasions the veterans lose hope. Panic starts to build, and one of the clearest signs of this is the cold sweat syndrome, that feeling in the pit of the stomach that tells them the game has ended. Like a walker on a high wire they look down and see the abyss; they lose their balance and take the plunge. This was what happened in April.

The Dow closed at 686 on April 12, giving what Dow theorists considered a "sell signal," which would mark the beginning of a bearish phase. The steel confrontation was on, and one might have expected a selling wave the following day. Remarkably, prices held, and on Tuesday, April 24, the Dow ended at 693. The news out of Washington was favorable; Kennedy had assured the business community that the depreciation tax credit measure was very much alive; automobile sales were excellent, up by close to 50 percent from the 1961 period; first-quarter earnings reports were surprisingly good. On Wall Street several analysts spoke guardedly about "false signals" given by the Dow twelve days earlier.

As it happened, the signal had not been false. The market dropped by more than 9 points on Wednesday, lost 6 on Thursday, and on Friday gave up 7, to close the week at 665, its lowest point in more than a year.

The Kennedy Crash had begun.

Five

THE PIT AND THE
PENDULUM

RUE FINANCIAL PANICS and major crashes occur rarely. In recent times, when like most other things language itself has been devalued, the terms have been applied loosely to phenomena which three or four generations ago would have been considered little more than medium-sized ripples. Few Wall Streeters active in the spring of 1962 had ever experienced what a half century earlier would have been termed a major panic, though many had lived through minor dislocations.

Transient fears, the failure of grand manipulations and speculative ventures, reverberations from foreign crises, and simple disillusionment might result in sharp declines of a few days' duration. By themselves such periods would not lead to long-term declines and depressions. Rather, they resulted from temporary weaknesses in the economy and banking systems, a sudden switch in investor psychology, or unexpected political news.

Mainstream economists of the early 1960s held that the nation had solved the problems of economic stagnation. Furthermore, through the proper use of fiscal and monetary policy, the worst excesses of the business cycle might be avoided. It followed that without depressions, there would be no serious financial panic in Wall Street's future. Should it appear that things were coming apart, the experts would apply the proper medicine and make things right.

Walter Heller, the head of the Council of Economic Advisors, believed this. He had worked in the Treasury and other federal agencies during the New Deal. James Tobin, another member of the CEA, had served with the War Production Board and the Office of Price Administration (OPA). Kermit Gordon, an original member, had extensive wartime service. H. Gardner Ackley, who arrived on the board in 1962, was an OPA alumnus.

All four men were born between 1915 and 1918. Like John Kennedy (born in 1917) they had no direct memories of the way the nation's economy had functioned prior to the New Deal, though of course they had learned of it through their studies (begun at a time when that system appeared to have failed). They were members of the first generation of professional economists called into government service with a mandate to solve major national problems. These men understood power and believed they could use their knowledge and skills to create what amounted to permanent prosperity.

In view of their experiences and outlooks, this was not surprising. They had been trained in techniques of economic recovery and considered full employment and optimum usage of resources major goals. The leading economists in the Kennedy administration did not believe inflation—provided it was controlled and moderate—was too high a price to pay for these benefits. In his memoir of these years, *New Dimensions in Political Economy*, Heller chided Eisenhower's economists. "Even after inflationary forces had ebbed," he wrote, "the continued fear of inflation kept policy thinking in too restrictive a mold in the late 1950s." A collection of essays by new economists edited by Heller was entitled *Perspectives on Economic Growth*. It contained two index columns devoted to "economic growth" and not a single entry for "inflation."

Economists such as these did not fear the consequences of a business slowdown; they believed Washington could stimulate the economy whenever such action proved necessary and desirable. Inflation was another matter. Their only direct contact with this phenomenon had come during the war when they worked for government and had wielded great power. This experience provided an answer: wage and price controls. Given the ability and willingness to foster economic expansion and this simple technique to hold prices in line, there seemed no reason to have a serious recession or depression at any time in the future. And without an economic decline of this nature, there could be no old-fashioned stock market panics like those of 1937, 1929–33, 1919–20, and 1907.

Few of the new economists understood how Wall Street allocated funds or its other functions. None had written extensively on the subject or at any time shown much interest in or knowledge of it. Galbraith, who was not a CEA member, was the exception on both counts. He had indicated a belief that in the 1920s the district had been dominated by charlatans and crooks and, in the 1950s, second-raters and mossback reactionaries—and he wasn't certain which were more dangerous. Throughout the 1950s he had warned of a possible new stock market panic and crash resulting from unrealistic prices and wild speculation—clearly a replay of the 1920 experience was imminent, he suggested. Of course there had been no such crisis during the 1950s, though stock prices appeared quite high at times and speculation increased toward the end of the decade. Now that a Democrat was in the White House and Galbraith a member of his administration, there was no more talk of collapses from that quarter.

In the spring of 1962, many analysts thought prices would decline due to a profits squeeze. Writing in the *Times* on May 2, Burton Crane said that economic problems "coincide with a growing belief that the rates of earning growth for some of the glamour stocks were no longer justifying the high price-earnings multipliers conferred by the markets in the past." As though to illustrate this, IBM dropped 55 points in two days when its first-quarter profits were no better than those of the previous year, and although the stock quickly recovered, its gyrations troubled owners of other, less substantial growth issues. At the same time the newspaper announced that steel production had hit an eight-month low, and this was interpreted as an indication that the economic recovery from the 1960–61 recession had slowed down.

The international news was troublesome, too. A shaky ceasefire in Laos collapsed, and with the resumption of war in that country Kennedy had to reassess the American role in Vietnam, where 5,000 American troops were helping support the regime of Ngo Dinh Diem. Wall Street feared this would lead to a new confrontation with the Soviet Union and lower stock prices. From Europe came news that the Swiss were selling American shares. "We are skeptical but not pessimistic about the U.S. outlook," said a Zurich banker. "The United States is facing a psychological rather than an economic crisis."

The Street agreed. But outside of a few eccentrics, misanthropes, followers of bizarre market theories, Marxists, and believers in conspiracy theories, no one anticipated a major panic or crash.

The stocks that comprised the Dow Industrials held firm during the first week in May, but many glamour issues declined steadily on heavy volume. Then, on Monday, May 7, the Dow fell by more than 6 points to close at 671. Trading broadened, volume increased, and stocks continued to slide the rest of the week, with the Dow ending at 641 on Friday. *Times* columnist Clyde Farnsworth wrote, "A full-scale reappraisal of market values is under way," but stocks rebounded the following Monday and Tuesday to close above 655. Then the selloff resumed. The Dow went below 650 on the 16th and on the 21st closed under 640. The next session, which was Tuesday, the Index lost more than 12 points, and close to 10 was sliced from the Dow on Wednesday, when the N.Y.S.E. reported 460 new lows for the year against 5 new highs.

That day, at his regularly scheduled press conference, Kennedy said the economy remained strong and refused to offer much of a statement regarding what was happening on Wall Street. "I believe that the stock market will move when—in accordance with the movement of the economy as a general rule," was his only reference to the decline.

On Thursday astronaut Scott Carpenter was launched successfully into space. In the past such spectacular feats would be reflected at the exchanges in higher prices for science-based issues. This time the Dow gave up 4 points, though it was strong toward the close.

Edwin Posner, head of the Amex, told reporters that "this definitely is not panic selling. We have had a ten-year bull market, and this evidently is the time for an adjustment. Stocks are now getting down to a realistic level." Keith Funston agreed; there was no slump in sight. George Mitchell of the Federal Reserve thought the market's decline reflected an increasingly sluggish economy, but little more than that. Burton Crane, who quoted them and others, observed that conditions usually were dangerous when reporters ran around asking important people their opinions of the market and economy.

On Friday, May 25, the Dow closed at 612, having lost close to 39 points for the week. Market statisticians calculated that the value of all stocks listed on the N.Y.S.E. had declined $30 billion, more than the combined gross national products of Australia, Sweden, and Ireland. Brokers were troubled by the late tape, which ran on for 32 minutes after the close on Friday. More than 6.3 million shares changed hands, which though not a record was unusually high.

That night and over the weekend the newspapers carried stories about the decline and advice from experts. *Times* financial writer John Forrest remarked that thus far at least there had been little evidence of panic. Funston agreed; he noted a "considerable diminution of confidence," but little else. Crane wrote, "Stocks went down for five days in a row last week, five days that carried the market averages back to the levels at the end of 1960, and 15,000,000 shareholders suffered from unusual demands to their minds." As for advice, he said, "The professional would say, get out." The Dow Jones News Service report was ominous. "Should the industrial average be able to hold around the 610 level, brokers say the dramatic effect alone may prove of near-term help to the market generally—if it should not, however, these sources say that the technicians would be groping for a clue as to where a solid bottom might be found."

Stocks opened with a rush of selling on Monday, May 28, and from the first it was evident that a major collapse was taking place. The 610 barrier fell quickly; by noon the Dow was at 601, and still falling on heavy volume. Every group participated in the decline, with the glamours leading the way. The ticker couldn't keep pace with transactions on the floor, and "flash prices" of 30 key stocks were being sent out at 10:20. An hour and a half later even these were dispensed with by harried operators. Slightly after midday the tape ran almost an hour behind floor transactions, so that clients couldn't obtain quotes from their registered representatives. by then the market's crash had made headlines in afternoon newspapers, and radio and television stations were scouring Wall Street and the local universities for "experts" who could tell the public what was happening. Of course there were anticipated comparisons with the 1929 crash—some commentators called it "Blue Monday" and others "Black Monday" while trading continued on the floor.

But there were differences, and the most important of these involved the aforementioned cold-sweat syndrome. It was remarkable by its relative absence, considering the decline and the trading volume. "It was as though some great natural calamity had occurred to some far-distant people," said one broker after the day was over, "and we watched with horror and fascination, but not fear."

The market closed at 3:30 as usual, but the ticker continued on until 5:58. Shortly thereafter the N.Y.S.E. announced that more than 9.3 million shares had been traded, making this the fifth most active session in history to that time, and the busiest since 1933. The Dow ended at 577, down by 35 points, a 5.7 percent drop. At the Amex a shade less than 3 million shares were traded, and the decline was 6.3 percent. The OTC market was in shambles, with quotes on some stocks unavailable until the following day.

As the floor personnel and back office workers worked overtime to set things in order for the next day, industry, press, and government figures started the postmortem. Funston blamed the decline on the government. "There has been a growing disquiet among investors because of Kennedy's steel action," he said. The *Times* noted "the rather cheering picture presented by current economic indicators" (but didn't say which of that week's crop offered hope) and suggested investors remain cool. The president rejected a recommendation that he go on television to soothe the nation. Walter Heller called the collapse "a disturbing situation." Quite correctly Secretary of Commerce Luther Hodges observed that most large companies were self-financing, and so the market's action wouldn't have too great an impact on the economy. Henry Ford and Thomas Watson of IBM refused to comment, but J. Paul Getty said he was buying stocks.

So were Walter Benedict, Dwight Robinson, and Joseph Fitzsimmons, and they were more important in some ways than all the others insofar as determining the market's future. Robinson headed the Massachusetts Investment Trust, Fitzsimmons Investors Diversified Services, and Benedict Investors Planning Corporation. These men and others in the mutual fund industry told those reporters smart enough to ask them that they would be in the market picking up bargains. The same situation existed at the trust funds and pension organizations. The large institutions, which had become so important in this bull market, were in a liquid position and ready to go in on the buy side.

News of the funds' actions spread through the district in the early morning of Tuesday, May 29, but had no discernible effect on opening prices. Stocks fell rapidly on heavy volume; by the end of the first hour the Dow was down by 11 points. Then, as fund-buying pressure took hold, prices turned around. It is not clear just when this happened, for the tape was late once again, but by noon the market had made up the loss and was headed upward more rapidly than it had declined during the morning. At 1:00, for example, the Dow Jones ticker showed a loss of 14 points when in reality the average was up by around 8 points according to actual floor transactions at the time. Brokers had a difficult time convincing clients that prices truly were advancing and that they should ignore the ticker. They did come around, much more rapidly than might have been anticipated, and in large numbers. Quickly the mood turned bullish.

By 1:30 Wall Street was experiencing its greatest rally since the end of World War II, and the most remarkable turnabout in N.Y.S.E. history. From a low of 554, stocks surged forward to 613 in late afternoon, for a range of close to 60 points, an unequaled record. The Dow ended the day at 604, for a gain of slightly more than 27 points. Volume was 14.7 million shares, making this the second busiest day on Wall Street—the first being October 29, 1929.

Commenting on the two-day experience, *Business Week* wrote that "for the first time, a whole generation saw with its own eyes and felt with its own pocketbook the impact of real panic selling in the stock market." This was only part of the story. There had been relatively few margin calls, and no fear of bank failures or mass defections at the brokerages. As far as has been recorded, no customer's man or client jumped out of a skyscraper window due to this crash that saw the Dow lose slightly less than 100 points from the Friday high to the Tuesday low.

In this period there had taken place a variant of the classic panic—in fact, the mirror image of one. On Tuesday afternoon the Street underwent a buyers' panic the likes of which hadn't been experienced since the late 1920s. These take place when cash-rich investors and speculators conclude that stocks are dirt cheap, and that unless they fill their portfolios quickly they will miss out on the feast. The cold-sweat syndrome that appears during sellers' panics result from fears that all may be lost; its counterpart in buyers' panics is the product of greed and an awareness that conditions are much better than had been believed.

Wednesday was Memorial Day, and so the markets were closed. Most firms asked employees to work, however, and clear up the large amount of paper that had piled up during the two previous days. Almost all the analysts agreed that the buying wave had sufficient momentum to carry into the following session, perhaps longer.

Trading was wild on Thursday morning, the ticker was late, and prices were higher. There was selling during the afternoon, which brokers attributed to profit taking. Still, the Dow managed to close at 613, up by close to 10 points on volume of 10.7 million shares. Conditions were back to normal on Friday, when 5.7 million shares traded and the Index ended at 611.

Fortune blamed the "Kennedy crash" on the president, whose "double-barrelled blast hit the expectations of the average investor and businessman alike," and most of the postmortems agreed. Eisenhower spoke critically of "the reckless spending programs of the Kennedy Administration." Undersecretary of Commerce Edward Gudeman found that his former business colleagues were irate. "You son of a bitch," one of them screamed. "You guys down there are to blame for the market collapse." And so it went.

Few said much about the amazing recovery. Clearly the president wouldn't get credit for that. There had been little in the way of foreign buying, and small investors came in late. The large funds had been responsible for the rally, though their efforts received little attention at the time. All that was remembered was the crash. Yet the rally was more important, for it demonstrated that "another 1929" hardly was possible. Not only had the system survived its greatest shock since the 1937 collapse, but it had done so without much damage and within a few days was back to where it had been prior to the disaster. The crash had left some emotional scars, but within a year the Street would come to understand that it had been a powerful test of the market's ability to take a blow, one that was passed successfully.

Kennedy said little publicly about the collapse, but soon after, in his famous Yale University speech, he spoke of myths regarding the economy, where "illusion may prevent effective action." One of these was that an unbalanced budget automatically results in inflation; this he denied, but at the same time he added that all attempts to keep expenditures in line with income should be made. Another myth involved "the matter of confidence," and on this subject the president said, "The solid ground of mutual confidence is the necessary partnership of Government with all of the sectors of our society in the steady quest for economic progress."

Schlesinger, Heller, Galbraith, and others had helped write this speech, which was meant as both an indication of where the government was heading and a gesture of friendship and conciliation to the business community. It was followed by suggestions by Commerce Secretary Hodges that additional tax credits to stimulate the economy were being considered. Despite this, Kennedy continued to be viewed as the most anti-business president since Franklin Roosevelt.

There was a growing sense of paranoia in many board rooms and brokerages regarding the administration. Literally hundreds of new issues were withdrawn from registration even though there was no evidence they couldn't be distributed. Several small underwriters and OTC houses folded. Reynolds & Co. announced a temporary suspension of its trainee program, and the New York Society of Securities Analysts reported that 50 of its 400 members were out of work.

There was much talk of a possible mass exodus from the market throughout the month of June, when volume was high and prices declined steadily. The Dow dipped below 600 on the 4th, rallied, and went under that level again on the 11th. The Index fell 15 points the following day and another 6 on the 13th, when it ended at 574, which was below the panic-day closing of May 28. This triggered another wave of selling, which brought the Dow to 563 on June 14. This was followed by a rally and a further collapse. On Tuesday, June 26, the Dow closed at 536.

The carnage was impressive, enough to sicken and shake the confidence of any bull. The glamours had been especially hard-hit. In late 1961 IBM had sold at 607; now the stock was slightly over 300. Minneapolis Honeywell had fared worse, going from 170 to 75 in the same period. Polaroid had topped out at 238 in 1961, and in June it was sold at 81. Xerox went from 171 to 88. Few groups had been spared or investors left unscarred. In less than half a year more than $107 billion in stock values had melted away. (To appreciate better what this meant, the gross national product that year would come to $500 billion.)

Throughout the decline the large institutions picked up blocks of stock. They hadn't been able to halt the collapse, but the general feeling was that their actions had prevented an all-out rout from developing. In late June several general-interest and financial magazines ran articles on this demonstration of their power. Earlier in the bull market there had been talk that the institutions might contribute to some future collapse; the typical question then had been, "What will happen if they all decide to sell at once?" The Kennedy crash answered the question and ended such talk. The funds would not run away from the market. They had become its solid underpinnings. New money was continually entering their accounts; and these large amounts of capital would be channeled into Wall Street. In 1962, many analysts came to the conclusion that such funds had no other place to go.

What the manipulators had been to the 1920s market, the fund managers would be to that of the mid-1960s: figures of prestige, power, and trust.

On June 25, H. J. Nelson told his readers in *Barron's* that while prices might decline further, "the series of convulsive shocks of the past month may not be expected to continue indefinitely . . . it is illogical for investors to grow increasingly bearish with every fresh decline." Along with a growing number of his colleagues, Nelson was convinced a moderate correction was in order. But there would be no new bull market, or resumption of the old one, until the political and economic climates were altered in some dramatic fashion.

There was an advance in late June that continued through July, followed by stagnation in August and a quiet selloff on lackluster volume in September. The economic outlook was uncertain, wrote *Business Week* in mid-October. "With few dissenters, economists forecast: No Boom, No slump. Most leading economic advisors to U.S. corporations predict a mild decline in 1963, followed by recovery. Others see steady growth, but no great upswing in business activity." Nelson agreed and saw in the stock markets a reflection of this kind of economy. "The fact is that the public is either distrustful of, or bored by, equities," he wrote on October 15, and the *Barron's* columnist complained of a "sleepwalking market."

That day Kennedy and his advisers sorted out news of a Soviet missile base in Cuba, and planned a response to the threat. Of course, the entire matter was kept secret. "I now know how Tojo felt when he was planning Pearl Harbor," wrote Attorney General Robert Kennedy.

On Monday, October 22, the Dow closed at 569, off 5 points for the session. That evening the president informed the nation of the existence of the bases and called the Soviet action in establishing them "a deliberately provocative and unjustified change in the *status quo* which cannot be accepted by this country, if our courage and our commitments are ever to be trusted again by friend or foe."

Did this mean war? It was impossible to say, but the combination of Soviet and American moves, together with the general belief the president could not afford another diplomatic setback, resulted in the most dangerous direct confrontation since the beginning of the Cold War.

In the past stocks generally moved higher when analysts and investors concluded that defense appropriations would increase but that actual warfare was remote. Such was not the case in late October. The Dow lost more than 10 points in heavy trading on Tuesday, October 23, as the Street buzzed with rumors regarding a Soviet-American confrontation off the coast of Cuba. If anything, conditions had worsened by Wednesday morning, as the newspapers and television shows concluded that Kennedy would not be budged in his stand against Khrushchev. The market opened lower, hitting bottom in late morning at slightly below 550. Then followed a strong and somewhat puzzling rally, something completely unorganized and unanticipated, as the Dow added more than 25 points in the afternoon to close the day at 577.

That evening and the following morning analysts offered two explanations for the advance. The first and most obvious was a rumor that made its way through the district of a compromise worked out by French President Charles de Gaulle which both parties would accept. This proved false, but some investors might have been influenced by it. The second was more important. The investment community approved of the way Kennedy had handled the situation, even though his methods carried risks. The president appeared strong, determined, and skillful. The Street was gambling that he would carry it off—that the Soviets would back down. In the aftermath of the crisis there would be additional military spending, of course, and this would stir a lagging economy. As a bank trustee put it, "I think there was a fundamental change in the business outlook on Monday night. A week ago I would have bet the economy a year from now would have been lower than it is today; now I think it will be higher." To this was added a signal from the Federal

Reserve. The central bank cut the reserves member banks were required to retain against time and savings deposits from 5 to 4 percent, which meant an additional $767 million could enter the loan stream. This led to a revival of rumors that the discount rate would be cut from 3 to 2¾ percent.

Prices fell back somewhat on Thursday and Friday to finish the week at 569. Volume was back to normal, however, and by Friday most of the initial fears had been dissipated. On Monday, October 29, the news ticker carried the story that Khrushchev had agreed to remove his missile bases; Kennedy had his victory. The market celebrated by advancing over 10 points on good volume, to which was added another 10 points the following day, when the Dow closed at 589.

Analysts and brokers talked of a new psychological atmosphere in the nation and on the Street. Now Kennedy had demonstrated he could be "leader of the free world." More than any other single action of his administration thus far, the missile confrontation had won him support and admiration. "It would appear the Cuban crisis has changed the setting and direction of the market," said Stanely Nabi of Schweikart & Co. According to *Business Week*, "The Cuban crisis seems to have ridden the stock market of much of the mood of black pessimism that had prevailed since the crash at the end of May." A week later, with the Dow over 604 and the market clearly in a new bull move, Lucien Hooper of *Forbes* wrote, "There is little room to debate that there has been a favorable change in investment and speculative psychology," while Sidney Lurie of Josephthal said, "Now the mood has changed—and proper recognition is being given to the fact that business by and large is quite good, if not exhilarating. . . ."

Stocks moved up steadily now, as the Cuban euphoria was reinforced by optimistic projections and good economic news. Automobile sales and steel production picked up, and several corporate executives predicted a good year for 1963. George Katonah and W. H. Locke Anderson, both of the University of Michigan, thought consumer spending would remain strong for at least 6 more months, and Anderson forecast a 1963 GNP of $575 billion, against an estimated $552 billion for 1962. On November 15, Treasury Secretary Dillon promised a major tax cut for the following year, and this time the news was applauded on the Street, even though it might mean a temporary widening of the deficit. A few days later *Business Week* editorialized, "The year 1962 should go down as the one in which leading representatives of business, labor, and the public finally demonstrated that they both comprehend and will support a modern fiscal policy. Such a policy aims at a combination of tax and expenditure programs to bring the economy up to optimum levels of employment and production." For years the magazine had considered inflation to be the prime economic danger. Now it adopted a different line. "The real argument for reducing the tax burden today is that this is the only way to correct the nation's slow rate of economic growth."

The Dow moved up by more than 50 points in November to close the month a shade below 650; in the 26 sessions after the October 23 selloff it had risen by 94 points. The advance had been led by the old-line industrials, solid blue chips like General Electric, du Pont, and General Motors. The well-established glamours—IBM, Polaroid, Xerox—outperformed the rest of the list. The new-issues market remained quiet, and many of the flashy new electronics, office equipment, and defense issues continued their declines and showed few signs of life.

This had been the most unusual year on Wall Street since the end of the war. The Dow had closed 1961 at 731, and then collapsed to a low of 536 in late June. It rallied to 616 in August, only to decline again, this time to 558 during the Cuban Crisis. Then followed the strong November rally, and the Dow ended 1962 at 652. The loss for the year was slightly more than 79 points, making this the worst year since 1931 in this regard.

Seldom does a market undergo two completely separate and unrelated traumas on the order of the Kennedy crash and the Cuban crisis in a single year. When it does, the debris is worth investigating, and analysts busied themselves in this pursuit at the end of the year. By then they had concluded the institutions indeed had been behind both rallies, a sentiment supported by a SEC investigation the following year. In June and October the funds had purchased large blocks of high-grade investment stocks—IBM, GE, RCA, Eastman Kodak, and others. These performed fairly well during 1962, despite the sharp loss posted by the Dow.

The district took note of the fact that many small investors had left the market and gone to the sidelines. This conclusion was drawn

Trading Range of Selected Old-Line Blue-Chip Stocks, 1962

STOCK	HIGH	LOW	CLOSE
Allied Chemical	57	34¼	44
American Can	47¼	38⅛	45¼
American Tel & Tel	136¼	98⅛	116¾
Chrysler	75¼	38½	45¼
Du Pont	254¾	164½	238¾
Goodyear Tire & Rubber	44¾	24⅞	32⅝
Procter & Gamble	92¼	56⅜	70½
Sears, Roebuck	88¾	59	76¾
Standard Oil (N.J.)	59¾	45⅜	59¼
U.S. Steel	78⅞	37¾	43⅞

SOURCE: *Barron's*, December 31, 1962.

Trading Range of Selected Blue-Chip Glamour Stocks, 1962

STOCK	HIGH	LOW	CLOSE
Beckman Instruments	152¾	62⅛	104
Eastman Kodak	115⅞	85	109
General Electric	78½	54¼	77
IBM	578½	300	392½
Litton Industries	74½	37⅜	65⅛
Minneapolis-Honeywell	133¼	70⅛	84¾
Polaroid	221	81½	142⅝
RCA	63⅞	38⅝	57
Texas Instruments	100⅜	39¼	63½
Xerox	166¼	87½	157¼

SOURCE: *Barron's*, December 31, 1962.

Trading Range of Selected Speculative OTC Stocks, 1962

STOCK	HIGH	LOW	CLOSE
Acoustica Associates	10¼	1⅞	2⅛
Barden Corp.	24¼	11¼	12¼
Cove Vitamin	22	3	3½
Digitronics	35½	13	17½
Electronics Capital	31¼	8	10¼
Itek	31½	9⅜	12⅝
Kalvar	635	240	255
Mite Corp.	13¼	3⅛	3⅜
Savin Bus. Machines	20¾	6	7
Taylor Instruments	48½	26	32¼

SOURCE: *Barron's*, December 31, 1962.

from brokers' comments, a decline in odd-lot dealings (usually a good measure of activity on the part of that segment of the community), and generalized hunches of seasoned observers. Still, the mutual funds managed to retain their clients. Sales for 1962 came to $2.7 billion, down by $350 million from the previous year but still the second best showing in history. More significant perhaps was the statistic indicating that redemptions also were down—$1.1 billion against 1961's $1.2 billion. Fund sales organizations reported that purchases rose and redemptions declined during the two sell-offs, and they took this to indicate that small investors were more certain than before that professional management had its virtues and was worth the price, that in an uncertain market it was best to have the diversification and expertise provided by mutuals with long records of accomplishment.

The leading advisory services and business publications offered guarded predictions that December. All of them seemed to think the new-issues boom had ended, with most appearing to believe it would not be reborn in that generation. *Financial World* suggested that while many high-grade stocks might perform well in 1963, "the bloom is off the speculative rose," at least for the foreseeable future. *Business Week* echoed the thought. "Speculative demand meanwhile is light," was its post-Christmas report. "The betting is that stock prices will have trouble sustaining their fast November rise." Writing in *Barron's*, H. J. Nelson noted that "stocks offer few demonstrable bargains, and the spring upset shows the danger in a market that long ignores abnormally high earnings multiples." Yet he observed that the Dow's P/E ratio was "about the average that prevailed in 1958 as the market was moving up from the 1957 break." Perhaps there was some reason to hope for higher prices after all. Nelson concluded that "the outlook for earnings is so mixed as to call for the utmost care in embarking on new equity investment."

All agreed, implicitly or explicitly, that the economic and financial situation in 1963 would rule the price levels. Martin Gainsbrugh of the National Industrial Conference Board was troubled about inflationary pressures. "We have built fewer excesses into this recovery with nearly two years of it under our belts than in any postwar recovery." Fed Chairman Martin talked about several problems—the outflow of gold, the wisdom of the Kennedy tax program, and most of all, the large budget deficit. He warned that the central bank would go to a restrictive monetary policy in 1963 if inflation got out of hand.

In the past large segments of the American business community would have applauded such talk. But the situation had changed in this regard during 1962. With differing degrees of enthusiasm, many conservative organs had concluded that the economic outlook was fairly good, and that the Kennedy tax reform package would prove beneficial to business. The situation was rather unusual. For years these same businessmen had argued in favor of balanced budgets and against tax cuts if the latter would contribute to large deficits. In effect, they had opted for an approach that would mean lower net profits for their companies in return for a stable price level. Now they had come around to the idea set forth by the new economists—that lower taxes would mean greater economic activity, and that this in turn would be translated into still higher profits.

The *Wall Street Journal* and *Business Week* embraced the concept, as did the *New York Times* and the *New York Herald-Tribune* (though both were temporarily silenced due to a newspaper strike). In December the First National City Bank commented, "Fears of a business recession this winter, so widespread six months ago, have been largely dispelled, and hopes have been aroused that tax cuts can be worked out to revitalize our economic growth."

Moody's and the *Dow Theory Newsletter* recommended a cautious investment stance for the coming year, as did most services. They suggested purchases of blue chips, especially chemicals and well-established growth issues. Standard & Poor's *Outlook* recommended Alcoa, Celanese, Commercial Credit, and General Motors, among others. "Essentially, the economy is marking time, buoyed by rising Government outlays and by large private capital spending," it wrote early in 1963. "The postwar boom has long since ended; economic growth has slowed down; and industry, operating in a state of manifest overcapacity, makes little profits headway, and then only sporadically." The service concluded that "the investor who buys discriminatingly and times his purchases well will find rewarding opportunities."

The 1962 experience had led investors and the services to conclude that a major bull market hardly was likely, but that the economy was resilient, and the market had the capacity to take severe blows and then recover. The safety net had been tested—twice in fact within a period of a few months—and had held. Young and middle-aged investors now felt they had gone through the fire and survived. To a generation that had not known the pains of a truly severe panic and crash, the 1962 experience seemed vivid and frightening, but quite bearable. Was this the worst they might expect? Had this been what Galbraith warned them of a few years earlier? If so, they had little to fear. Psychologically at least, the Street was in good shape, prepared for good news and further advances.

Emotionally, ideologically, and even economically, many of the preconditions for a market advance were in place in early 1963. In fact the beginning of one had occurred in October and November. That January, analysts searched for signs that the old bull market was reviving; not until much later would they realize that the move already was underway, that Wall Street was well into in the fifth and most dynamic stage of the great post–World War II bull epoch.

Six

THE FIFTH STAGE

I N THE 43 months following the June 1962 market low, the Dow-Jones Industrials rose by close to 460 points. Several earlier moves had been sharper or lasted longer, but in none of them—not even during the fabled 1920s—had the market moved upward so steadily and uniformly.

Once this fifth and penultimate stage of the great bull market got under way, the Street became enveloped in euphoria. Stocks moved upward almost effortlessly, with no truly serious correction until spring 1965, and that was of short duration. By then a cult of growth had become so ingrained in the collective mentality of the Street that it appeared incapable of being shaken. There was a brightness and newness about the investment scene in this period unlike anything the Street had known since the 1920s.

As had been the case during that period, the investment world threw up a group of men who became the *Wunderkinden* of the district, whose ideas were listened to carefully by big and small speculators and investors, and whose buy and sell orders caused ripples throughout the markets. Many were young by Wall Street standards, which is to say they were in their thirties and early forties. Although respectful to their elders, they hardly considered any of the antique wisdom of the district worth their while. Rather, they would create new sets of rules by which to play the game, and they were supremely confident of success. "We aim at a 30 percent growth rate for our clients' assets," said one money manager in 1965, adding quickly, "Of course we expect to do better than that overall, but 30 percent is the rock bottom." Such a person had never gone through a long bear market and, more importantly, never expected to do so. Veterans who spoke of "preservation of assets" and "safety of principle" were replaced by younger men, who by mid-decade were known as "gunslingers" in recognition of their daring and penchant for fast action.

It was a time for youth and excitement. Perhaps without meaning to do so, John Kennedy had established the tone early in the 1960s, with his looks, his style, and his policies. A few years later, some antiwar activists would cry out, "Never trust anyone over the age of 30," directing their barbs against several Kennedy appointees. Although on Wall Street the figure was upped to 40 or 45, the idea was pretty much the same: older people simply were incapable of dealing with serious matters in the modern world—be it foreign policy or investments.

The Wall Street atmosphere in this period bore some resemblance to that of the fantasy-filled fourth stage. The difference was comparable to that between dreaming and awakening to find the dream had come true. For example, not even the most sanguine new-issues underwriter expected any of his stocks to enter the Fortune 500 in his lifetime. Rather, they were viewed as trading vehicles, to be brought out at one price and then sold thereafter at a higher one, creating profits for clients that could be used for further purchases. Kletz, Lomasney, and others of that class were small-time operators, albeit highly successful ones, and they understood they never could hope to be anything more than that.

In the fifth stage, the dawn of the age of conglomerate building, it became common for medium-sized companies with $100 million or so in revenues to grow to billion-dollar corporations in two or three years through takeovers and mergers. Anticipating these developments and buying and selling stocks involved in such transactions occupied much of the gunslingers' time, and success could result in 100 percent profits overnight.

Veterans of the new-issues boom often did as well, but there was quite a difference between making money from purchases of shares of a speculative high-technology company with a few thousand dollars in assets and a dozen employees and getting in at the right time in the stock of a company with close to a billion dollars in sales and a striking record of earnings growth. The former situation appealed to small investors and speculators willing to buy several hundred shares of a $5 stock, while the latter attracted large investors who often put many thousands of dollars into the paper of growing conglomerates.

Even more important was the attitude of major institutions, several of which in this period came under the management of gunslingers. While some mutual funds purchased blocks of stock in new, chancy companies, most preferred to invest in proven performers or stocks with "proper sponsorship." The pension funds and life insurance companies rarely touched stocks not listed on the N.Y.S.E. and would have nothing to do with new issues or most OTC and Amex shares. These organizations took on or developed gunslingers who were supposed to seek out and purchase "turnaround opportunities," which often meant developing conglomerates or companies about to be absorbed by them. The 1962 traumas had worked to the advantage of the large institutions, increasing both their assets and followings. But they could keep neither unless they advanced more rapidly than did the Dow—at a time when that index was rising steadily. This translated into acceptance of the "cult of performance" by many large institutional investors, meaning they cast aside the last vestiges of seeking dividends and steady earnings growth for capital gains and explosive price action.

The expansion of institutional ownership of N.Y.S.E. stocks was a major aspect of the fifth stage; in 1962, the institutions owned $70.5 billion worth of these stocks; by 1969, the figure was $162.5 billion. More impressive, however, was the way these institutions came to dominate trading—and the establishment of prices—at the central market. This was due in part to their enlarged portfolios, but even more to the rapid rate at which the institutions turned over their portfolios as the gunslingers and their followers and imitators jumped from stock to stock in their search for faster capital gains. In 1961 the large institutions accounted for $12.3 billion worth of transactions at the N.Y.S.E., or 22 percent of the total; by 1969, they dealt in slightly less than $80 billion, which came to 60 percent of the dealings.

Giganticism and novelty were important factors in the investment world during this fifth stage. It was a period in which new people organized important deals for big money involving major corporations and did so with a sang-froid that astonished many old-timers. Combinations and restructuring operations that would have occupied J. P. Morgan, John D. Rockefeller, and James Hill for months or even years were carried off in days or weeks by men who a few years earlier had been in graduate schools of business administration or in laboratories.

Wall Street always has been closely attuned to outside political and economic events. The fifth stage of the great bull market coincided with and for a while was stimulated by activist administrations in Washington. John Kennedy and Lyndon Johnson moderated taxes, sought the understanding of businessmen if not their enthusiastic support, and spent enormous amounts of money on social programs and the Vietnam War. These contributed to economic growth and higher profits, which in turn meant rising stock prices. The New Frontier and Great Society programs also helped awaken inflationary forces and created economic dislocations. Eventually both the economy and the markets would pay a large price for this boom era, but of course this was not evident in early 1963.

The fifth stage was a complex phenomenon. Not only did it possess a central unity of its own, but also it recapitulated aspects of those stages that had preceded it.

The investment community's mood in January 1963, for example, bore resemblances to what it had been in 1949. Many businessmen mistrusted Kennedy as they had Harry Truman. Leon Keyserling, Truman's head of the Council of Economic Advisors, had advocated economic stimulation, and Walter Heller would do the same fourteen years later, though his program was different; both men were labeled inflationists. Yet each got what he wanted, and in the end both programs resulted in higher growth and greater profits.

In 1963 Heller attributed the yearning for balanced budgets to old-fashioned views on how the economy actually functioned and "the Puritan ethic"; Keyserling had held the same view in the late 1940s, when he suggested that faster growth would result in lower inflation rates.

In both periods investors were licking wounds after suffering through market declines, but it was here that differences were more important than similarities. In January 1963, the Street read of major purchases by institutions during the fourth quarter of the previous year, and despite some slowdown in the tempo of buying, it appeared many funds remained bullish. The market hadn't had this kind of institutional underpinning in 1949. Furthermore, Truman-era investors had been troubled about talk of a repetition of the 1929 crash, while their descendants in 1963 knew that the declines of the previous year hadn't been too bad. Consumer confidence was high, as shown by department store sales, orders for new cars, construction statistics, and other relevant data. Millions of investors and speculators who had done well for themselves in the immediate past were prepared to take risks for similar gains in the future.

There was no important foreign policy news in early 1963. Instead, attention was focused on rumors of changes in the tax laws and the performance of the economy. Businessmen and their advisers were divided over the tax cut recommendations set forth by Kennedy in January. "Rates have too long been in the confiscatory area," said Glidden Co. Chairman Dwight Joyce, "and this is long overdue." John Ballard, an economist for the Mellon Bank, thought the proposals "are heavily biased toward tax relief in the lower income brackets—which by itself will not solve the problem of sluggish economic growth." DuPont economist Ira Ellis wrote that the program had been "very much oversold," while an anonymous Pittsburgh corporate treasurer, quoted in *Business Week,* said that opposing tax cuts was "like biting Santa Claus."

On the whole, Wall Streeters applauded the program. A spokesman for Walston & Co. noted, "For the first time since 1935, major tax changes have been proposed that don't involve higher taxes for upper income groups and for business." All approved of the president's intention to reduce the maximum capital gains tax from 35 percent to 19.5 percent, though many of the same people criticized the suggestion that the holding period for capital gains be lengthened from six months to a year. In general, the district thought enactment of the package would mean higher prices for many common stocks.

The debate continued through the first part of the year, while the economy recovered and the market followed suit. H. J. Nelson of *Barron's* continued to warn his readers of the perils of inflation, but even he turned bullish in late May. "Stocks are high on all traditional approaches," he said as the average topped 720, "but the profits outlook under Welfare State planning is not to be disregarded." At the same time James Dines, whose lively market letter had a wide following, told subscribers that "the bull market is alive and young." "Where do we go from here?" asked *Business Week*

and, answering its own question, said, "Higher, by most indications."
One of the major reasons for this was the creation of a spirit of har-
mony between the White House and the business community. "Despite their continuing disagreement on this key issue of government
spending, more and more businessmen are beginning to accept the
new look on the New Frontier as a genuine change."

All the elements for a substantial advance were in place by
early June—good economic news, growing business confidence,
and higher corporate earnings. For the moment, however, all of this
was negated by rumblings out of the central bank. Chairman Martin
warned the nation against inflationary pressures, suggesting the
Federal Reserve would boost the discount rate unless Kennedy
made serious attempts to eliminate the deficit, or at least cut it
down somewhat. Already there were indications that Martin was
tightening up on credit through open market operations. Bond
yields were rising, luring some institutional money away from
stocks. News of this and a suspicion that a showdown soon would
take place between Kennedy and Martin caused prices to dip at the
N.Y.S.E. Brokers reported that many clients already had sold their
holdings and were in strong cash positions. Mutual fund liquidity
was at a two-year high. Analysts were upgrading second-quarter
earnings projections; they thought business was excellent and
profits were expanding nicely. The foreign trade figures were turning around. Gold sales were easing. Once the situation at the Federal Reserve was resolved, investors would return to the market and
prices would rise.

On July 17 the Federal Reserve announced that the discount
rate would go to 3½ percent. Stocks sold off, and now the bulls and
bears squared off for a confrontation. The bulls pointed to higher
earnings and dividends, the bears to tight money and the possibility
of more of the same. The bulls won this contest, with analysts at-
tributing their success to the growing confidence in Kennedy,
whose popularity on Wall Street as in the rest of the nation was rising.

There was a summer rally that year, as investors and institutions picked up blue chips and glamour stocks. The sentiment in
this period resembled that of the second stage in the early 1950s,
when investors started to switch out of income stocks to seek established growth issues.

The Dow crossed 700 on August 5 and a month later cracked the old 1961 high to post a new one at 737. Good earnings reports and an expectation the tax package would be enacted in the autumn contributed to the advance, but there also was a rosy glow to other news stories. The Street talked about a new era for railroads brought about by regional mergers and technological innovations. A congressional committee debated at $5.3 billion space program, which certainly would have a major impact on high-technology companies. Automobile sales were better than anyone had thought possible earlier in the year. Steel production was firm, and the companies instituted price increases. Significantly, Kennedy said and did nothing about them, and this was interpreted as another peace gesture from the White House. Finally, Congress moved closer to enacting a Kennedy-sponsored bill providing a 7 percent investment tax credit, which was designed to encourage business expansion, and in effect was a federal subsidy.

Not all of the skeptics had been converted. One mutual fund officer was troubled by the fact that "stock yields are very low, multiples quite high," and for this reason he thought a pause to be in order. Supporters of this approach noted that the P/E multiple for the Dow was close to 19, while a year earlier it had been 16. Dividends hadn't risen as rapidly as had earnings, so the yield on the Index was 3.1 percent, which was 0.5 percent lower than it had been in the second quarter of 1962. The bulls responded by observing that the P/E multiple had been as high as 24 only a few years earlier, and they took this to mean prices had a way to go before topping out. As for yield, they anticipated a spate of dividend increases and special payouts in the fourth quarter and thought these would boost prices to new highs. In any case, they claimed, investors were becoming more concerned with growth than income, and so the yield factor was no longer of prime importance.

Stocks moved upward steadily in September. The investment tax credit went into effect the following month and provided additional stimulation to the market. Volume rose, in large part the result of stepped-up institutional activity. A *Business Week* survey released in late September indicated that most fund executives believed the Dow would rise at least another 10 percent before any serious correction took place. "We are finally in the Soaring Sixties, and most people don't realize it," complained one investment banker. "It's almost frightening," said a broker quoted in the *Wall Street Journal*, "but the party line is that there's no place to go but up."

The Dow went over 750 on October 17, but by then investor interest had shifted from the blue chips that comprised that index to the more speculative stocks, many of which were traded at the Amex or over the counter. Barnes Engineering, Electrographic, National Video, and other little-known stocks had impressive run-ups, while such N.Y.S.E. issues as Xerox and Control Data gyrated as though out of control. "This kind of irresponsible speculation is frightening some of the more seasoned pros," said Bradbury Thurlow of Winslow, Cohu & Stetson though that was hardly likely. Rather, the advent of such a market reminded many analysts of the situation during the third stage, which was being repeated in October and early November. While the Dow blue chips marked time, the glamours staged their own version of a bull market.

The Federal Reserve took note of this development and on November 11 raised the margin rate from 50 to 70 percent. At the time the Dow stood at 754. The central bank's action did put a crimp into the blue-chip sector, which by November 21 had fallen to Dow 733. The glamours and less known issues kept rolling along, however.

Rumors, the spice of all market advances, spread through the district. News of an AT&T stock split led to talk that other firms were considering the same step, so that a great many issues selling

Per-Share Earnings for Selected Common Stocks,
Second Quarter of 1973 vs. Second Quarter of 1972

STOCK	1972 EARNINGS	1973 EARNINGS
Bethlehem Steel	0.46	0.61
Chrysler	0.28	1.07
Ford	1.28	1.41
General Dynamics	1.22	1.77
General Motors	1.41	1.62
IBM	2.17	2.56
Litton Industries	0.41	0.56
Merck	0.60	0.87
Socony Mobil	1.19	1.38
Standard Oil (N.J.)	0.89	1.18
Dow Industrials	8.84	10.25

SOURCE: *Moody's Handbook of Widely Held Common Stocks, 1974.*

above 60 or so had runups. Xerox, Perkin-Elmer, and Foxboro posted large advances in mid-November, each on news of new products about to be announced. Now many other new-technology issues moved higher, on similar stories. Dennison Manufacturing was said to have perfected a copying machine that was better than Xerox's, and that stock jumped ahead by 3 and 4 point bounds.

There was a touch of wildness in the air that November, and this was taken as a sign that the Dow stocks would soon join the rally. After taking a survey of fund managers and analysts, the *Dow Theory Newsletter* reported that a majority of them were bullish. "We expect a definite breakout after the old high is topped," it wrote. "The Dow should have an easy time getting to 800."

On the morning of Friday, November 22, Funston and other N.Y.S.E. officials discussed the possible failure of Ira Haupt & Co. and Williston & Beane. Both firms were involved in the fortunes of Allied Crude Vegetable Oil Refining Corp., which three days earlier had filed a bankruptcy petition. If Allied failed, Haupt and Williston & Beane might have to follow suit. Between them, these two brokerages had 30,000 customer accounts. What might happen to them under these circumstances?

The Exchange officials attempted to deal with this issue that morning, and shortly before the lunch break had developed a plan whereby Merrill Lynch might rescue Williston & Beane. The Haupt matter was more complicated, and at the time it appeared it might erupt into a major scandal.

Shortly thereafter Wall Street learned of the assassination of President Kennedy. After recovering from his shock, Funston tried to round up enough board members for vote on a suspension of trading. As staff members and messengers manned telephones or ran through the district seeking enough members to constitute a quorum, trading accelerated and prices plummeted. There were rumors of Soviet involvement in the murder and talk of Texas extremists who planned to seize political power. Many feared the outbreak of World War III. The Dow, which had been rising in the morning, now lost more than 24 points in a half hour of hectic trading. The Haupt matter was forgotten, as brokers talked knowingly of an impending Cuban invasion of Florida.

The board finally met at 2:00, by which time a measure of relative calm existed on the trading floor. Seven minutes later the

N.Y.S.E. closed down. The Dow ended at 711, for a loss of more than 21 points. Volume had been high—6.6 million shares—but clearly there had been no panic. That evening brokers, analysts, and clients knew that if the transition to a Johnson presidency went smoothly, the Dow would regain all that it had lost in the first hour of trading.

Over the weekend, while much of the rest of the country pondered the meaning of the assassination, Funston and the board worked out a settlement of many of the issues regarding the Haupt situation. The Exchange remained closed on Monday, in observance of a national day of mourning, during which the final matters were concluded. At the very worst, no client would lose money for having a Haupt account. Of course, the country hardly noticed any of this, given the unusual circumstances of the funeral.

The news was released Tuesday morning, but at that time brokers and investors talked more of the way Lyndon Johnson had handled the transition to a new administration. The Dow opened higher and continued to rise for the rest of the session. Volume was 9.3 million shares, making this the busiest day in the year, and the Dow closed at 744, up 32 points, the largest one-session leap in Exchange history. Gratified, Johnson called Funston to congratulate him. A major bull move seemed in the offing.

During the next few weeks academicians, businessmen, and market analysts considered the prospects for the coming year. Most were generally impressed by the way Johnson had taken command at the White House, and all believed he would push ahead vigorously for legislation proposed by Kennedy, the tax cut in particular. They differed on the economic outlook and were troubled by the collective state of mind of the American people. Gabriel Hauge, president of the Manufacturers Hanover Trust, remarked, "The basic strengths of the economy that have been lifting it to higher ground remain generally unimpaired," while Raymond Saulnier of Columbia University said, "I think we're at a high point," and wasn't sure that any important further advance was possible. Walter Heller, who remained at the Council of Economic Advisors, spoke of the "basic strength of the economy" and said he felt certain that passage of the tax legislation would provide it with a new impetus. Robert Turner of Indiana University was troubled by the idea that the assassination had "undoubtedly shaken the confidence of the American people," but added that "Mr. Johnson's succession to the Presidency will remove some of the less rational obstacles to the acceptance of Pres. Kennedy's policies." Finally, William Butler of the Chase Manhattan Bank said, "There will be some hesitation until people figure out what it means."

Wall Street did not hesitate. Confidence in Johnson grew rapidly, and with it stock prices moved upward. The Dow hit a high of 767 on December 18 before pausing, and it closed the year at 763. "Wall Street is calling it the Johnson bull market," wrote *Business Week*, while the *Journal* added that "investors show more confidence now than they have in recent years."

The McGraw-Hill year-end survey was as sunny as possible. "In 1964 the U.S. economy is due to set records in gross national product, industrial output, and in the durability of an upward movement. If the year fulfills its promise, this will become the longest sustained peacetime expansion the U.S. had ever recorded." Edward Rubin, president of Selected American Shares, flatly predicted that "the coming year will be the best this country has ever had." In the *New York Times* National Economic Review Thomas Mullaney opened his article thusly: "The United States appears poised on the brink of a great new economic era that is taking form slightly behind schedule."

Wall Street's analysts were somewhat skeptical of this view. Joseph Humphrey of Calvin Bullock Ltd. noted that plant capacity was strained and that inflationary pressures were bound to increase. John Harriman of Tri-Continental Corp. was troubled by the rapid rise in credit buying and the balance of payments situation. Also, he noted that foreigners had started hoarding gold, and he predicted that the outflow of this metal from the United States would prove troublesome in the future. A majority of mutual fund managers surveyed said they expected a good year, but few thought the Dow would perform as well as it had in 1963. Even the optimistic Edward Rubin said, "The advances are likely to prove more subdued than many enthusiastic predictions now making their appearance would indicate."

Wall Street approved of Lyndon Johnson, and so did many big businessmen. Harding Lawrence of Continental Air Lines said, "Johnson appeals to businessmen because he operates his office in a way that businessmen understand." A Montgomery Ward official, noting that the new president made it up the ladder the hard way, added that Johnson "knows the importance of a buck, has lived with the oil industry for years, and has a knowledge of big business and its problems." Another businessman summed up a general sentiment: "Johnson's a hell of a lot more like me than Kennedy was." Apparently most Americans were satisfied with their new leader. In early January a Gallup poll indicated that 79 percent of them thought he was performing well in office.

The first of the 1963 annual earnings reports started appearing in the newspapers in mid-January, and they made pleasant reading. When all the figures were in they showed net corporate profits that year of $29.4 billion, a new record that was $3.5 billion more than had been earned in 1962. Other good news appeared at the same time. There were many dividend increases and stock splits, though no new marks were set in these categories. On the other hand, a McGraw-Hill survey indicated that capital spending in 1964 would establish a record.

Some businessmen remained troubled regarding the impending tax cut. Was such stimulation truly necessary? Would it not prove inflationary? Lyndon Johnson was considered a "spender," and the combination of new federal programs and lower tax revenues easily might set off a new wage-price spiral.

Mixed feelings on this issue were insufficient to keep the market down. Prices rose on good volume in early January, as White House reporters noted that Johnson had come to view the Dow as a measure of his popularity. The glamour issues led the way, followed by stocks of those firms that were increasing dividends or splitting their shares. The aluminum industry boosted prices, and so Alcoa, Reynolds, and Kaiser moved upward. Each favorable story was good for a few additional points, while bad news had less of an impact. For example, a government report linking cigarette smoking and cancer sent the tobaccos into a tailspin, but two months later these stocks were back to their old levels, and some actually set new highs.

The key news, however, came out of the White House and the Capitol, where Johnson was revising the Kennedy budget and Congress completed work on the new tax bill. In early January the president hinted that the public would be surprised by the budget, that he had managed to keep spending below the limits established by Kennedy prior to the assassination. Johnson orchestrated the presentation carefully. On January 20 the White House released a report indicating that the gross national product that year would be $34 billion more than it had been the previous year. The following day he sent his budget to Congress. It had been common knowledge that the Kennedy draft had called for over $100 billion in spending. The Johnson proposal was for $97.9 billion, well below that magic triple digit mark, and more than $13 billion less than actual expenditures in 1963. Veteran analysts didn't expect Johnson to keep to his projections; rarely had presidents ever succeeded in this. Moreover, Johnson had achieved his goal by slashing heavily into the military budgets, and pressures from that quarter would be difficult to overcome. But Wall Street appreciated the gesture. More than Kennedy, Johnson knew the value of a buck, or at least so it seemed.

The Dow closed at 773 on January 20, and a week later was at 785, as volume expanded and trading became more hectic. The following week General Motors raised its quarterly dividend from 50¢ to 65¢, and stocks spurted ahead once again, coming within hailing distance of Dow 800.

Meanwhile members of Congress met to put the final touches on the Kennedy-Johnson tax cut bill, also known as the Revenue Act of 1964. In its final form the measure sliced $11.5 billion from the nation's tax bill. Corporate taxes were to go from a maximum of 52 percent to 48 percent in two steps, and the nation's business also would benefit from a variety of stimulative programs designed to encourage capital investment.

Taken by itself, the Revenue Act might have troubled some Wall Streeters, who still didn't accept the idea that a deliberately unbalanced budget could come into balance through the magical devices of economic growth. Eisenhower always had placed a budget surplus above tax cuts in his order of priorities; he had been willing to sacrifice growth for stable prices. Kennedy had appeared to reverse the priorities. Now Johnson was blending what many businessmen thought were the best elements of both. The nation would have its tax cut, and so the economy would grow more rapidly than otherwise might have been the case. But the president would put a lid on spending—or at least so it appeared in late February of 1964—and this would keep the deficit within manageable limits.

Johnson would have to fight off attacks from both left and right in order to do this. Congressional liberals and some members of the Cabinet argued for new social programs, and Johnson appeared to support them. The conservatives, led by Senator Barry Goldwater, were distressed at cuts in the defense budget, and they vowed to fight for their restoration.

Everyone realized that a good deal depended upon the economy's performance in 1964 and 1965. If Walter Heller and the new economists were correct, economic growth would accelerate, there would be little in the way of additional inflation, and in fact prices actually might decline. Even at the new reduced rates a full-employment economy would produce record tax revenues. What was needed for all of this to work was time. The staunchest tax cut advocates conceded that net revenues initially would be lower than would have been the case under the old schedule. Then they would rise, as the fiscal stimulant worked its way through the economy. What was required, then, was tight controls on government spending in 1964 and perhaps part of 1965 as well. Then, assuming all went well, Johnson might implement some of his new programs and even offer sops to those who wanted to see increased military spending.

The president refused to await the results of this experiment in taxation, and this would prove one of the more important decisions of his administration. Temperamentally he was unwilling to sit aside and watch the unraveling of history. Also, Johnson had to bow to political pressures, seeing that he was an accidental chief executive in an election year. Even before he signed the Revenue Act, he prepared new spending programs. Additional sums were earmarked for military ordnance; Johnson quietly restored most of his cuts in this area. There were supplemental appropriations for Southeast Asia, and a $962 million anti-poverty program. The president indicated that more of the same might be expected.

In 1964 the government took in $47.6 billion from individual income taxes and $21.6 billion in corporate taxes, which were respectively $2 billion and $1 billion more than the previous year. Heller and other new economists were gratified by this showing, but conceded that the figures would have been higher had not the tax cuts gone into effect. The stimulus was working, however; the full impact would be felt in 1965. Total federal revenues for 1964 came to $112.7 billion. As expected, Johnson was unable to keep spending below $100 billion. Outlays came to $118.6 billion, about the same as in 1963. The 1964 deficit was $5.9 billion, the third highest since 1946.

That there would be a deficit in 1964 became evident in the spring of that year. Wall Street had been presented with a curious mixture of stimulative actions and restrictive talk and tried to sort it out. The tax cut and the spending program would accelerate growth and enhance earnings in the short run, while Johnson continued to use the language of fiscal moderation and engaged in symbolic acts as though to prove he was prudent. In the morning he would recommend multi-million-dollar welfare programs, which, whatever their merits, would further unbalance the budget, while in the afternoon he would stroll through the White House putting out lights so as to save on electricity. The public was delighted by the human interest story, while most people didn't understand the implications of the spending programs. The president's popularity remained high. All seemed well.

The stock market behaved erratically that spring and early summer. The Dow crossed the 800 level on February 28, and by March 30 was over 830. Then followed a long pause, and by April the Index was back to 810. Favorable first-quarter earnings statements renewed the bullish sentiment, and the Dow went over 830 on May 7, fell back to 800 a month later, and in late June again was over 830.

Analysts attributed this up-and-down-and-up behavior to noneconomic developments. Senator Goldwater scored surprising victories in several key primaries and by mid-June seemed capable of winning the Republican presidential nomination. While many Wall Streeters approved of his political philosophy, they also seemed to think Goldwater was a naive extremist who if elected would try to implement his programs, and this would send the economy into a tailspin.

Also, there was distressing news from Vietnam, where it appeared the Viet Cong might win major victories unless the United States intervened. Both Johnson and Goldwater had spoken out on that issue. The president believed in a "moderate" approach, which meant additional American military and economic aid to South Vietnam but no major commitment of troops. Goldwater preferred a stronger stand, indicating that he was willing to take any step that would ensure victory.

Fears of Goldwater were credited with keeping stock prices down. But that spring most Americans believed Johnson could defeat anyone the Republicans nominated, and few thought the United States would become involved in an important land war in Asia. Carl M. Loeb, Rhoades & Co. told clients that the market was behaving erratically for psychological reasons. Conditions were so good that investors felt some sense of shame. "There is a peculiar mixture of superstition and residual puritanism, the desire not to defy the gods by too great a show of satisfaction and the guilty feeling that it is positively sinful to be so well off." Reynolds & Co. was decidedly optimistic. "Based upon the foreseeable future, it is difficult to see how the current market decline can carry substantially further." Donaldson, Lufkin & Jenrette, noting the first-quarter statements, said, "The extent to which corporate profits are increasing has come as a surprise to investors," and that firm too looked for higher stock prices.

The Dow closed at 840 on Monday, August 3. Volume came to 3.8 million shares, the lowest in more than a month. Then came news of what was described as an attack by North Vietnamese torpedo boats on the American destroyer *Maddox* in the Bay of Tonkin. The following session, on a volume of 4.8 million shares, the Dow lost 7½ points. Johnson told the nation that he had ordered retaliatory attacks, and in the first hour of trading Wednesday the Dow dropped close to 10 points. There was a rally in the afternoon, however, enabling the Index to show a slight gain for the session. Volume was 6.2 million shares, with the tape falling behind on several occasions. The selling resumed on Thursday, with the Dow closing at 823, for a loss of 9½ points. That day the Senate adopted the Bay of Tonkin Resolution, which authorized the president to take military action against North Vietnam and which the administration later claimed was the equivalent of a limited declaration of war.

It was a popular move. A Harris poll taken in July indicated that 58 percent of the public had disagreed with the way Johnson had been handling the war. After the Bay of Tonkin episode and resolution, the president received an approval rating of 72 percent.

Stocks rallied, with the Dow rising above 840 in mid-August. There was no major military buildup in Vietnam in this period, or any indication that Johnson intended to embark upon a large scale war there. Those who later on would be called "hawks" approved of the Bay of Tonkin resolution; the "doves" could note that nothing much had changed since then and that, in any case, Johnson's position on the war was far more moderate than that of Barry Goldwater. The economic news continued to be good, and so the market rose on increased volume. In late September the Dow was over 870, with analysts predicting that 900 would fall before the end of the year.

Stocks marked time in October, and on November 2, the session prior to the election, closed a fraction above 875. As expected, Johnson won a smashing victory the following day, and shortly thereafter a rally got under way. By November 23 the Dow was at 889, with the 900 level apparently within easy reach.

The next day, the Federal Reserve raised the discount rate to 4 percent. The move caught many Wall Streeters off guard. When questioned about it, FRB officials spoke of inflation, unbalanced budgets, and the importance of fiscal restraint. The Board mentioned the need "to maintain the international strength of the dollar" as well. Clearly this segment of the financial community did not believe that all was well as far as the economy was concerned.

Stocks declined, bottoming out at 857 on December 15 before rising once again. There was a year-end rally in 1974; the Dow ended up at 874. Brokers congratulated themselves and their clients for a price rise that added over 111 points to the Dow. The talk on the Street no longer was of Dow 900, but of 1,000 and beyond. A year-end survey of analysts conducted by *Business Week* indicated that a large majority of them were bullish, with the consensus being that the Dow would end 1965 at 950–75.

If there were flaws in the design, they could not be seen by the bears. Those few who remained talked about stocks having too high a P/E ratio, of the need to pause after so large a gain, and of declining profit margins. Inflation seemed less of a problem; the Consumer Price Index rose by only 1.2 percent in 1964, and the Federal Reserve was counted upon to keep it at that level. However, none of the pessimists paid much attention to the erosion of the dollar's position in international trade, and of course the full impact of the budget deficit had not been felt as yet. The American commitment to Vietnam remained unclear.

The nation's strengths were apparent in late 1964; its weaknesses were masked, or at least not in the foreground. The tide would turn in 1965.

Seven

FLAWS IN THE DESIGN

MARKET ANALYSTS paid little attention to international economic and financial issues during the Eisenhower era. This continued to be the case in the Kennedy years, though even then there was talk of balance of payments deficits, pressures on the dollar, and a possible revival of the gold standard. These matters became increasingly important in the mid-1960s and soon would be the talk of the boardrooms.

By then sufficient time had passed to obtain a perspective on the nation's development in the post–World War II period, to draw up a balance sheet of strengths and weaknesses, and try to guess where America was headed.

In addition to possessing the world's most powerful economy in the late 1940s, the United States had its strongest currency. The dollar remained supreme through the 1950s. One reason Eisenhower had been willing to submit the nation to three recessions was his defense of the dollar and of the system that had been erected upon it at the Bretton Woods Conference of 1944. Under the terms of the agreements, the Allied and other nations agreed to fix the price of their currencies in terms of dollars, and to intervene in the money markets should their prices rise or fall above or below certain limits. The United States, in turn, was obliged to tie the dollar to gold at $35 an ounce, and to stand willing to buy or sell at that price to any central bank. The assumption was that through the judicious management of the federal budget and timely interventions by the Federal Reserve System, America would create sufficient dollars to keep the system afloat, but not so many as to swamp it. Eisenhower considered a strong dollar one of the key ingredients in the Western alliance, and so did Federal Reserve Board Chairman William Mc-Chesney Martin. A decline in the purchasing power of the dollar, any indication that the United States would not honor its commitments, would have caused an international financial panic greater than any in history.

In large part the power of the dollar relied upon the strength of the American economy, and during the Cold War a significant portion of that economy was devoted to the production of military goods. The United States shouldered most of the costs and responsibilities involved with defending the West and Japan against the Soviet Union. In contrast, Europe and Japan spent relatively little on defense, and so were able to devote larger shares of their national incomes to social welfare programs and capital investments. Often this situation helped their economies vis-à-vis that of the United States. For example, the Korean War provided a stimulant for the American economy, but also drew capital away from the consumer-based sector, created dislocations, and increased the national debt. American military procurement programs relating to the war sparked a boom in Japan, where industrial production shot up by a startling one-third from 1950 to 1951—and under the terms of their constitution, the Japanese were forbidden from maintaining a defense establishment. Almost 15 percent of America's increase in gross national product during the 1950s went into defense spending; West Germany earmarked less than 3 percent of its increase for defense. While the United States was becoming the world leader in sophisticated military and space hardware, the Germans and Japanese were able to concentrate their attention on goods for the civilian markets, and to a lesser extent so did France and other Western nations. Thus, the United States led the West in aviation, weaponry, and missile propulsion systems in the 1960s—while European and Japanese exports of automobiles, cameras, steel, television sets, and a variety of other products made important inroads into world markets.

More than any other Western nation, the United States had become a large, powerful, complex garrison society, and even though its evidences were everywhere, most Americans hardly seemed to notice this new state of affairs. President Eisenhower perhaps had as complete an awareness of the situation as any person. In 1946, as chief of staff, he had urged "cultivating to the utmost the integration of civilian and military resources and of securing the most effective unified direction of our research and development activities." Fifteen years later, in his Farewell Address, he warned against some of the consequences of the kind of condition he had helped fashion. The president spoke of "the acquisition of unwarranted influence whether sought or unsought, by the military-industrial complex," and of how military considerations were fashioning the economy. "Akin to and largely responsible for the sweeping changes in our industrial-military posture has been the technological revolution during recent decades. In this revolution research has become central; it also becomes formalized, complex, and costly. A steadily increasing share is conducted for, by, or at the direction of the Federal Government."

Eisenhower described what for some was a subtle change in the nature of American capitalism. Before World War II, economists and reformers were concerned with the dangers posed by monopoly, situations where one company or aggregation of power controlled a product or market, and these concerns carried over into the postwar period, when a new antitrust crusade began. In retrospect, however, one can see that monopsony—the domination of a product or market by a single purchaser—had become more a hallmark of a major segment of the economy by the 1950s. That consumer was the federal government, and the sellers and suppliers were hundreds of firms of various sizes eager to obtain secure long-term contracts for military hardware and services.

In general the profit margins on such sales were lower than those available for similar transactions in the private sector, and government contracts could be renegotiated after their conclusion. On the other hand, it was possible to obtain government contracts that ran for several years, to which were attached aid programs of various kinds, and once a company had the proper connections with one or more federal agencies, follow-up contracts were easier to obtain. What the company might have lost in profit margins was more than compensated for by volume and security. Furthermore, the technologies and techniques acquired through government contracts might be employed in the creation of products and services that could be sold in the private sector. As Eisenhower indicated, the government had become the sponsor of much research and development in the 1950s.

That there would have been a bull market in the 1950s and early 1960s without these kinds of federal programs is beyond serious doubt. Given America's pre-eminent position in the world after the war, its large internal market eager for consumer goods, its powerful and intact industrial machine and well-trained and motivated work force, the economy was bound to expand. The nation's technological superiority in most areas would have enabled it to remain ahead of foreign competitors no matter how great an effort these could have mounted. Corporate profits would have risen sharply and with them, eventually, stock prices as well. Had there been no Cold War and related complications, such a major bull market might have been led by stocks of companies that produced consumer goods, machinery, and raw materials, or were involved in leisure-time activities, construction, and new technologies geared to public needs. In fact, such a market did develop in the late 1940s, spearheaded by stocks of television companies. In 1949, the year the bull market began, the best-performing groups were the utilities, food chains, and cement stocks, followed by those of finance companies, glass, steamship, and baking, which hardly could be classified as important segments of the military-industrial complex.

Without the Cold War this bull market would have resembled that of the 1920s, a period when government spending—especially for war-related goods—declined most years, the economy expanded greatly, inflation and unemployment were relatively minor problems, the dollar was secure, and the United States had the strongest economy in the West. The glamour stocks of that earlier period were in such fields as automobiles, radio, motion pictures, and electric power, all of which might be classified as being in the "consumer" sector.

As it was, the bull market of the late 1950s and 1960s was led by stocks of firms involved directly or indirectly with government spending, and in fact a large part of the general economy was dependent upon government for its well being. The planning for and expectation of a sizable government contract sufficed to enable a small electronics firm to float its first stock issue, while many giant corporations grew even larger as a result of such work. Among them were firms one ordinarily didn't consider in this category. AT&T was among the ten top recipients of military contracts in 1960, and these accounted for 10 percent of the company's sales. General Electric was a top ten company, with 20 percent of its sales to the military. So were Westinghouse (13 percent), RCA (16 percent), and Food Machinery (21 percent). Pan American World Airways, a major airline, also ran government testing facilities and had important contracts for military transport; some 44 percent of its sales were government related. Dozens of companies born in the postwar period, or which had been small and insignificant in the mid-1940s, entered the $100-million-a-year category in the 1950s as a result of such contracts, and their stocks became stars of the bull market. Such issues as Aerojet, Collins Radio, Control Data, General Precision, and Teledyne came to the public's attention because of defense contracts. Sales and profits rose rapidly, and their stocks took off.

These and other military-industrial companies benefited hugely from technological spinoffs into the civilian market, and some used their knowledge and connections to obtain federal, state, and local contracts in nonmilitary areas as well. Lockheed ran drug abuse programs and created curricula for public schools; North American attempted to become an important factor in transportation planning. Both sold computers in the civilian market that had been developed under military contracts. General Dynamics became involved in water purification programs, using technologies created when the firm constructed atomic submarines. Aerojet diversified into computerized teaching systems and related informational areas. The technologies involved in space programs were used by Communications Satellite Corp. to create a service that enabled television to become a global utility. Ceramics developed for military nose cones were transformed into dinner ware. In this way, the federal government's programs, especially those relating to the military, became an important part of the general economy, and certainly provided much of the glamour for Wall Street in the two decades following the end of World War II.

By the early 1960s radical critics of America's world role charged that the nation had become dominated by an unwholesome alliance of government officials, businessmen, academics, and military officers, and some even quoted Eisenhower in support of their view. Clearly this was a gross exaggeration and oversimplification, and many people dismissed the idea that such a conspiracy existed. But there was some truth to it. Due to the world situation after the war there developed major tensions between the United States and the Soviet Union, and demands created by this phenomenon shaped the economy in ways that otherwise would not have been possible. These changes in turn were transmitted to Wall Street and helped give birth to the bull market and then enabled it to flourish. Even those investors and speculators who hadn't given a thought to such matters instinctively appreciated the impact federal spending had upon the market. The temporary "heating up of the Cold War" might result in a dip, but invariably stock prices would recover. Then, as new defense programs were announced, shares of companies that would benefit from them would bound upward. Through the 1950s and early 1960s, the market sold off on "peace scares," while warlike noises out of Washington or Moscow meant higher prices on Wall Street.

Analysts and investors had by then come to understand that there really were three markets for stocks. The first, related to federal procurement programs, consisted of the aerospace issues, many electronics, some construction stocks, and perhaps a majority of the new issues. Then there was the "civilian market," led by the electric utilities and industries that had only a marginal involvement with federal programs, such as cosmetics, bowling, tobacco, foodstuffs, and leisure time and fast food. Finally, there was a third kind of market, this one in stocks of companies that neither were completely government-oriented or had most of their business in civilian markets, but whose activities overlapped both. Most office equipment, automotive, petroleum, and electronics stocks fell into this category. For example, IBM was not a major supplier of goods to the federal government; less than 10 percent of its sales were related to military procurement. But IBM computers were purchased or leased by most military-industrial companies, as were its typewriters and other equipment. Without the demands of the Cold War, IBM could not have grown as rapidly as it did; without assured sales to military-industrial firms it could not have generated the funds for research and development for the production of new machines. If "peace broke out," IBM would continue to grow, though perhaps at a slower rate than before, and the same held true for other companies whose stocks fell into this third category.

In 1964, however, all three groups rose simultaneously. The Cold War persisted, and in fact there would be increased military spending for the war in Southeast Asia. President Johnson's desire to place an American on the moon by the end of the decade assured larger appropriations for space. The expansion of Great Society programs meant more spending at home. And the new economists assured the nation that lower taxes would mean higher returns to the Treasury, more than ample to pay for it all.

These massive federal outlays since the end of World War II had been financed by the collection of taxes and the creation of debt. In 1945 the gross federal debt stood at $260 billion, more than five times what it had been in the last peacetime year, 1940. In 1964 the debt was $317 billion, and although it sounded enormous, economists observed that it was a smaller percentage of the gross national product than it had been in 1945, and in any case was quite manageable. Also, it was money Americans owed themselves; the nation had only a small foreign debt. Furthermore, it was a small price to pay for peace, security, freedom, and prosperity.

Wall Street was confident about the present and secure in the belief that the future would be better. Analysts and financial writers commented favorably on the record of economic growth, the magic of the new economics, the potential of novel products and small companies, and the wisdom of the nation's political and business leaders. Some academic and government economists were troubled by trends and statistics, and a handful of them saw dangers ahead. Their sentiments appeared in print, usually in specialized or fringe journals, but generally these people were ignored, or read and quickly forgotten. That invisible screen which 15 years earlier had filtered out the good news leaving investors to ponder the bad, had by 1964 been completely reversed.

After World War II the American economy had been powerful, while confidence in it was low. On the eve of the Vietnam War buildup, most Americans believed their economy to be strong, resilient, and capable of great expansion, when it fact it was flawed and vulnerable.

Part of the problem derived from the enlarged role of the public sector, which stimulated the economy and helped effect a redistribution of wealth, but at the same time diverted assets from capital formation in the private sector and greatly added to the national debt. Indirectly related to this was the increased challenge from overseas. Between 1952 and 1960 Western Europe's industrial production increased by more than 60 percent, while Japan's output rose by an amazing 144 percent. Neither Europe or Japan was seriously affected by the three American recessions of this decade, and in fact their exports actually increased somewhat during the American slowdowns. By the late 1950s it was evident that West Germany and Japan had powerful economies, while France was not far behind and would do even better once extricated from colonial wars. Internationalists rejoiced at this demonstration of free world might, while at the same time some economists and businessmen noted that foreign goods were selling well in the United States, often at the expense of their American counterparts, and that the Europeans and Japanese had become major competitors in world markets as well. This situation, they said, meant that the growth of the American economy in the future might not be as rapid as it had been in the past.

Throughout this period the United States enjoyed a substantial favorable trade balance. But at the same time America posted regular balance of international payment deficits, the results of foreign aid programs and military spending overseas, as well as private investments of various kinds. In 1958–59 alone the deficit came to more than $5 billion. By then there no longer was talk of a dollar shortage. Instead, international economists spoke ominously of a dollar glut.

Throughout the 1950s foreign governments had converted some of their dollars into gold, thus reversing the situation that had existed immediately after World War II. Outside of governmental and banking circles, however, this move back to gold was hardly noticed. Those who wrote on the subject tended to think that it was quite normal, even healthy, in that it signified a growing strength of the European currencies. But as the balance of payments deficit widened—it came to $3.4 billion in 1960—these gold purchases increased. Late in the year the pressures and rumors of a run on the Treasury caused the open market gold price to rise above $36. Some economists started to talk of a revaluation of the dollar, or removal of the 25 percent gold cover for the American currency. From France came Charles de Gaulle's solution: the gold price should be increased, toward the end of having the metal replace the dollar as the international measure of value.

Incoming President Kennedy dismissed these ideas out of hand. He had promised during the campaign, "If elected President

I shall not devalue the dollar from its present rate. Rather, I shall defend its present value and soundness." Kennedy's determination to do so played a major part in his yearnings for a balanced budget and early opposition to deficit spending and a tax cut; on several occasions he told advisers that the two things he most feared were nuclear war and a balance of payments deficit.

The deficit declined to $1.3 billion in 1961, but the Treasury had to sell $719 million worth of gold on balance that year, much of it to France, while talk persisted on devaluation and/or an end to the gold cover. Kennedy continued to swear that neither was being considered, and he promised vigorous action to bring an end to the deficit. All he did, however, was to recommend an interest equalization tax under which Americans who purchased stock from foreigners would have to pay a temporary tax of 15 percent—and even this minor measure to discourage capital outflows did not go into effect until 1963.

Still, the gold outflow did decline. Treasury net sales came to $230 million in 1962 and only $159 million the following year. The French appeared to have abandoned their plan for an international gold standard and the new economists claimed the tax cut would rectify the balance of international payments situation as well, and so make the entire issue academic.

These problems vaguely troubled Wall Streeters, but had little impact upon market movements. Instinctively analysts and investors felt deficits of any kind were undesirable, and they were unhappy about the outflow of gold, though most weren't certain why this was so. Of all the district's major publications, only *Barron's*, the most conservative of the lot, seemed to believe the dollar was in trouble.

Those who bothered to investigate the situation and peruse the literature understood that the rest of the world still wanted American goods, and that the balance of trade remained favorable—it came to $8.3 billion in 1964, a postwar high. Whatever difficulties the United States had in terms of international payments derived from the nation's position as leader of the free world, and no responsible political figure of either party cared to alter this situation. Nor would the government of any Western European nation, not even France, care to see a drastic change in its relationship to America.

In 1964 American foreign aid programs and military spending

overseas more than wiped out the trade surplus and left the nation with yet another balance of payments deficit. That year the nation lost more than $381 million in gold, and buying had accelerated in the fourth quarter.

What did all of this mean as far as the average investor was concerned? Those who followed gold mining stocks knew they had risen every year from 1960 to 1964, in anticipation perhaps of a boost in the gold price. Other than that, the erosion of the dollar's position had no significant effect on the market's behavior. Foreigners seemed quite willing to go on absorbing dollars; de Gaulle's attitude appeared more motivated by anti-Americanism than economic dogma, and in any case he hadn't much of a following outside of his own country.

This, then, was the situation in the first months of the Johnson administration. The economy seemed to be in fine shape. The prime lending rate stood at 4½ percent, where it had been since 1960. Most economists predicted another good business year, the fifth in a row. Such a performance would result in an increase in tax revenues, which could mean smaller deficits and enable Johnson to initiate more of his Great Society programs. At this time there were fewer than 24,000 American servicemen in all of Southeast Asia, and it appeared few additional ones would be required there. "War in Vietnam, however, will drag on," concluded *U.S. News & World Report* in its 1965 preview edition. "That war could move to a climax, with a U.S. pull-out not inconceivable before the end of another year." The Johnson budget, presented to Congress in January, actually projected a small decline in total defense spending for the coming fiscal year. Still, there would be a deficit of more than $9 billion.

On Wall Street a majority of analysts thought the gross national product would expand by 5 to 6 percent, while corporate earnings would be up by slightly more than that. The financial district was concerned over weakness in the British pound, and betting was that another devaluation would take place in 1965. There was no thought the dollar would come under pressure, despite continued news of Treasury sales. In an unusual move the government warned speculators that any attempt to inflate the price of gold would fail, but this had no impact upon foreign buyers. The flight from the dollar continued.

The Dow had closed 1964 at a fraction below 875, and a small number of analysts thought a correction overdue. Anthony Gaubis warned that the price/earnings ratios of many leading issues were out of line with economic reality and recommended a move into fixed income securities. Benjamin Clark of White, Weld, was troubled about corporate profit margins and related problems, and he thought the Dow could fall 100 points or so early in the year. But none of the bears offered arguments based upon the declining position of the dollar, the gold situation, or budgetary imbalances. As for the bulls, most of them were convinced by then that America could weather any storm. "Wall Street bears have been wrong for a long time," said Robert Johnson of Paine, Webber. "They've been wrong because they have consistently underestimated the tremendous strength of our economy."

In late January the Treasury announced that as a result of continued gold sales, it had only $1.8 billion of the metal above the 25 percent cover for the dollar required by law. Not since the days of Grover Cleveland had the American currency appeared so vulnerable in the international arena. Charls Walker, a prominent administration insider, agreed that this situation "threatened the sustainability of the economic advance and may hurt the dollar internationally," but he went on to say that retention of the cover was necessary, and that it should be "relaxed, not removed." President Johnson told interviewers that he intended to remove the gold cover "in stages," and he clearly indicated by his attitude that this matter was not of primary concern to his administration.

In January, as corporations reported 1964 earnings and several large ones raised their dividends, the market moved ahead on good volume. Late in the month the Dow crossed 900, and with the fall of this psychological barrier the way to 1,000 appeared wide open. Several commentators, led by Gaubis and Anthony Tabell, warned that prices had risen too fast and that a correction was overdue. As though in answer to this, a chorus of statements were made expressing complete confidence in the economy. *Business Week*, which by then had emerged as a leading voice of the bulls, wrote, "The financial community simply is taking account of the fact that the outlook for business is strong. Investors are saying, in effect, that even though the current upswing in business has gone on longer than any peacetime expansion, it can continue."

In February both the gold and Vietnam issues erupted and combined to put a crimp into the bull move. Outgoing Undersecretary of the Treasury for Monetary Affairs Robert Roosa became a rallying point for the skeptics, though he hadn't sought such a role. He delivered a speech in which he warned against "a further weakening of our national balance-of-payments position" and in a magazine interview added, "It is vital that any elimination of the gold cover on bank deposits must be accompanied by a strengthening, not an impairment, of the Federal Reserve as defender of the gold reserve." Wall Street took Roosa's message to mean that he had little confidence in Johnson's ability and willingness to deal with the issue and that all hopes for monetary salvation had to rest with Chairman Martin. Roosa went on to join the investment banking firm of Brown Brothers, Harriman, and in the months ahead continued to sound alarms of this nature, most of which were heard on the Street and helped undermine Johnson's credibility on such matters in that part of the nation.

On February 9 the president asked for a series of "voluntary" restrictions on gold outflows. The exchange equalization tax would be extended, and American banks were to make fewer and smaller foreign loans. Corporations were asked to cut back on overseas investments. That same day the Viet Cong mounted a major attack against South Vietnamese and American positions, and newspapers carried stories of meetings between Chinese and Soviet diplomats. Was this a sign that these countries were about to unite to intervene directly in Southeast Asia? The news and fears engendered by these monetary and foreign policy developments caused the market to fall by more than 8 points the following session, to close at 893. Volume reached 7.2 million shares, the highest since the Kennedy assassination. The selloff continued into the next day, when the Dow gave up more than 11 points, and the bears remained in control until the morning of the 16th, at which time the Dow struck bottom at 877.

By then it appeared the Johnson plea had been taken seriously by banks and large corporations. To the surprise of almost all concerned, the programs seemed to be working, and in fact the balance of payments problem eased a trifle in February, and in the second quarter the nation experienced a payments surplus. Still, the gold outflow continued, though it no longer seemed as serious as before. In addition, there was no Soviet or Chinese intervention in Vietnam, and the Viet Cong withdrew and for a while the area seemed calm. The market rallied, to close the month above 900 once again.

Wall Street had been provided with a preview of the shape of the young bear. An end to the unique position enjoyed by the dollar since the finish of World War II, combined with a deepening involvement in Vietnam, would soon cause the massive bull market to climax and then end. As it turned out, these two forces were interrelated, and each possessed a psychological as well as an economic dimension. Working in tandem, they undermined the bulls and finally converted them to negativism.

It was not supposed to finish this way. Throughout the 1950s social and economic critics had warned against problems of various kinds on Wall Street, comparing the situation then to what had transpired during the 1920s. That there were excesses in the early 1960s, and even more after 1964, was evident. More important than any of them, however, was the recovery of Europe and Japan and all that entailed, and the military and political miscalculations in Vietnam, and neither had any direct relationship to the prices of stocks at the exchanges and markets.

Stocks declined in early February but rallied toward the end of the month. The selloff was attributed to fears of an accelerating conflict in Southeast Asia, the recovery to optimistic news out of Washington that all was going well there. News of an extension of the steelworkers' contract and increases in orders for capital goods were balanced against signs of continued erosion of the pound sterling and warnings from the Federal Reserve that credit tightening might be needed. The result was a standoff market in March, with the Dow closing a fraction below 900.

The *Wall Street Journal* carried articles indicating that business confidence was high. The *Times* and the *Herald-Tribune* celebrated the Johnson approach in Vietnam. *Business Week* admired his prudence in having refused to "let himself be stampeded" by those who wanted all-out war and others who called for a complete withdrawal from the area. Alan Abelson of *Barron's* saw matters differently. "Now, one doesn't have to be a grizzled bear to sniff out potential sources of trouble for the market," he wrote on March 1, and he cited excess business inventories as one emerging problem. This was not the key element for a decline, however. "Sooner or later, moreover, Washington is going to have to admit that warnings and good wishes aren't enough to cure the nation's balance-of-payments ills; comes that apocalypse, interest rates will go up and, temporarily at least, equity prices will go down. Then, of course, the war in South Viet Nam may blaze into something much bigger."

Stocks broke out on the upside in mid-April and crossed over 920 late in the month. Brokers attributed this performance to expectations of excellent first-quarter earnings and continued indications that the balance of payments deficit was narrowing. On April 28 Johnson ordered the marines to intervene in a revolutionary situation in the Dominican Republic, and for several days it appeared the United States might become involved in two military actions simultaneously. The following week he dispatched more troops to the Caribbean and in addition sent a paratroop brigade to Vietnam. Johnson asked Congress for $700 million to support both ventures, and he received this money after little debate.

Business Week reported that "A thriving stock market, fed by lush corporate earnings and the prospect of a capital-spending boom that could top last year's 14% rise, took off last week. The popular Dow-Jones industrial average climbed to 932." Leading the way were the military-industrial stocks—electronics, weapons producers, and the like. As had been the case through most of the post–World War II period, news of increased military engagements resulted in higher prices on Wall Street.

The Index peaked at 945 in the afternoon of May 14 before closing 940. Volume came to 5.8 million shares that day. A week later the Dow was down to slightly better than 922, and some analysts warned of a further correction. Fundamentalists said that earnings might not be as good as previously had been believed; technicians thought there was a need to test the 910–15 level before the market could resume its upward climb.

The news that month was bad. There were rumors the Communist Chinese were moving troops into North Vietnam and soon would intervene in the war. While a slowly accelerating engagement in that part of the world was seen as being bullish, the Street knew that a major confrontation between America and China could result in serious dislocations of all sorts, and so stocks fell. Conceding that the budget would be badly out of balance, the Treasury asked Congress to increase the national debt limit. The gold outflow continued, and administration leaders began speaking of the need for a new international conference at which both the dollar and pound sterling problems would be discussed.

On June 1, with the Dow at 908, Chairman Martin warned about "disquieting similarities" between the current situation and the one that had existed in 1929. Stocks sold off, falling below 900 on the 4th, rallying, and then dropping by more than 13 points on the 8th to end the session under 890. The following Wall Street was swept by rumors that President Johnson had suffered a stroke. On heavy volume the Dow plummeted, winding up a fraction under 880.

As it turned out, Johnson was healthy, and he told reporters there was no reason for "gloom and doom." Treasury Secretary Henry Fowler met with a group of senators and informed them there would be no difficulties for the rest of that year or even for 1966. Commerce Secretary John Conner said "business is great, and getting better." Gardner Ackley, chairman of the Council of Economic Advisors, said economic expansion "seems destined to continue many, many months." He challenged Martin's assumptions, claiming that the international monetary system was strong, the dollar was secure, the gold outflow was being afforded too much attention, and the United States was moving "vigorously—and so far successfully—to restore equilibrium to its balance of payments."

Through all of this the market continued its steady decline. On June 14, for no apparent reason, the Dow dipped 13 points to close below 860. Then, after a week's rally, the selling resumed. Now it was called the "Martin market," with analysts blaming the chairman for the selloff, the sharpest sustained selloff since 1962.

Martin offered no direct response but instead sounded new warnings and alarms. On June 25 he spoke of the need for changes in the international monetary system, and, with what for him were sharp words, he criticized the administration for sympathizing with "those who say in effect that international money will manage itself." Martin said time had come for the creation of a new form of international reserves, that the dollar no longer could be counted upon to carry the burden and gather the rewards of being the sole measure of international value, and that a major adjustment was needed if trade were not to break down. Thus, he joined Roosa in signaling the erosion of the Bretton Woods agreements, and strongly implied that the blame rested with the administration's fiscal policies.

The market responded with another selloff, and on June 28 closed a fraction above 840. In two months the Dow had lost close to 10 percent of its worth. Once considered a hero on Wall Street, Martin now was castigated as a villain, the man who slaughtered the golden bull.

But the decline already had run its course. Inexplicably, the market staged a rally, which in the next four trading days added close to 35 points to the Dow; on July 2, when the district closed down for the long Independence Day weekend, the Dow stood at 875.

As usual analysts tried to rationalize this behavior. Some talked of "bargain hunting" by institutions. "Stocks seem demonstrably good," thought a pension fund manager, who was picking up blocks of Eastman Kodak, Sears Roebuck, and Merck. Wellington Fund said it was taking "a constructive but not aggressive" position toward the market. Stuart Silloway of Investors Diversified Services was cautious, but also in the market on the buy side, looking for bargains among the blue chips, which he acquired "in a major way on a selective basis." There was an unusually high level of interest in such old favorites as Xerox, IBM, Motorola, Polaroid, and Lockheed. The market chugged ahead, so by July 14 it was over 880.

In late July, after visiting the Vietnam warfronts, Secretary of Defense Robert McNamara told Congress that it was likely he would need an additional $1–2 billion that year for Vietnam-related expenditures and that his request for the new money would be appended to the more than $45 billion defense appropriations bill then before the legislature.

Everything was falling into place. The war psychology was building, while at the same time the position of the dollar was eroding. As McNamara prepared to deliver his requests, the Red Chinese claimed that American planes had violated its air space; the *New York Times* and other newspapers noted that such charges had preceded China's intervention in the Korean War. On July 14 the House had approved a new coinage bill, which eliminated silver from dimes and quarters; conservatives observed that the degradation of the coinage was a certain sign of impending monetary collapse, and some predicted the gold cover for the dollar would be removed before the end of the year. James Dines, now a leading "gold bug," told his followers that the metal would go to over $75, and he suggested they accumulate shares in South African mines.

The market's response was predictable. Gold and silver mining stocks shot up, but they were overshadowed by defense-related issues. Analysts drew up lists of companies that would benefit from the stepped-up fighting in Vietnam, and that sector of the market led the July advance. At a press conference held toward the end of the month, the president told reporters that he planned to increase the American commitment to Southeast Asia, and, while he spoke of his willingness to negotiate a settlement, American planes smashed North Vietnamese missile sites.

A few days later McNamara revealed that the increase in military spending that year would come to $1.7 billion, but that an additional $3 billion would be required for 1966—unless the war came to an end before then. He added that this would not cause undo strain upon the rapidly expanding economy, and McNamara discounted all talk of inflation. On July 30, Johnson signed the medicare bill into law, a clear indication he would not allow the war to interfere with the realization of his Great Society programs. Apparently he thought the nation would be able to enjoy a great deal of butter along with its new guns. The costs of neither were measured very carefully.

Wall Street believed him. By mid-August the Dow was close to 895, with the May high of 940 within reach. Some analysts predicted the 1,000 mark would be topped before Christmas. McNamara spoke of the need for helicopters in Vietnam; Boeing and United Aircraft posted large gains. The president told reporters that the medicare program might be extended; Upjohn, Eli Lilly, and A. H. Robins led the drug stocks higher, while a small boom started in shares of hospital supply and management companies. What all of this meant, wrote *Business Week,* was that "investors have increased faith that the Johnson Administration will do all it can—via monetary and fiscal measures—to keep the economy on course."

Chairman Martin, who had more influence over monetary policy than anyone else in the nation, stepped up his campaign against excesses in the economy. He continued to warn against deficit spending, talked about the gold outflow, and offered thoughts regarding international actions. And starting in late July he issued a series of warnings regarding the fiscal and monetary consequences of continued involvement in Vietnam. Martin said the FRB's Open Market Committee had to consider that "while there had been no declaration of war, a war-time psychology might be developing more rapidly than was generally realized," and that this could result in shortages, greater demands by government and the private sector upon the capital markets, and the creation of new strains on the central bank's resources. Martin urged Johnson to deal promptly with this situation, intimating that in the absence of White House action, he would feel obliged to come out in favor of tighter money and higher interest rates.

In this period only a handful of congressmen and senators spoke out against the political and military ramifications of the Vietnam War. Several of the new economists were certain the nation had the resources both for the war and the Great Society. The gross national product in 1964 had come to $632 billion, and it appeared the $680 billion mark would be topped in 1965. Preliminary forecasts for 1966 were in the $700–710 billion range. Given this increase, they said, an additional $3 billion for Vietnam shouldn't be difficult to raise or for the economy to absorb. Martin doubted that this would be the case, and in the autumn of 1965, he was the only important official in Washington to talk so boldly about what effects the war might have on the economy.

If Martin had few supporters in America, he apparently had many among Europe's central bankers. The gold sales continued through the summer and into the autumn and early winter. The total outflow for 1965 was $1.18 billion, the largest loss of the metal in American history. At year's end the gold stock stood at $13.8 billion, the lowest since before World War II. The postwar world financial system was showing severe strains, as America marched into Vietnam and the market soared ahead.

Eight

WUNDERKINDEN

A s has been indicated, fantasy was metamorphosed into reality on Wall Street during the fifth stage of the bull market.
Analysts who in 1960 had pondered balance sheets, and
three years later spoke guardedly of "concepts," by mid-decade
had concluded that the former were irrelevant while all the latter
required for realization was imagination, daring, and vigor.

All three qualities were possessed by the conglomerateurs,
who through their activities helped reshape several aspects of
American business organization and operation. On Wall Street their
counterpart was the "new breed" of analyst and asset manager, who
set about creating a novel way of obtaining capital gains that cap-
tivated investors and speculators and enabled them to enjoy several
seasons of power and notoriety.

This was not a new phenomenon; the last stages of almost all
bull markets feature such characters. In the post–Civil War period
the glamorous entrepreneur-speculators included Jay Gould, Jim
Fisk, Daniel Drew, and Cornelius Vanderbilt, while Wall Street's
speculator heroes were Anthony Wellman Morse, John W. Tobin,
and Henry Keep. Addison Jerome, the "Young Napoleon of the
Open Board," made and lost several fortunes in speculation and had
a large and enthusiastic following; this colorful grand-uncle of Win-
ston Churchill would have been destitute at the end were it not for a
birthday present of several hundred thousand dollars he had given
his wife during the lush times. In the late nineteenth and early
twentieth century, when such investment bankers as J. P. Morgan
and Jacob Schiff were reorganizing and shaping giant enterprises,
James Keene and Bernard Baruch were lions on the Street, and
hundreds of speculators were convinced that Thomas Lawson, the
leading soothsayer of the day, knew precisely when and how far cer-

tain stocks would take off and go. In the late 1920s the entrepreneur-heroes were led by automobile, radio, and motion picture tycoons, along with the new faces at the old investment banks—such as Paul Warburg, Thomas Lamont, and Mortimer Schiff—while the speculators followed the machinations of Arthur Cutten, Jesse Livermore, and Baruch, and Mike Meehan was the "hot" broker.

Such was the situation in the mid-1960s, when it appeared that what was old had to be discarded, or at best employed as raw material from which would come new and better forms. In the past, leading businessmen had the "right" parentage and religion, attended prestigious universities, belonged to exclusive clubs, and had come up the ladder at old corporations. Assuming their private lives were in order and they had some luck, such people might aspire to the leadership of a firm high on the Fortune 500 list. By and large they were faceless; their names were unknown to the general public, even while the products turned out by their factories were quite familiar. Such businessmen usually did competent jobs at conserving and extending whatever it was they had inherited. They were links in a long chain.

These individuals played no important role in the fifth stage, and in fact many of them were ousted by the new men, the organizers of large conglomerates. These newcomers were young, and most had indistinguished parentage. Many had been raised in the South or the trans-Mississippi West; a goodly number were foreign-born. While several had Ivy League credentials, none were truly "social," in the old sense of the word. Most were self-taught or products of technical or business schools. Few had important experiences with the familiar corporate ladder.

They were mavericks. To the old guard such men seemed alien, perhaps because they were not inheritors, but instead innovators and founders who liked to boast of their less than auspicious origins. Also, they tended toward self-advertisement, due in part to their personalities and the times, but also because it was good business practice. It appeared their corporations really were extensions of their egos, and this was anathema to conventional executives who claimed they existed to serve the corporation and its stockholders.

Critics charged the new conglomerateurs were not builders, but only slick organizers. Whether this was wholly or partially true cannot detract from the fact that they shook the foundations of some industries, fashioned billion-dollar corporations in a matter of months in some cases, and altered the conception of American business.

James Ling of Ling-Temco-Vought and Harold Geneen of International Telephone & Telegraph were the superstars of the fifth stage. These men and other conglomerateurs did not build enterprises from the ground up, as had Henry Ford and Andrew Carnegie. Rather, they acquired operating companies through the issuance of a variety of corporate paper, and then instituted managerial and operating changes, usually geared to demonstrate that earnings were rising rapidly. Additional takeover candidates then would be approached, and the process would be repeated. Noting this pattern, critics claimed the conglomerateurs merely were shuffling the economic deck—no new cards were being added, no important business advantages were being realized. This was an exaggeration, but whatever the facts of the matter insofar as productivity and innovation were concerned, the activities of these men and their creations made for good reading on Wall Street, and subsequently higher stock prices.

Several factors combined to create the movement. After World War II a number of large firms engaged in defense work sought acquisitions in the civilian sector. Government contracts declined in 1946–48, and the tax laws of the time encouraged them to diversify. A revival of antitrust activity that began in 1945 with the Justice Department's successful suit against Aluminum Company of America and reached a climax with passage of the Celler-Kefauver Act of 1950 indicated that conventional methods of expansion might result in legal actions, and this caused businessmen to seek opportunities in nonrelated areas. From the business schools came several new concepts regarding the nature of the firm. Peter Drucker and others urged executives to rethink all of their old beliefs in a time of rapidly changing technology and expanding markets. "It is management's responsibility to decide what business the enterprise is really in," Drucker wrote in 1949, and he went on to suggest that all truly were engaged in what he termed "the business of opportunity," which is to say that entrepreneurs should enter into free-form activities. Then there were the new electronic technologies of various kinds. In the past the development of major innovations such as this had spawned new companies and businessmen; it was no different during the 1950s and 1960s. The increased importance of government procurement contracts also made a contribution to the mix. A firm had to be large and possess a wide variety of capabilities in order to be in a position to bid for a prime contract. Growth by conglomeration was the fastest method of achieving this status.

Finally, the nature of the securities markets in this period enabled the conglomerateurs to pull off some of their more elaborate deals. Glamour and growth were assets on Wall Street in the early 1960s, and the conglomerate stocks seemed to have both in great abundance. Each company had its own investment banker, who would help arrange takeovers, put together bundles of securities used in the deals, and provide marketing facilities for the sale of new paper to the public. Through the use of "creative accounting," firms were able to show large leaps in earnings, which were reflected in the prices of the common stock the bankers printed for use in their transactions. Institutions and individual investors sopped up these shares and demanded more of the same. "The market is suffering from a severe case of conglomeritus," said one skeptical analyst in 1965, "and it appears the affliction will become permanent."

As has previously been indicated, Wall Street knew of conglomerates in the 1950s, and toward the end of the decade two of them, Textron and Litton, had attracted sizable followings. Investors were intrigued by their many acquisitions, while Royal Little of Textron and Tex Thornton of Litton were colorful, even flamboyant promoters. Still, Litton's high P/E multiple—over 50 at times in 1960—was credited to its position in several new-technology areas and its government contracts. As for Textron, it too had major government contracts and in addition was represented in growth segments of the civilian market.

Litton had listed its stock on the N.Y.S.E. in 1956, at which time it had sales of less than $15 million. Quickly it became a speculative vehicle, but trading volume was low, and the company's name was no more familiar than those of hundreds of other firms in its category. This changed as acquisitions multiplied and when Thornton's activities became a staple for financial reporters. A large number of analysts discovered Litton in 1959; the stock doubled that year, and redoubled in 1960, when sales were $250 million. Litton's 1964 sales came to $686 million, and despite the absence of dividends, its stock rose seemingly without effort. By then Thornton was being publicized as the exemplar for managers of the future, and graduates of the Litton organization were leaving the mother company to go off on their own and help create new conglomerates of their own. Hunt Foods acquired William McKenna from Litton, and George Scharffenberger left Thornton to take over at City Investing. Western Union lured Russell McFall from Litton in the hope he could work magic at that moribund firm. Similarly, Seymour Rosenberg went to Mattell and Frank Moothart to Republic. Henry Singleton, a Litton alumnus, helped form Teledyne in 1961. The stock was listed on the N.Y.S.E. two years later, where it doubled in price in six months. It seemed by then that new conglomerates were being formed and their stocks floated every week, while old firms were rushing to become conglomerates, usually beginning by acquiring one or more "Lidos."

Despite all of this, Litton was soon overshadowed by larger conglomerates and Thornton by more audacious executives. The stock continued to soar after 1964, but leadership passed to a new generation that year.

In 1956 former coffee trader Charles Bluhdorn joined the board of directors at Michigan Plating and Stamping Co., a minor factor in the automotive aftermarket, which posted sales of little more than a million dollars. After a short apprenticeship he assumed leadership of the company and immediately set about making small acquisitions, most of them for cash. In 1958, when Bluhdorn changed the firm's name to Gulf + Western, its sales were over $8 million. G + W passed the $100 million mark six years later, an impressive showing but hardly spectacular as such things went. Some of this growth resulted from takeovers, almost all of which were of companies involved with automobiles in one way or another. What was Bluhdorn trying to do? In 1965 *Steel* magazine offered an answer in an article entitled: "Gulf & Western's Goal: Become the GM of Partmakers."

If Bluhdorn had ever entertained that ambition he appeared to relinquish it late in the year, when he announced the purchase of New Jersey Zinc, a firm that had sales of over $135 million the previous year. Bluhdorn said his company had "reached the size and financial position where, for the long term, it should broaden the base of its operation to include major participation in basic industries, such as those in which Zinc Co. is engaged."

Wall Street thought otherwise. Investors interpreted the move as a sign that a new conglomerate had been born. G + W stock rose from 36 to 99 in the last three months of 1965, and by the summer of 1966 was over 120.

Harold Geneen, a British-born former accountant, left his post as executive vice-president of Raytheon to accept the presidency of International Telephone & Telegraph in 1959. On the announcement Raytheon's stock fell more than 6 points and ITT's leaped ahead by 3, for Geneen was considered one of the ablest managers in American industry. He took over a company with sales of $766 million, more than 80 percent of which was overseas, and he set about increasing the domestic share, while at the same time diversifying away from telephones and telegraphs.

At first ITT's acquisitions were of relatively small companies, most of which were in electronics and related businesses; General Controls and Bell & Gossett were taken over in 1963, for example. Then, in 1965, Geneen wooed and won Avis Rent-a-Car, a major factor in an industry completely divorced from ITT's original base. Frustrated in an attempt to acquire American Broadcasting, he turned to Levitt & Co. in 1966, and then set about investigating a wide range of firms within a broad spectrum of businesses. By then ITT was recognized as a major conglomerate; its sales that year topped $2 billion. Yet the stock did not perform as well as did those of others in its category, in part because there were signs the government might institute antitrust actions against ITT and also as a result of Geneen's growing reputation as a harsh wheeler-dealer. Still, ITT sold at 79 in the autumn of 1966, after having risen more than 30 points in less than a year.

James Ling, the creator of the third great conglomerate of the mid-1960s, possessed a natural flair and daring that amazed conventional businessmen and delighted investors and analysts. Where Geneen appeared methodical, Ling was brash, often acting intuitively and reversing field without much of a warning. An Oklahoman who was a self-confessed "bum," Ling founded Ling Electric Co. in Dallas in 1947 with net capital of $3,000 and an ambition to obtain government contracts. The company did fairly well; in 1955 it grossed $1.5 million. Because of this and to raise capital for expansion, Ling decided to sell stock to the public, which he did by going door to door and operating out of a booth at county fairs.

Armed with new funds, Ling started to make small acquisitions, the first of which was L. M. Electronics, a manufacturer of testing equipment. Now he changed his firm's name to Ling Industries, and purchased United Electronics and Calidyne. With these in tow, he sold $2.2 million worth of convertible bonds and with the proceeds purchased Altec Companies, University Loudspeaker, and Continental Electronics. Once again he changed names, this time to Ling-Altec Electronics.

By 1959, in a series of swift moves, Ling had created a $48-million-a-year electronics company and in the process had learned techniques of finance and mergers. His stock was listed on the N.Y.S.E., and while trading in it was not particularly active, he knew that once its price rose, he could use the paper to obtain additional companies at advantageous prices.

In 1960 he acquired Temco Electronics and Missiles, and his company now was called Ling-Temco. Then came Chance Vought, a large but ailing aircraft company and his largest merger to date. Ling-Temco was thus transformed into Ling-Temco-Vought. Its chairman sold off some of Chance Vought's assets, sought new financing, and set about making new deals.

In 1964, a year in which the company's sales were over $320 million, Ling announced "Project Redeployment." Ling-Temco-Vought would be radically restructured into three separate, and for the time being wholly owned, companies: LTV Aerospace, LTV Electrosystems, and LTV Ling-Altec. Now Ling-Temco-Vought became little more than a holding company, with an office and staff and a portfolio of stocks. It was a conglomerate—or at the very least a "multi-industry company"—and prepared to make additional acquisitions,—and so would its three operating companies.

Next, Ling announced a tender offer for his stock; for each share of Ling-Temco-Vought offered to the parent company, the stockholder would receive a half share apiece in each of the three subsidiary companies plus $9 in cash. The offer would establish public markets for the three stocks (and then they could use their paper for acquisitions), lower the number of Ling-Temco-Vought shares outstanding (and thus increase its earnings per share), and enable him to borrow more money than ever before (through four companies instead of three).

Ling was engrossed by the concept. In 1965 he took over Okon-

ite Corp. and repeated the process, and he gave every indication of
continuing to add to his stable indefinitely. Clearly a celebrity and a
favorite among analysts, Ling came to typify the new kind of entre-
preneur the business magazines said was transforming the face of industry. He was an open, attractive individual, willing to explain his
machinations to the most obtuse reporters and analysts. Additional
acquisitions were in the works, he said, and eventually he expected
"LTV" to become the largest industrial firm in the nation.

Many stockholders agreed. From a low of 17¼ in the summer
of 1965, LTV went to 75 in the spring of 1966, at which time the
Street was talking about Ling's proposed takeover of a half dozen
companies with sales of over a billion dollars each.

Ling, Bluhdorn, and Geneen were quintessential outsiders as
seen through the eyes of most leaders of old, established firms.
They were called shady and ruthless manipulators, more adept at
fashioning paper empires than turning out needed goods and services. But they were feared more than they were despised. The
chairmen of many large, sluggish corporations looked upon the conglomerateurs in much the same way as captains of treasure galleons
viewed pirates during the years of the Spanish Main. Ling and his
kind were swift and wily corsairs, who swooped down with a flotilla
of lawyers, accountants, and bankers to engulf companies several
times their own size. No firm whose stock had a depressed
price/earnings ratio and a low concentration of ownership seemed
safe from their raids. In the mid-1960s, their exploits, plans, and
visions made good reading on Wall Street, and their stocks became
the darlings of the bull market at its height.

Wall Street's counterpact for industry's conglomerateurs was
the "new breed" of money managers, also known as "hot shots" and
the "go-go boys." Not all of them were new to finance in the 1960s;
in fact most had had several years of training before going off on
their own. Several had undeserved reputations for wizardry; they
simply followed trends or imitated the leaders. A few were adept at
ferrating out new growth issues, while a handful perfected techniques of dubious honesty or merit.

They did not fall into any single pattern, except that all were invariably optimistic regarding the future. These men operated out of
perches at mutual funds, often named after them or at the very least
of their own creation. Thus, they managed large pools of money

without having to answer to any individuals on a day-to-day basis. In order to attract new investors (and lure old ones from rivals) they had to be expert at public relations and know how to garner publicity. The new breed provided good copy for journalists and would go out of their ways to locate magazine staffers in the hope of becoming the subject of a feature piece or two. Such men were always prepared to appear on television to explain their magical ways or conduct seminars on investments at Palm Springs and other watering places. Some were quite prominent socially; they became members of literary or artistic sets, contributed to and joined political movements then in vogue, and associated with the "beautiful people." Others seemed to avoid the limelight—except that they became famous for so doing. On the periphery were a few eccentrics who worked in dungarees, grew beards, and in other ways affected lifestyles that troubled Wall Street's old guard. But most of these new men looked pretty much like junior partners on the way up. They were tanned, lean, and tough-minded, respectful toward their elders but vocal in their conviction that most knowledge and experience obtained prior to the early 1960s was of little value.

These money managers were well known on the Street in the early 1960s, but to owners of mutual fund shares they were only names on prospectuses. In 1961, and after the Kennedy crash of 1962, a number of new funds appeared that seemed willing to take greater than normal risks in pursuit of capital gains, while several old mutuals switched to that approach. Their clientele consisted of two groups. First, there were new investors who found the market exciting but quite complex. These people had heard and read about great profits to be made by being in the right situation at the right time, but they knew they lacked the time, experience, and temperament to take the plunge on their own. They learned of the new "performance funds," which did far better than the Dow due to a penchant for trading and an ability to obtain inside information. And so they purchased shares.

The second group was comprised of more experienced investors who had seen such stocks as Polaroid, Xerox, Control Data, and Syntex double and redouble, and somehow never seemed to get on or off at the proper moment. These new funds were headed by men who appeared to possess that knack. Some individuals in this second group might have owned mutual shares in the late 1950s, only to sell them a few years later to get into the market on their own. Now they purchased shares in performance funds. Perhaps they suspected the market was rigged and that only by going along with purported insiders could they make large profits. It might have been that they did so out of disgust with the ways they had managed their own portfolios. Clearly a large number of people were lured into the performance funds by tales of their bright, efficient, coldly scientific managements.

Mutual fund assets rose from $17 billion in 1960 to $29 billion in 1964, and the following year they topped $35 billion. There were more than 6.7 million shareholder accounts in force at mid-decade, by which time the performance funds comprised the fastest-growing segment of the industry.

At this point the industry produced its first superstar. Gerald Tsai, Jr. had been born in Shanghai in 1928, the son of the manager of Ford's operations there who himself had been educated at the University of Michigan. Although many on Wall Street viewed him as exotic and inscrutable, Gerry Tsai was as Westernized as any broker or analyst in the district. He had been educated at Wesleyan and Boston University before taking a variety of jobs, some involved with stocks and bonds. In 1952, at the age of 24, he joined the Fidelity Fund as a junior stock analyst. This fund, headed by Edward Johnson, had a fairly good record, but hardly was a leader in its field. Johnson, one of the most respected figures in the industry, came to view Tsai as a protégé, and the young man rose rapidly in the organization. By 1957 Tsai was asking Johnson to be placed as leader of a new fund that concentrated on growth issues. Johnson agreed, and soon after Fidelity Capital Fund was established under the Fidelity umbrella.

Tsai operated differently than most fund managers of that period. Instead of spreading his risks, he concentrated much of his capital in shares of a few high flyers, such as Texas Instruments, Polaroid, Litton, and Xerox. Also, he did a good deal of his own research, not only in archives but through visits to the offices of leading executives such as Thornton, Geneen, and other conglomerateurs, who understood that if Tsai purchased their stocks, other funds would follow, and so the paper would command premium prices.

The Capital Fund soon became one of the fastest-growing speculative vehicles available. Its price declined sharply in the 1962 selloff, however, at which time hundreds of shareholders liquidated their positions. But it bounced back the following few months, and grew rapidly during the ensuing bull phase. Now Tsai became a wheeler-dealer, buying large blocks, holding them for a few months, and then selling out positions so as to take new ones in stocks few outside of his own organization seemed to know much about. Tsai had a following among fund managers and analysts as well as the general public. Stories about his exploits appeared in the *Journal, Business Week, Fortune,* and *Newsweek.* The *New Yorker* ran a profile on him. Gerry Tsai was a full-fledged celebrity.

In 1965, when Edward Johnson approached the retirement age of 65, Tsai asked if he would take over as head of the Fidelity Group. Johnson replied that the chairmanship was reserved for his son, Edward, Jr. "Fidelity is a family business and Mr. Johnson's wishes were very understandable," said Tsai later on. "But I wanted to be number one, not number two." He sold his holdings in the company for $2.2 million and set about organizing his own fund.

The financial and business journals kept track of Gerry Tsai, and in late December it was learned that his new operation would be called Manhattan Fund. In January 1966, he announced that an initial offering of $25 million would be made the following month by his new entity, Tsai Management and Research. As soon as they could do so, investors sent checks to Tsai, in such volume that the offering had to be quadrupled in size, and even that wasn't enough to absorb the demand for shares. On February 15, when Manhattan Fund spun into operation, Tsai had over $247 million in cash to invest, and all attention was focused on the 37-year-old wizard who was about to toss a quarter of a billion into the market.

No one had followed Tsai's activities closer or better than Fred Alger, who at the age of 30 was the head of his own research operation. Alger's career to that point had been checkered. The son of a Michigan politician, he had graduated from Yale and then gone to work at a Detroit brokerage house where his father had connections. Then followed short stints at a variety of banks and funds. In early 1965 Alger was a portfolio manager for Winfield funds, a relatively small San Francisco-based organization, which he left after a series of squabbles with top management. He then formed Fred Alger & Co., which initially had only one client, whose fee came to $100 per week.

Alger was close to giving up when part of the Winfield group was sold to Security Benefit Life, a small Kansas insurer, and some of his old friends there got him a job as portfolio manager. This was an important assignment, and Alger moved cautiously. "I tried to avoid hot-stocking it with crud," he later said. "I wanted to do well with the big companies that everyone owned by buying them at their bottoms." This he did, racking up an appreciation of close to 80 percent for the year. Now Alger was considered one of the hottest managers in the business.

Toward the end of 1965 Alger was approached by representatives of Bernard Cornfeld's Investors Overseas Services (IOS) and asked if he would be interested in managing a $5 million fund under Cornfeld's Fund of Funds umbrella organization. Alger quickly accepted. "We'll call it the Alger Fund," Cornfeld reportedly said, "so we'll know the schmuck to blame if it goes wrong."

Other accounts followed, so that by the time Tsai was ready to invest his quarter of a billion in the market, Alger possessed the vehicles with which to spar with the giant Manhattan Fund.

Alger had correctly concluded that Tsai would fashion Manhattan in the mold of Fidelity Capital—that he would buy for his new portfolio the same kinds of stocks he had accumulated in the old. "Now, if you assume an average price of $50, that made an imputed short interest of a hundred thousand shares in each of the stocks Gerry was going to buy. So that's what *we* bought." Alger outguessed other fund managers in this game, and by successfully tracking Tsai and anticipating his moves, the new Security Equity Fund and Alger Fund were able to turn in excellent performances.

Cornfeld was pleased with his capital gains, and so he turned over another, larger fund to Alger, and a number of important private accounts followed. By late 1966 Alger & Co. was considered one of the sharpest research outfits on the Street, and its president, usually followed by a reporter or two, prowled the Western world for hot new stocks. Yet Alger was more modest than most go-go managers. He admitted that occasionally Alger & Co. picked stocks that performed poorly but added that this was the risk associated with his line of business. Later on Alger said, "We have the best sense of timing in the market. Our stock selection is no good—I can't think why—but our timing is superb."

Dave Meid, who arrived at Winfield shortly after Fred Alger departed that fund, was 31 years old in 1965. He had been raised on a small farm near Fort Wayne, Indiana, and attended De Pauw University in nearby Greencastle, where he was introduced to business subjects. A summer spent as a runner for the Wall Street Journal convinced Meid he could not be happy on a farm or in a small town and that only on Wall Street could he experience the kinds of excitement he craved. But he returned to De Pauw to complete his studies and then went on to take a master's degree at Indiana University. Then followed a tour of duty with the Air Force, after which, in 1961, Meid was taken on by Smith, Barney, a medium-sized brokerage, as a portfolio trainee.

Apparently he didn't do well at the job, or perhaps he couldn't get along with his superiors. In any case he was transferred to the San Francisco office, where he worked as an institutional salesman. Meid did fine at this; by 1965 his salary was $35,000. But he knew that research and management, not sales, were his true interests. "Picking stocks was the most fun of anything I'd ever done," he later said. So when he learned of an opening as a portfolio manager at Winfield, Meid resigned from Smith, Barney, and was taken on at a salary of $12,000.

Meid turned in a phenomenal performance in 1965. "By the end of that year I had made more money than the whole payroll of the Smith, Barney research department," he gloated. Meid had an eclectic approach to the market, gathering as much information as he could find, then letting it roll around in his mind, and finally relying upon hunches as to which stocks to buy and when to sell. "The best word is flexibility," he said. "You want to make money as reasonable risk." Meid was not a wild speculator, for he insisted upon following trends, not initiating them. Somewhat disingenuously, he later told a writer that he would "try to concentrate on the things that can go up the most." In a major bull market, this simple advice took on shadings of profundity.

Winfield was experiencing management problems at this time, and the fund was up for sale. Fresh from his successes, Meid now wanted to run his own operation. He joined with Bob Hagopian, a 31-year-old securities salesman, and put together $250,000, offering to purchase Winfield at that price. After some dickering, the sale was concluded in the autumn of 1966. Now Meid started to shuffle his portfolio, and once again his instincts served him well. Winfield's assets rose sharply, as did its list of shareholders.

Meid joined Alger as a performance fund star, followed by analysts and interviewed by reporters. He boasted that if he couldn't beat the Dow Jones Industrials by at least 20 percent in any given year he would step down. Meid's performance in 1966 indicated he would be around at least through the bull market.

Fred Carr, who was 36 years old when Meid purchased Winfield, was a portfolio manager in the Fletcher organization at that time. Like Alger and Meid, Carr was an outsider as far as the Wall Street Establishment was concerned. Born of immigrant parents in a lower-class neighborhood on the outskirts of Watts in Los Angeles, Carr worked at odd jobs to support himself through high school and later attended City College of Los Angeles for a while. After serving in the Army during the Korean War, Carr dabbled in real estate, construction, and gas stations.

In 1957 he took a job as broker's assistant in a Los Angeles office of Bache & Co., where he also learned the rudiments of securities analysis. From there he went to Ira Haupt & Co. as director of research for the West Coast. After the Haupt collapse Carr became director of research at Kleiner, Bell & Co., known as "the hottest underwriter in California." He quit his $100,000-a-year position there to become manager of Fletcher's California Fund, which had less than $21 million in assets and whose investments were restricted to firms based in that state. "I saw an opportunity to build a business and to create a quality product instead of just making a lot of money every year," explained Carr, who continued to do his own research. "I was never pointing to become a money manager," he later explained. "Being an analyst is a fruitful occupation. You have the excitement of discovery, being right sends you up to the sky and being wrong bounces you on your can."

Together with Fletcher and others, Carr organized Shareholders Management Co. (SMC), a firm whose major asset was a group of men in the Carr mold who managed mutual funds. Later known as "The Dirty Dozen" and "Twelve Angry Analysts," these men were, said Carr, "relatively young—in their late twenties or early thirties—bright, intense guys, usually loners who are frustrated by the investment committee process. I don't think they would work very well together." With their help Carr made one of his funds, Enterprise, the hottest performer in the industry. Carr proved adept at sniffing out new growth companies, whose stock he placed into Enterprise and other SMC operations. What followed was a variant of the relationship between Tsai and Alger in 1966. Analysts and speculators would receive the fund's quarterly report and from it learn of new investments. Then they would rush to make similar purchases. In this way, Enterprise's net asset value would rise sharply, as would its following.

There was no better time to be young, brash, irreverent, and a portfolio manager. "It was a beautiful period," Fred Alger later would recall. "We were impressed with the war babies. There was a new individualist sense, a greater sense of competitive enterprise, a sense of armies of entrepreneurs. You could *see* them." Alger and his sort fitted in well with the conglomerateurs, who as a group were only slightly older and also were outsiders. Ling would tell reporters that old accounting methods were inadequate to the task of understanding what he was doing. "As for those who can't keep up with our changing financial structure," he said, "well, that's their problem." Old-time investors might have thought these words applied to them, especially when they perused an Alger Fund quarterly report and discovered they didn't recognize the names of quite a few of the holdings—usually the stocks that had risen the fastest.

Many of these portfolio managers and conglomerateurs of the new wave had links with Bernard Cornfeld, who in 1965 still was something of a mystery man, but who Wall Street already recognized as a potent force in the field of international investment. Carr and Meid would soon join Alger as managers of IOS mutual funds. Carr's old company, Kleiner, Bell, maintained a close relationship with Cornfeld. James Ling, Charles Bluhdorn, and other conglomerateurs utilized his services in making some of their more important acquisitions. Perhaps more than any other person, Cornfeld symbolized the apogee of the fifth phase of the bull market.

In what to the new men of the mid-1960s seemed prehistoric times, N.Y.S.E. President Keith Funston had spoken of "People's Capitalism" as it applied to the World War II veteran and his family, who might own a few shares of stock in leading American corporations and hope to accumulate more. Cornfeld, in contrast, thought hundreds of millions of people throughout the world should own mutual fund shares sold by his agents, and that his portfolio managers should control funds with assets in the billions of dollars. He saw himself as a major force in international affairs, the creator of what he termed "world-wide People's Capitalism."

Cornfeld was a true exotic at a time when many bizarre and un- usual characters attracted attention on Wall Street. Even his origins were romantic. His father was an actor and stage manager who had settled his family in Constantinople in the mid-1920s, and it was there that "Bernie" was born in 1927. Shortly thereafter the Corn- felds moved to Providence, Rhode Island and then, after the father's death, to Brooklyn. Later on he attended Columbia's School of So- cial Work, and he labored for a while in that field. Almost by acci- dent he drifted into mutual fund sales.

In 1953 Cornfeld became a salesman for Investors Planning Corporation, one of the thousands of people working for commis- sions during the first flush of Funston's drive for People's Capital- ism. He enjoyed the work, earned a good income and lived well, and became convinced that those in charge of mutual fund sales were short sighted and not terribly intelligent. Why sell fund plans only to Americans? Everyone in the world knew the United States had the strongest economy in the world, that the American dollar was supreme, and that owning shares in American corporations was a sound investment. Why not give foreigners a chance to buy funds? Armed with these insights and truisms, Cornfeld set out for Paris in 1955, with a plan to sell mutual funds to American servicemen stationed in Europe.

It was a good idea, and Cornfeld possessed the talents to make it work. His organization, Investors Overseas Services, began by selling Dreyfus Fund and other mutuals to soldiers and sailors. Then it expanded to include other Americans working in Europe. Finally, Cornfeld peddled the funds to Europeans as well. Further- more, his salesmen made deep forays into Asia, Oceania, Africa, and South America—some even tried to get to Antarctica to uncover in- terested investors among explorers, scientists, and servicemen.

In 1962 Cornfeld organized the Fund of Funds, which existed to invest capital in shares of other mutual funds. By then he had set up a few of these on his own, and others would follow. The rationale for such an entity escaped those in the field, but the Fund of Funds proved successful. A good part of its portfolio consisted of shares of other Cornfeld funds, which meant that the IOS collected a man- agement fee on top of other management fees. And it worked. Corn- feld appeared to have the golden touch. By 1966 he was managing more than $1.5 billion in assets, and predicting that within less than 10 years he would have over $15 billion in his various projects.

That year he organized IOS Development Company, and took on as its chief James Roosevelt, the son of FDR. The purpose of this company wasn't made clear at the time, but later on Cornfeld announced that it would sell mutual fund shares to "the lower economic elements in the major urban areas of the underdeveloped world . . . office clerks, hotel attendants, taxi drivers, vendors, and thousands of other low-income wage earners who can afford to save only in small amounts." One of the Wall Street jokes of the time was that Cornfeld would not rest until every beggar along the Ganges had shares in one or another of his funds.

Americans, however, could not purchase these shares, because Cornfeld knew his funds could not pass the screening established by the Securities and Exchange Commission. If this bothered him, Cornfeld had his compensation elsewhere. He was undisputed king of the mutual funds in all other parts of the world. By 1966 he was setting up deals for American conglomerates in Europe, dabbling in investments in the Middle East, and planning new forays into the underdeveloped areas of Asia and Africa. The increased American presence in Vietnam interested him. Was it true that eventually there would be a million soldiers there? If so, he thought, that could mean a new major market for shares managed by IOS and sold by its salesmen.

Cornfeld liked to talk of the fine records established by his funds and the intelligence and sophistication of his sales methods, and of course the rhetoric regarding world-wide People's Capitalism continued. In fact, however, much of the money he managed came from foreigners who wanted to squirrel away assets in American securities, or from Americans who for tax or other reasons sent their money abroad, and then repatriated it through the purchase of Cornfeld's funds. Thus, they were given the opportunity to participate in the great bull market by indirection. "Talk about hot money," said Cornfeld to one of his associates. "We've got a million clients, and if any major proportion of these million clients represents hot money, there must be a lot of it about."

He knew this to be the case. In addition, the various Cornfeld funds became vehicles by which the undergrounds in Europe and Asia could "launder" their money and keep it from the prying eyes of the police. Some people opened numbered accounts in Swiss banks; others purchased shares in Cornfeld's funds. Many did both.

Two-tenths of one percent of these million accounts owned approximately 20 percent of the fund shares. Sophisticated investors do not purchase shares in mutual funds; they invest directly, unless there is some tax advantage or other principle involved. The Fund of Funds did manage to skirt the American tax laws, and all the Cornfeld vehicles could be used to hide assets. Cornfeld's salesmen in Asia and Africa were far less interested in hotel clerks and taxi drivers then they were in military officers and politicians anxious to have nest eggs comprised of American securities.

In 1966, the high noon of the bull market, such approaches seemed not only worthwhile, but sensible and prudent. Like Harold Geneen and Charles Bluhdorn, Bernie Cornfeld was both an outsider and a hero on the Street. In the past the appearance of such characters in these roles had been signs of coming troubles. But in 1966, as had been the case in previous euphoric years, the bulls ignored the signs. And at that time, they were in complete command.

Never again would the outlook seem so bright, or would hopes be so high.

Nine

THE CRIPPLING BLOW

I N AUGUST of 1965 Defense Secretary McNamara asked for and received a $1.7 billion emergency appropriation to help pay the cost of the Vietnam War. The money was voted in a routine fashion, for at the time most citizens and most members of Congress supported the U.S. role in the conflict. Also, it generally was believed American involvement was close to its peak, and the economy might easily accommodate such an additional expenditure. Wall Street still thought the war was good for business. On news of the supplemental appropriation the Dow rose 5 points, with defense and electronics issues leading the way.

John Stennis of Mississippi, one of the Senate's leading experts on military affairs, warned President Johnson that spending would rise sharply in 1966 unless something was done to end or at least contain the war. Gardner Ackley, chairman of the Council of Economic Advisors, agreed, and three months later he told Johnson that he could not have the war, the Great Society programs, and a stable price level all at the same time. Something would have to give; an economic and political price would have to be paid. Ackley urged the president to ask for a tax increase. This would put a damper on economic growth, but higher taxes would help hold down inflation while at the same time impressing the nation and the world with the seriousness of the war. Johnson understood this, but for the time being refused to act, fearing that to do so would kill all hopes of passing his social welfare program. The president's decision would have many repercussions. One of these would be a crippling of the great bull market on Wall Street.

Total defense expenditures for 1965 came to $50.3 billion, only $1.1 billion more than they had been for the previous year. But spending rose strongly toward the end of 1965, and McNamara knew even then there would be a major jump forward in 1966 if the war continued that long. In mid-1965 he had thought there would be 300,000 American troops in Vietnam by the end of 1966. In November his estimates had risen to 400,000. Earlier he had told Johnson he would need $10 billion to fight the war in 1966. Now the figure had risen to between $15 billion and $17 billion.

In August 1965, when McNamara received his additional appropriation, the government announced a balance of payments surplus for April and June of $132 million on a seasonally adjusted basis. Treasury Secretary Fowler hailed this as a sign the administration's policy of voluntary restraints on American investment overseas was working. Federal Reserve Board governor James Robertson, in charge of the program, thought the surplus only "a little less then terrific," making him "proud to be an American." But Commerce Secretary John Connor told reporters that American corporations were planning to invest record amounts of money overseas and that this, coupled with rising tourist expenditures, meant a deficit in international payments could be anticipated. Federal Reserve Board Chairman Martin agreed, and he warned against "an overly optimistic assessment" of the April and June figures. Senator Stennis found himself in rare agreement with Martin. He noted that the administration's forecast of a $46.8 billion defense program for 1966 was "unrealistic" and thought additional funds would be required later on. A good deal of this money would be spent overseas, said Stennis, and thus the balance of payments difficulties would increase.

Automobile sales had been at a record clip in early 1965, and the showrooms had been filled with customers in the spring and early summer. In all, 9.3 million cars would be sold that year, an all-time mark that eclipsed the old one of 7.9 million set in 1955. In August, however, dealers reported inventories of 1.4 million cars, the highest on record, at a time when the 1966 models were being released. The initial reaction to the new Ford and Chrysler cars was poor, and advance notices for the General Motors products were mixed.

The market for new housing had peaked in 1963 and then declined for two consecutive years. The industry picked up somewhat in the spring of 1965 but then slumped once again. By autumn it had become evident that the falloff would continue for a while longer, perhaps through the summer of 1966. Ripples were felt in a variety of industries, from appliances to copper to lumber. Manufacturers and warehousemen started to work off inventories, and the flow of new orders slowed appreciably.

Important segments of the economy were on the verge of recession. This was not surprising or unusual, considering the length of the recovery from the last economic decline. None of the new economists called for a tax cut, as they had in 1961, however. Ackley and his colleagues knew that this time spending in the public sector would increase by more than the decline in the private, and a tax increase was needed to finance it. For example, the steel mills might sell less of their products to the automobile manufacturers in 1966, but demands for their products from those firms specializing in military hardware would compensate for that. Thus, Ackley would tax consumers and use the money to help pay for the Vietnam War.

The unemployment rate would not rise; in fact it declined from 5 percent in February 1965 to 4 percent by year's end, this a result of hiring by military-industrial companies, acceleration of draft calls, and the flight of young men from the labor market to the colleges so as to avoid the draft. But all this—declining production of civilian goods, a growing tightness in the labor market, large deficits, and a negative balance of payments—meant inflationary pressures would be intensified. Ackley did what he could with the president. Chairman Martin tried to contain the upward price movement through both open market operations and by raising the discount rate, but this was not enough to do the job. In 1965 the Consumer Price Index rose by 1.9 percent, hardly frightening but still 50 percent more rapid a move upward than had been the case the previous year. By early 1966 the inflation rate was over 3 percent, the highest for the decade thus far.

The outlines of these problems were visible in August 1965; later on Wall Street could not claim it had been caught unawares by political, social, and economic dilemmas that surfaced the following year. In the late summer and early autumn of 1965, however, analysts and investors preferred to concentrate on good news and overlook the bad. Sparked by increased military spending, factory orders were rising. The success of the Gemini V space flight prompted Johnson to announce a plan for a manned orbiting laboratory, and this resulted in a rally in the defense and space stocks. Rumors of a settlement to contract discussions in the steel industry that would mean higher prices prompted stockpiling for that product. Was the economy headed toward a combination of inflation and recession? Perhaps, thought *Barron's*, though the idea seemed somewhat bizarre in 1965. In any case, wrote H. J. Nelson, "Continuation of the wage spiral can only lead in due course to compensatory higher prices, constituting a powerful underlying inflationary force. Against this, and regardless of intermediate price movements, the only protection for investors, in the light of the historical and accentuated postwar decline in the purchasing value of the dollar, is still in common stocks."

In late August the Dow closed only a handful of points below the 900 level. Volume was strong, and the market had good leadership. The steel talks ended successfully on September 7, which is to say there would be no strike. On the other hand, the settlement clearly was inflationary and would provide the basis for other, similar settlements in contract negotiations throughout the economy. The Dow closed that day at 910, and by September 20 was over 930. After a brief pause, news of administration plans for increased military spending resulted in renewed buying of stocks in defense-related companies. According to the *Wall Street Journal*, "Prospects are for much bigger military spending than officially intimated from any source," while *Barron's* wrote of the stimulative effects of "the future upward trend of social welfare expenditures from new 1965 laws" and warned, "All this means spending on such a scale that its effects might logically be considered as possibly leading to an overheating of the economy."

Alan Abelson of that magazine was troubled by this, as well as by indications that tighter money was on the way. In mid-October, with the Dow over 942, he wrote of "the difficulty of seeing what's ahead after the turn of the year," and asked investors to "tread carefully." Already he saw signs of a topping-out process. "With its strong speculative tinge, the market for some weeks hasn't been exactly suited for widows and orphans. Nor is it likely to become so in the foreseeable future."

At the close of October, the Dow was 961, having shot up by more than 100 points in two and a half months. Analysts attributed this showing to signs that auto sales were picking up and to good third-quarter earnings reports. It was difficult to find an analyst who didn't believe the Dow would top the 1,000 mark before the end of the year. "Short of catastrophe, seemingly nothing can dispel Wall Street's sunny mood," said *Business Week*. *Barron's* added, "The refusal of investors, usually a fairly skittish lot, to push the panic button in recent weeks, despite some strong provocation, is based partly on the conviction that there's plenty of life in this old business boom yet."

Stocks went into a holding pattern in November, as fears of inflation overcame faith that still better profit statements were on the way. All indications were that industry was operating at peak levels, and while this implied full employment and excellent earnings, it also meant that signs of strain were bound to appear soon. On November 21 Treasury Secretary Fowler warned that the administration would oppose wage and price increases deemed inflationary. Fowler pledged that the president would "blow the whistle impartially" against both unions and companies, but on Wall Street his words were taken to mean the White House was planning a new anti-business crusade as part of the Great Society.

It was against this news background that the Federal Reserve increased the discount rate to 4½ percent on December 6, and leading New York banks promptly responded by posting their prime rate at 5 percent. The news set off waves of selling at the N.Y.S.E. Volume that day was 11.4 million shares, making this the most hectic session in more than three years. The Dow gave up more than 6 points to close a fraction below 940. Still, the rate increases had been anticipated for almost half a year, ever since Martin had warned against a repetition of the 1929 experience. Prices picked up the next session, and the Dow was back over 960 on December 22, closing the year on December 31 at an all-time high of 969.

The forecasts for 1966 were mixed that holiday season. Analysts had been burned when the Dow failed to top 1,000 in December, and now some of them concentrated on weak spots in the economy and market. The vast majority of them predicted the Index would go over that mark sometime in the first half of the year, but they were uncertain as to what would follow, and it was here that a wide divergence of opinion developed. The gold bugs, whose numbers increased as the dollar weakened, called for a pullback to 800 or lower—James Dines thought 600 a distinct possibility. Harris,

Upham told investors, "It would take a blind man not to notice the many signs that have presented themselves which have been typical of the last stages in past major bull markets—pronounced profit-taking in high flyer, glamour stocks; renewed interest in safer blue chip issues, coupled with demand for the steels, which have been late-stage movers in the past." The company went on to predict the Dow would see 900 "sometime later in the year."

There appeared to be a consensus that capital expenditures would rise in 1966, that there would be a sharp increase in government spending, and that consumer purchases would be at record levels. "All three points constitute the logic underlying the standard forecast of a Gross National Product around $710 billion for 1966 against an estimated $670 billion for 1965. This would have been bullish news were it not for the fears regarding inflation, uncertainties about wage and price controls, and the growing sentiment that the United States had ventured into uncharted waters in Vietnam. Ragnar Naess of the consulting firm of Naess & Thomas said that if the war escalated "we are in for controls of manpower, materials, and wages, and for higher taxes," the combination of which would kill all vestiges of bullish sentiment. But he didn't think it would happen, and so he predicted a continuation of the bull move.

Several money managers were having second thoughts regarding the market, however. Given the eroding international trade situation, the growing budget deficit, and most of all, increases in the inflation rate, they concluded the economy was in for a rough time. In preparation for this, the Dreyfus Fund accumulated a cache of $100 million in liquid assets, which its president, Howard Stein, said would be used to purchase stocks "under the proper conditions." By this he meant some kind of conclusion to the Vietnam War. "If the war does not end," he said, "we will need our cash position—and then some—in self defense." The *Wall Street Journal* reported that many fund managers had taken the same stance. Stuart Silloway of Investors Diversified Services said, "This is the time to be alert and cautious." John Cooper of the Massachusetts Investors Trust told a reporter there were "a number of decent values in the market," but Stein's approach was more prevalent among money managers.

Was the war bullish or bearish for investments? Stein had come to believe the market would rise if the fighting ended. But *Business*

Week continued to have mixed feelings on the matter. In its first editorial of the year the magazine observed that "the rapid increase in military spending . . . has forced all the economists to raise their sights for 1966." While fearing strains in the economy, it noted that "an abrupt truce in Vietnam would raise disquieting questions as to whether the civilian economy could keep growing lustily on its own without the push of military spending behind it." The economy should not be afraid of peace, the magazine believed, but at the same time it implied that an end to the fighting would mean dislocations and perhaps help trigger a recession.

This attitude would change as 1966 wore on. Increasingly stock prices would respond to higher levels of fighting with sharp declines, while rumors of peace would result in rallies. Even before the organized protests and marches on Washington began and the antiwar movement erupted on the nation's campuses, Wall Street realized the war had become an economic liability, though many analysts and large investors continued to believe the American role was justified in the light of political and international considerations.

Could the market continue its upward drive in the light of economic problems and a changing national mood toward the war? Edson Gould of Arthur Wiesenberger, one of the leading market theoreticians for many years, offered suggestions that it could not do so. In late December Gould wrote that the Dow could move as high as 1,040 to 1,160 in the spring of the new year, but then it would decline sharply, perhaps to a low of 650. Gould based this prediction upon his technical studies of market behavior, as well as the nature of the money supply, taking almost no note of other economic considerations. "Unfortunately, market projections are not that simple," Gould conceded. "Also, monetary factors are just one of the variables in the stock market equation. Equally important—especially at major stock market peaks—are the psychological factors. And economic factors are always important; some imbalances in the economy always make their appearance prior to a major market peak."

On January 8, Carl M. Loeb, Rhoades & Co. told its clients not to fear a possible truce in Vietnam. "Should it be possible to resolve this conflict peaceably, the blueprint . . . for the Great Society is sufficiently well defined and our economy resilient enough to permit the prompt reallocation of productive means without triggering a recession."

The president's 1966 budget called for increased Vietnam spending, but Johnson also indicated his expectation that a peak for such expenditures would be reached in midyear, after which they would decline. He also wanted additional funds for Great Society programs. The economy could bear it, said presidential spokesmen. The Council of Economic Advisors forecast a 1966 GNP of $722 billion, much higher than that anticipated by private economists. In any case, according to supporters of the president and the war, defense spending would consume less than 8 percent of the GNP, in contrast to the 13.5 percent taken by the military during the Korean War in 1952. Expenditures for that conflict hadn't harmed the economy, and there was no reason to anticipate major dislocations this time.

The situation was different in 1966, however, and the president knew it. Ackley continued to urge White House support for a general tax increase, and now Johnson made his first, tentative move in that direction. In his State of the Union message, delivered on January 12, he called for a temporary restoration of automobile and telephone taxes and accelerated collection of corporate and personal taxes, which he said would increase the total tax burden by some $6 billion. Congressional reaction was good, but the president, who understood the mood on Capitol Hill, didn't feel he could press further on this front. Nor would he take actions that might cripple business confidence. When U.S. Steel raised prices on its products, there was little more than a vague stirring from the White House. Other firms followed suit. Inflation was in the air.

Through all of this, Wall Street awaited the debut of the Manhattan Fund, with analysts certain the "Tsai rage" would impel the Dow over 1,000. Technicians noted there was nothing magical about that figure, and yet all recognized it was a major psychological barrier. If the market could push through confidently and in fine style, there appeared no reason why additional gains could not be made. But if the market faltered, then a correction might be expected. Still, all of this was deemed a matter of emotion rather than economics; in January 1966, the nation's businesses appeared in good shape, and most of the projections were optimistic.

The market closed at Dow 987 on Friday, January 14, but in interday trading it had gone over 994. That weekend newspapers and business magazines celebrated the coming of the quadruple digit Dow, which they felt would be realized early the next week. During the morning of Monday, the 17th, the Dow hit 997, but then retreated to close at 990, up three points for the day. Stocks opened higher on Tuesday morning, and in the early afternoon the Dow finally went over the mark, reaching 1,000.50. But a selling wave developed in the afternoon, and so the Index closed at 994, a new high but hardly one the bulls could celebrate. By then there was no doubt that strong selling pressures existed, and the bulls turned skittish. "It was the N.Y.S.E.'s version of the showdown at O.K. Corral," a specialist later remarked.

Stocks rose smartly on heavy volume Wednesday morning, so as to cause the tickers to run late and the bulls to rejoice. In early afternoon the Dow Jones wire reported the Index at 1,000.55, and a roar went up from the floor. This was a critical moment. If the bulls were confident and present in large enough numbers, the prices should have taken off, while timidity would be an indication that bearishness was growing. Whatever happened at this point would be followed by the unraveling of a self-fulfilling prophecy—the market was destined for either a major push upward or a serious correction.

That afternoon's contest was won by the bears. Leading issues weakened. Led by General Motors, General Electric, and du Pont—all stocks that were included in the Dow Index—the market started to slide. The Dow closed at 991, off a fraction more than 3 points for the session.

So the first major assault on Dow 1,000 had failed. During the next few days, some bulls claimed that the interday marks, and not the posted closes, should be considered for the purposes of establishing or breaking records. Few took the idea seriously. Many more noted that the Standard & Poor's and Value Line indexes were far stronger than the Dow and urged clients and colleagues to switch their attention to them. There was truth to this charge, but the Street had become so accustomed to using the Dow as well as to hearing arguments against it that this came to nothing. Besides, this was a psychological rather than a financial barrier, and thus irrational forces predominated. In any case, the Dow Rails established a new high on January 26, and bulls who criticized the Industrial Index rushed to point this out. The same day, however, the Dow Utilities posted a two-year low, and this encouraged the bears to think the Industrials would follow. By then that Index was at 990, drifting downward.

On February 1 one of several Johnson bombing pauses came to an end, and the district buzzed with rumors that this "peace offensive" had born fruit. Such was not the case; that afternoon the president ordered a resumption of the bombing, and the following session the Dow lost 8 points, to close a fraction above 975.

Clearly investors were becoming jittery, what with uncertainties in Vietnam and the inability of the market to rise above 1,000. *Business Week* thought the situation unhealthy. Secondary stocks and those of small Amex-listed firms were gyrating wildly while the old standbys were being neglected. "Trading has had to be stopped on numerous issues, and rumors abound of buy-out bids, tin strikes, and new contracts. Credit in the market is rising. 'Peace scares' bounce stock prices about like yo-yos."

The following week the bulls staged a second attempt to crash through the 1,000 barrier, and this time the omens were not favorable. The failure of the initial drive had left scars and shaken confidence, and in addition, the financial and political situations had eroded. Interest rates were rising, and, as was usual at such times, money flowed from stocks into bonds and short-term Treasury obligations. The growing awareness that the Vietnam War would continue indefinitely was a sobering thought, and there were rumors that McNamara would ask for a new supplemental appropriation to pay for that conflict.

The poor behavior of leading blue-chip stocks troubled technicians. Both General Motors and Standard Oil of New Jersey reported good earnings and raised their dividends, but their stocks fell. Chrysler turned in a record performance; the stock dropped 3 points. "The question naturally arises, in view of the impotency of past achievements to influence top stocks, whether the always forward-looking stock market is developing skepticism over corporate ability to sustain earning power, if the economy eventually becomes strained," wrote H. J. Nelson in *Barron's*, as he pondered the effects of increased military spending upon an overburdened economy. At the same time, Eisenhower's former CEA Chairman Arthur Burns told a Washington audience of troubles ahead due to the "overheating" of the economy resulting from Johnson's expansionary monetary and fiscal policies. On Wall Street the poor behavior of leading issues troubled both fundamentalists and technicians. Both took note of rising prices and tighter money, and said stocks could not continue to advance in the face of these factors.

The Dow closed just over 991 on February 8, up a point and a half on the day. Volume was heavy. Late that morning, however, the Index had reached a fraction below 999, only to decline in the afternoon. The following session the Dow got to 1,001.11 three hours prior to the close but sold off to 995. On February 10 the Index went to 1,000.27 but ended at 991, down 5 points on the day.

This three-session battle took most of the steam out of the bulls. The second assault on Dow 1,000 had ended in failure, and while many talked of a renewed effort to be mounted the following week, veterans sensed some kind of turning point had arrived, though of course they weren't certain what it was.

A sign came from Walter Heller, leading theoretician of the new economics and father of the 1964 tax cut, who now warned against deficits and inflation. He urged suspension of the Kennedy investment tax credit and suggested that interest rates be allowed to reach a level at which they could begin to cut into consumer demands. In effect, Heller was asking for an economic slowdown—perhaps a recession—to dampen inflationary pressures. Daniel Ahearn, an executive at Wellington Management, told clients, "This is the time to be buying bonds." "It's still much too early to say the bull market is over," wrote Shearson, Hammill, but in such a way as to suggest that this indeed was the case. "Unless something comes along to renew investor confidence again, the stock market could be in for some further near-term irregularities." "For the first time in the business expansion," said another Wall Streeter to *Business Week*, "excesses are being built into the economy that some day will have to be worked off."

The financial district's mood in mid-February was grim, and it worsened through the rest of the month. By then investors had become convinced that 1966 would be a bad year for automobiles; GM, Ford, and Chrysler all sold off sharply. The Commerce Department disclosed that inventory accumulation in the last months of 1965 had been at record levels, a sign business anticipated shortages plus a higher inflation rate, both of which would be bearish for stock prices. Some steel shapes already were in short supply, and their prices rose. Goodyear announced that "advancing costs" necessitated price increases for replacement tires, and the other companies followed suit. Heller took to the podium again, arguing Congress should "lose no time in hammering out the general contours of a temporary tax increase" as well as taking other measures to deflate the economy.

Through all of this stock prices declined at an accelerating pace. The Dow went below 980 on February 17 and three days later was under 970. Within a week it was at 950. For three trading sessions, prices held steady, while technicians called for a "correction" to the 965–70 level, after which a reassessment might be necessary. But there was no rally. Instead, stocks continued to fall, on heavier volume. On March 1 the Dow gave up more than 13 points, to close at 938. AT&T, Standard Oil of California, Allied Chemical, Sears Roebuck, and other quality issues led the decline, and yet none of them had reported bad news, or even had been the victim of rumors. Rather, these blue chips and others had been dumped as a result of a growing conviction among investors that the great bull market was in trouble. "This is a very uncertain period," said Howard Stein of the Dreyfus Fund, who continued to maintain his large cash position, and even participated in the sell-off. "This is the first time in modern days that we have been at war in a period when we have had such a high level of business activity. We know how to turn on controls during a wartime period when business expansion has been limited. . . . Higher taxes could be a deflationary pressure that could brake the boom. All of this hangs over the market."

The Street by then agreed that higher taxes were needed to dampen inflationary pressures. The same men who during the Kennedy years had considered Heller a radical now approvingly quoted his remarks on the subject. To be sure, a major tax increase might stifle the boom and even result in a recession, but the financial district appeared to believe an economic decline preferable to accelerating inflation. Secretary McNamara, who as the market declined told a congressional committee that "the defense program should not be a major factor contributing to inflationary pressures" had lost much of his credibility. Analysts recalled McNamara's signal failure while at Ford and started referring to the Vietnam conflict as "the Edsel of wars."

Still, Johnson would not call for a tax increase. Later on it would be revealed that even then he knew defense spending was bound to rise through the rest of 1966 and well into 1967 and that the budget deficit would be far larger than most experts had anticipated. In his *Memoirs*, Johnson said nothing of this. Rather, he claimed that such legislation could not have gotten through Congress in an election year. Wilbur Mills, the powerful chairman of the House Ways and Means Committee, was opposed to a broad-based measure, and nothing in the form of taxes was possible without his approval. But Mills believed the deficit would be small; he was not privy to confidential White House information regarding war costs. Within the Cabinet only Commerce Secretary Connor spoke out for higher taxes. Even CEO Chairman Ackley started to hedge his bets—this most important of Johnson's economic advisers was working with incomplete information on defense spending. He warned the president that, once established, inflationary psychology would be difficult to uproot, but at the same time he told him, "We are not facing an explosive situation. A little inflation won't be fatal." Ackley assumed the fiscal 1966 deficit would come to around the same as the previous year, in the neighborhood of $1.6 billion. In fact, it would be $3.4 billion.

In late March Johnson hosted a White House dinner for 150 businessmen. "How many of you would recommend tomorrow a tax increase to the Congress for the purpose of restraining our economy?" he asked his guests. Not a single hand was raised. He repeated the question to a group of labor leaders several days later and had the same response. All of them were working on false assumptions regarding war costs and the nature of military and defense spending.

McNamara maintained a public silence on the issue. He met on several occasions with the Council of Economic Advisors, which urged him to recommend a tax increase to the president. This he refused to do, saying he lacked firm figures on war costs. Treasury Secretary Fowler continued to speak out on the essential strength of the economy and of how the administration was winning the struggle against inflation. Both men were disingenuous, to say the least, as was Lyndon Johnson. All three feared, perhaps, that if the American people and Congress knew of how much the war would cost, public opinion would turn against it. At the time the administration spoke of a "cutoff date" of July 1, 1967, for direct American participation; later on McNamara would admit that even then he knew this to be a deception.

So there would be no tax boost in 1966. Instead, Johnson signed into law the minor increases in excise taxes he had asked for in January. Government spending continued to soar, not only for war-related goods and services but also for Great Society programs. So did prices. Federal Reserve Board Chairman Martin kept his silence for the moment, knowing that monetary policy without the support of fiscal prudence could not do the job of restraining the economy. Perhaps he too believed the administration's figures, or he might have hoped Johnson would have a change of heart.

Afterwards former CEO member Kermit Gordon called the failure to work for and obtain a new tax bill in 1966 the worst blunder in American economic policy since the end of World War II. "Surely in any meaningful sense the Federal budget was the engine of inflation in the period from 1966 to 1968," wrote Arthur Okun four years later. And this inflation was an important factor in killing the bull market.

On March 7, the Dow lost 14 points to close at 918. As in previous declines this selloff had not resulted from bad news, but rather the continued erosion of confidence and the growing uncertainties regarding the war and economic policies. Stocks rallied this time, however, and at noon on Thursday, March 10, the Dow was a fraction below 940. Two hours later the Morgan Guaranty Bank increased its prime lending rate to 5½ percent, a level that had not been seen since the bleakest days of the Hoover years. Other banks followed, and now stocks plummeted, with the Dow closing just below 930. A new selling wave began, and the Index went below 906 the afternoon of March 13 before rallying to close at 911.

What did this imply? William Moses of the Massachusetts Investment Trust said, "There's no reason for pessimism. There's no major downturn in business just ahead," while A. Moyer Kulp of Wellington Fund said, "We are close to the point where institutions could buy stocks." But like McNamara, these men and others had suffered a loss of credibility. They managed huge portfolios loaded with hundreds of millions of dollars worth of blue-chip stocks. How could even a fraction of these holdings be sold into a weak market without triggering a panic? Should a major fund try to dispose of 10,000 shares of General Electric at a time when that stock was under selling pressure by small investors, for example, its price could fall by half a dozen points in a single session. What might happen if three or four funds decided to sell GE on the same day? multiply this by a half dozen key issues and the result would be pandemonium.

What about potential buyers? Dreyfus Fund, whose cash position had increased sharply in February, was one of these. But Howard Stein wasn't sure he wanted to enter the market at that time. As a nation, he said, "we seem at a loss on how to handle our problems," and such a period of indecision called not for major commitments to common stocks but rather extreme prudence—and liquidity.

Just as it appeared the Dow would slip below 900, the market turned around. Part of the reason was an increase in purchases of American securities by foreigners who came to the N.Y.S.E. with surplus dollars in the hope of getting into stocks at bargain prices. Then, too, the high prime rate, which by then had spread to other banks, convinced many foreigners that Americans were taking actions to hold down inflation and also encouraged them to invest in short-term commercial paper. Much of the heavy selling had ended, and some mutual funds and pension accounts had started to nibble at the harder-hit blue chips. Finally there were rumors out of Washington that the administration would push hard for a tax increase—though by then Wall Street wasn't certain this would prove bullish.

By March 18 the Dow was over 920, and three sessions later it went above 930. After a brief correction prices rose again, going to 950 in mid-April. The advance was fueled by good first-quarter earnings reports and an easing of the balance of payments deficit due to increasing foreign investments in the United States. Television, aircraft, electronics, and space-related issues paced the advance, as investors shrugged off reports of rising mortgage rates and higher than anticipated Vietnam spending. The new issues revived, as Kentucky Fried Chicken and Randolph Computer came to market. Electronic Memories and World Airways met with strong demand and quickly shot up to sell at premium prices.

With all of this, the rally lacked conviction. For one thing, it was paced by low-quality, speculative issues. This situation enabled some of the go-go money managers to turn in excellent results but troubled the old-timers. F. J. Miller, research director at Goodbody, warned, "When, as at present investors temporarily lose sight of some of the basic determinants of investment value, the market becomes vulnerable to unforeseen and adverse developments and . . . unreasoning fear." Monte Gordon of Bache saw "disquieting overtones" in continuing inflation. Abelson of *Barron's* wrote, "The American Stock Exchange has become the wildest game in town," with the tape running 20 minutes late and trading volume accelerating. Like many other skeptics, Abelson was certain it could not last much longer.

The money supply figures released in the second week of April indicated the Federal Reserve had begun tightening up in this vital area. Wall Street interpreted this as a signal the discount rate soon would rise, perhaps to 4¾ percent. Some enthusiastic bears said it would go to 5 percent, a level not seen since 1929. On April 21, in an attempt to curb speculation, both the N.Y.S.E. and the Amex announced that the minimum amount of equity required to open a brokerage account would go from $1,000 to $2,000, and three days later the exchanges imposed more stringent regulations on in-and-out trading. These rumors and moves contributed toward halting the bull move. The Dow peaked at 955 on April 21 and then started down once again, closing the month at 934.

On May 2 Chairman Ackley suggested that business profits were too high. Investors interpreted this as a sign that corporate taxes soon would be increased, and the Dow lost 10 points to close at 922 the following day. That morning Martin advocated an across-the-board tax increase, suggesting this would be the best way to deal with inflation and indicating that in the absence of congressional action he would push for a tighter monetary policy. With this, stocks fell again, the Dow giving up 7 points on heavy volume on May 4. The Index closed a fraction below 900 on May 5, as several analysts claimed to have perceived a signal for the beginning of a bear market.

The economic news contributed to the malaise. The big three automobile companies announced that due to large inventories they planned to cut back on production. Retail sales were not as good as had been expected. The Vietnam War continued to escalate, with hopes for a quick armistice all but gone. Later on McNamara would announce that additional funds were needed for the war. Administration insiders leaked stories to the press that even Johnson had concluded a tax increase was needed and that he would ask for one once the November elections were out of the way.

Could the economy be kept under control until then? More specifically, could the rate of inflation be maintained until fiscal policy eased tensions? In mid-May CEO member Arthur Okun told a Minneapolis audience that he saw no "significant possibility of the economy either running out of steam or bursting the boiler within 1966." But he did concede that pressures were being generated within that boiler, particularly in regard to labor costs. Unemployment was below 4 percent, and the labor market had become "exceedingly tight," said Okun. He warned that the country might have to expect "a marked acceleration in wage increases." This meant inflation, the kind that could be dangerous by the time Congress acted on a tax measure.

During the next four months the market declined steadily, as the bulls went into hiding. No rally of any significance interrupted the sickening collapse, but at the same time there were no signs of panic. After all, the economy remained strong, the labor force was fully employed, and corporate earnings were excellent. The massive selloff—the worst since 1962—resulted in part from a developing conviction that the war had gotten out of control, and inflation soon would follow. Administration spokesmen continued to offer optimistic projections regarding the fighting, but by then they sounded hollow. When they noted an easing in the balance of payments situation, critics charged them with telling half-truths, ignoring as they did the world-wide flight from the dollar and continued heavy gold sales, especially to France.

On June 29 several major New York banks hiked their prime rate to 5¾ percent, and at the same time the Federal Reserve accelerated its program of squeezing the money supply. "Money's tight and everyone knows it," wrote Abelson. "That's the big difference between today and last summer, or for that matter, four years ago." This situation, he believed, might cause the market to go into a tailspin. "Rapidly rising interest rates are unsettling the stock market," wrote *Business Week*. "Speculation is widespread that the Fed is about to harden its policy further, raising the discount rate once again to curb bank borrowing at the discount window."

The market sold off on these rumors; by the end of July the Dow was below 850. Then came some verification of inflationary fears. The steel companies announced boosts in prices in early August, with only a feeble protest from the White House. On the 16th the First National City Bank increased its prime rate to 6 percent and other major institutions followed. At that time the Dow was just over 823; four sessions later it was below 800, and on the 29th it closed a fraction above 767, at which point analysts finally discerned a "firming trend." In less than four months, the Dow had given up more than 160 points.

Volume had risen, but there still was no panic on Wall Street. Rather, investors were confused. What had this decline signified? Some analysts thought it meant investors believed a depression was on the way and were turning to cash in preparation for the decline. Others said the waves of selling signified opposition to tax increases. Perhaps Americans had altered their thinking regarding economic affairs, said several commentators. In the future, fears of inflation, and not recession, would result in major selloffs. To their way of thinking the market was indicating a lack of confidence in the president's ability or willingness to take strong actions to prevent price increases.

The statistics were more eloquent than the theories. In early September the Commerce Department released figures that showed the capital investment boom of the 1960s was drawing to a close. Housing starts also were down, and new car sales remained sluggish. Unemployment remained low, but most of the other major economic indicators pointed in the direction of recession. Analyzing these and other figures, Pierre Renfret of Lionel Edie & Co. concluded that at best the nation was in for a period of stagnation, while under the worst of circumstances there might be a serious recession the following year. There is, he said, "no growth at all" in the economy.

Bulls noted that factories were operating at full capacity, and it appeared third-quarter earnings reports would be excellent. Outside of the cyclical industries of housing and automobiles, they said, all was well. Furthermore, there were signs the Consumer Price Index was declining, largely as a result of lower food prices. In response, the pessimists said all of this would change as autumn turned into winter. "The market is saying that the state of mind of these people is exceedingly disturbed," editorialized *Business Week*. "Despite booming business and soaring profits, they do not like what they see. And they fail to take comfort either in the forecasts of the economists or in reassuring statistics that come out of Washington."

Optimism had been replaced by skepticism that summer, and now cynicism was coming into vogue. There was a crisis of confidence on Wall Street as well as in Washington that autumn.

A brief rally developed in mid-September, but analysts said it resulted from "technical factors." Then there followed another sell-off. Volume was low, and the *Wall Street Journal* interpreted this as a sign that the major dumping was completed, with perhaps hundreds of thousands of small investors in highly liquid positions. Would they return to the market later on? The newspaper didn't offer an opinion. The institutions also were liquid, their managers claiming prices were low, but their inaction demonstrated a lack of conviction that this was so.

Sometime in the summer of 1966, the champagne went flat on Wall Street. The joy and verve, the spirit of innovation and risk—and even the reckless daring—that had marked the fifth stage faded or changed into little more than a jaded opportunism.

Had the great bull market finally ended? There was little talk of this in the press, the business magazines, or at the brokerages. So powerful and prolonged an upward move hardly could be concluded by a simple decline on low volume, said Wall Street veterans, and they noted that obituaries had been released during similar corrections in 1953, 1957, 1962, and as recently as 1965. They were not prepared to write off this bull market unless and until it reached a dramatic climax similar to that of 1929, and in early autumn of 1966 this didn't seem possible. Government policies guaranteed the nation against a major depression, and while inflation was a serious matter, by itself it could not destroy all vestiges of bullishness. Prices might decline further, but soon they would find a bottom, bump along for a while to test it, and then turn up.

The Dow reached 794 on September 27, with technicials saying the market was due for a test of the low. It failed, and in the next two sessions gave up more than 22 points. By October 3 the Index was below 760, and it went under 750 on the 6th, as President Johnson told the nation the economic outlook was excellent and business never better.

Investors responded by selling stocks.

Ten

MAGINOT LINE ON
WALL STREET

THERE WERE few things Bernie Cornfeld liked better than to
talk about his boyhood in Brooklyn. He would settle himself
in a comfortable chair with brandy and cigar and reminisce
about how tough it had been to grow up in depression America. The
fact that this was done in a castle, with several Rolls-Royces at the
gate and an airplane awaiting his call, probably heightened his delight in telling visitors about the dark years of the 1930s.

Cornfeld was not alone in this. Throughout America tens of
millions of middle-aged people would become nostalgic about those
good old bad old days. Part of the joy in this derived from their having survived the period, and implicit in the monologues was a celebration of later good fortune. Still, they knew it had been a time of
great fear as well. Even while he planned his multi-million-dollar
deals, Cornfeld had nightmares of what it had meant to worry about
food, clothing, jobs, and a place to live. In this, too, he was not
alone.

A person who had entered the labor force in the early part of
the Great Depression might have been close to retirement in the
late 1960s. Such an individual probably worried about the possibility of a new collapse through most of his or her life. They were concerned about the Cold War but at the same time probably noted
that government spending on weaponry provided jobs for many
workers. The Depression had been ended by World War II appropriations; the postwar economy had been fueled by Cold War expenditures. War and prosperity seemed to go together.

An economic price of sorts had to be paid for this kind of prosperity. Inflation, which was part of the price, was a recurrent problem through much of the postwar period. A generation of Americans who had known depression were willing to accept some inflation if that meant full employment and steadily increasing wages; a generation of economists trained in the 1930s to combat depression by means of Keynesian techniques agreed with them, and so did the political leaders of the period. "Full employment" was the popular battle cry of these decades, and while some candidates gave lip service to "steady prices," they usually made it clear that they were of secondary importance. Even Dwight Eisenhower, easily the most anti-inflation-minded chief executive of the era, tended to tread cautiously on matters relating to unemployment during the first two of his three recessions. Only during the last decline in 1960, when he was freed from all political ambition, did Eisenhower squeeze the economy strongly and steadily in the face of rising unemployment.

Eisenhower's successors, Kennedy and Johnson, were committed to expansionary economic politics, in particular those that would create jobs for underprivileged Americans. Though both men paid homage to fights against inflation, neither seemed to consider it a major problem. In any case, they thought realization of social and foreign policy goals more important than a few extra percentage points in the Consumer Price Index.

These leaders subscribed to the belief that recession and depression constituted the greatest economic threat to the nation, and they erected a fortress of legislation and public policy to keep workers employed and factories busy. That they would do so is understandable, given the traumas associated with the 1930s and political pressures of the 1960s. But just as the French after World War I had constructed the Maginot Line to guard against a repetition of the kind of attack the Germans had mounted in 1914–15, so the establishment economists of the post–World War II period worked to prevent the outbreak of a new depression. Their values, instincts, and training enabled them to do so with great success, and they were aided by political and foreign policy decisions emanating from Washington.

Of course, the Maginot Line proved ineffective against the German blitzkrieg of 1940, for as the French awaited a frontal assault their enemy attacked from the rear and thus were able to overwhelm them. Similarly, the American economy in the 1960s, geared to provide full employment and keep factories busy, would be undermined by an inflation that wouldn't be dealt with effectively by government until very late in the game.

The Johnson administration considered strong economic growth the bedrock of domestic and foreign policies; without it Great Society programs would have had to be cut back, and the Vietnam War could not have been financed. Wall Street always had been more troubled by inflation than had been Washington, but even on the Street, advances in corporate earnings and dividends helped propel stocks to new highs in the mid-1960s.

Then the mood started to change. It happened in 1966. That year the gross national product increased sharply, going from $685 billion to $750 billion. Corporate earnings were up, as were dividends. Yet the Dow had fallen by more than 18 percent. Why had this happened?

Initially analysts attributed the decline to higher interest rates, tighter money, the Vietnam quagmire, and growing domestic discontent. Clearly Lyndon Johnson had lost much of his earlier popularity. All this, plus a suspicion that stock prices were too high anyway, had contributed to causing the selloff, the most serious since 1962. But most analysts and investors thought the decline would be followed by a smart recovery—as had been the experience in 1962. For decades, it had been said a bull market could not be killed by anything less than a major depression, and none was in sight that year, when the factories were humming and unemployment stood below 4 percent.

Today we know that the interday peak of 1,001.11 that the Dow reached on February 9, 1966, was the high point for this greatest of bull markets. Seven years later it would be topped, but by then the Index would be measured by dollars cheapened by inflation. (The Consumer Price Index rose by 8.8 percent in 1973 and would go up by 12.2 the following year.)

The bull market of the 1920s was climaxed by the beginning of the Great Depression. That of the 1960s would be ended by a far more insidious phenomenon, which might be called the Great Inflation. Americans of the 1920s and early 1930s had no difficulty recognizing the effects of depression, all of which were bad; they lost their jobs or took salary cuts, and saw savings shrink and homes lost to foreclosure. Those who experienced the onset of the Great Inflation had mixed feelings about it. Not only did they continue to work, but salaries rose steadily, savings accounts grew, and the values of their homes increased. Of course the purchasing power of their money declined, and so these apparent gains often were disguised losses. "Everybody knows that higher prices in our supermarkets and department stores are the result of inflation," said Arthur Okun. "When money income goes up, however, the cause is not so obvious."

When the man of the house brings home an 8 percent wage increase, he and his wife are confident that he earned and deserved that raise. If prices subsequently go up by 4 percent, the family is not happy with the 4 percent gain in real income; rather, it feels cheated that the wage gain was cut in half by inflation. In point of fact, of course, the husband's 8 percent wage increase may have occurred because of inflation. Nonetheless, nearly everybody feels that inflation leaves him with the short end of the stick. It is thus divisive and disruptive; and these social consequences cannot be ignored.

Still, these people were working, and if their purchasing power declined somewhat and their real income remained steady or actually declined, at least they had that. In this regard at least the Great Inflation did not strike as hard a blow as did the Great Depression, and its social costs were lower and not so sudden in their impacts.

Gradually, over a period of years, Americans came to appreciate what was happening. So did investors, and they left the market in dismay, using their savings to purchase consumer goods or putting the money into bonds, whose yields increased throughout much of the late 1960s. The great bull market of the 1950s and 1960s came to an end. It did so without a dramatic crash, a moment of truth, or the wipeout of fortunes. Because of this, the vast majority of analysts and related seers were misled. They had been on guard against another 1929 for decades, and while they awaited the earthquake the market was undermined by the dry rot of inflation. Thus, the Street was capable of staging one last blowout, a sustained one at that, a period of revelry and high speculation when it seemed all was well once again.

If nothing else, Keith Funston was a master of timing, or perhaps he was just extraordinarily fortunate. On September 12, 1966, he announced that as soon as a suitable successor could be found he would retire from the N.Y.S.E. presidency. Funston's term had another year to run, but he wanted to give the members sufficient time to find the right person. "I think I deserve a rest," he told reporters. Funston would travel, pursue his hobby of archaeology, and spend more time with his family. Then he might re-enter the business world. After all, he was only 55 years old and had much to contribute. Thus, the Street's "good luck symbol" prepared to exit.

That day the market rallied to close a fraction above 790, for a gain of 15 points. A selloff followed, so that by early October the Dow was under 750, with analysts predicting that a bottom soon would be reached. In the early trading on Friday, October 7, the Index dipped below 740 but rallied in the afternoon to close slightly better than 744. This was deemed a good omen. Johnson offered an optimistic prediction that weekend, but stocks opened lower on Monday, reaching 736 in the third hour of trading. Then, for no particular reason, the buyers returned. That afternoon the Dow advanced by more than 19 points to close above 754, for a gain of 10 points. Now some analysts were certain the bottom not only had been reached, but tested. The way seemed clear for a move back above 800—which was where the Dow wound up on October 26.

The rally resulted from a developing belief that the president finally would move against inflation. Johnson asked Congress to suspend accelerated depreciation allowances and the 7 percent investment tax credit—but only through 1967, as though to indicate his belief inflation not be a threat in 1968. In addition he would cut federal spending in some unspecified ways and ask agency chiefs to defer several ambitious programs. "At last we have something positive to work with—not just a rumor," said one analyst. David Rockefeller and George Champion of Chase Manhattan Bank said that "one practical and constructive effect of the President's program should be to contribute to a more settled atmosphere in financial markets," and so it did.

Would it be effective in curbing inflation? Representative Thomas Curtis of Missouri, the top Republican on the Ways and Means Committee, doubted the program would do much in this area, and in fact wasn't certain any serious attempts at balancing the budget would be made. "I don't believe these figures," he said. "I can no longer rely upon the President . . . why not tell the public where these cutbacks are?" Curtis went on to say the nation needed a prolonged period of tight money and high interest rates to "squeeze inflation out of the system" but conceded such was politically and perhaps economically impossible, since it would result in a recession.

Already some businessmen were complaining about restrictive Federal Reserve actions. "So far we've been all right," said Arthur Hyde of A. O. Smith, "but if we shrink credit it's going to hurt our business; 99 percent of our sales involve credit." Several market analysts agreed, but, for the short term at least, the way ahead seemed clear. "I think it could go up 10 percent" said Ralph Rotnem of Harris, Upham & Co., as the Dow closed October above 807. To be sure, earnings would drop as a result of the limited Johnson program, but so would prices. As the Street saw it, the president's medicine was somewhere between being a mild dose and a placebo.

H. J. Nelson of *Barron's* thought this might be just what was needed. The columnist had lived through the 1929 crash and the dismal 1930s, and while he warned against problems caused by inflation, his major fear was depression. "As a unit, the central bankers of Europe declare, 'never, never will there be a repetition of the 1929–1932 debacle,' " he wrote in mid-November, after the government released a report that new housing starts were at a 20-year low and Detroit announced automobile sales were 10 percent below that for 1965. "Despite the mixed stock market trends and cyclical weakness of the economy in a few directions, plus widespread predictions of a recession extending into a depression, there are plenty of good authorities yet to be convinced that even a full-fledged recession is in sight."

Stocks dipped in mid-November, the result of uncertainty; investors weren't certain of what to fear more, inflation or recession. Nelson too was troubled. "But the danger of a collapse in values evolving from a business recession developing into a depression later on is highly remote." He and others of his generation were certain the Maginot Line would hold against such an assault.

The Dow ended the year at 786, or approximately where it had been in mid-October. The consensus among analysts was that the bottom had withstood its test and that there would be an advance of sorts in 1967. Only the good bugs, led by James Dines, talked of a collapse. Edward Merkle of Madison Fund was considered overcautious when he wrote that it would be "a tough year to make money" in the market. "The stock market frequently moves in the opposite direction of business activity," said Gerald Tsai, who suggested the nation might be in for a period of stagnation. Yet he too was bullish; Manhattan Fund was buying stocks. Robert Johnson of Paine, Webber, Jackson & Curtis thought the market had "discounted about everything conceivable in the way of bad news," and he told clients to purchase shares in utilities and international oils. Ragnar Naess was an out-and-out bull; he expected "an exceptional buying opportunity which we see only every 5 or 10 years." "This is the year that promises to be the economic bridge to the adventurous Age of Space," wrote *New York Times* financial and business editor Thomas Mullaney. "Forecasters see 1967 as a period of consolidation between the great growth of the last six years and the trillion-dillar economies of the next decade." Alan Abelson thought he detected movement in space-age and related stocks, while the older, more familiar issues were being neglected. "Whatever happened to 1967?" he asked. "A lot of money these days seems to be going into stocks on the strength of what's coming up in '68."

Virtually all the analysts thought recession was a greater threat and problem than inflation. *Business Week's* year-end editorial opened with the following thought: "The year 1966 will go into the annals as the time when the longest and best balanced expansion in U.S. economic history began to run into trouble because of mistakes in economic policymaking." The most important of these errors was the uncertain monetary and fiscal policies pursued by the Fed and the Treasury. "Outlays for new plant and equipment may be throttled back more than is called for in 1967, unless fiscal and monetary policies are changed," the magazine warned. It recommended minor tax increases and an easing of the money supply, the one to compensate for the other, all in order to prevent an economic slowdown. "The risk of recession—or at least of lower profits and continued down pressures on some major sectors of the economy—is somewhat greater than it was. Still, it remains highly improbable that a general recession will occur in the midst of our military buildup—although we must certainly be prepared to shift our economic policies more drastically toward stimulation, should the Vietnamese war end or start to fade away later in 1967." *Business Week* concluded with the thought that if Johnson "can hold the increase in expenditures down to, say, $10 billion, there is a possibility that no tax hike will be needed."

The president had obtained almost all of his Great Society legislation by the end of 1966. The congressional elections were over and had resulted in minor Republican triumphs, but the Democrats still ruled in both houses of Congress. The word went out that Johnson was prepared to act against inflation and could count on legislative support for a new tax program. Shortly after New Year's Day Commerce Secretary Connor told a television audience that economic growth would be slower in 1967 than it had been the previous year, but that as a result of this inflationary pressures would ease. Finally, Washington heard new rumors of peace in Vietnam.

Two years earlier talk of an end to the war combined with economic recession or stagnation would have resulted in a major selloff at the exchanges. All this had changed by 1967. The Dow, which had closed at 786 on January 3, went to a fraction below 815 on the 10th. That day Johnson delivered his State of the Union message, in which he asked for a 6 percent surcharge on corporate and individual income taxes to help finance the war and balance the budget. Wall Street took this as a signal that the president would mount a campaign against inflation, and prices took off. For the rest of the month, trading volume fell below 10 million shares only twice, and the Dow ended slightly under 850.

The nation was about to enter what some economists later would call a "mini-recession," and stocks were booming. All the signs for a slowdown were present—unemployment was inching up, new factory orders declined, and there was slack in the money markets. In late January the prime rate was cut back to 5½–5¾, the first such decline since the great economic expansion of the 1960s had begun. And on the Street the celebration continued, with the Dow peaking at 860 in early February before a correction set in.

The promises and hopes of early January would not be kept or fulfilled. There would be no tax increase in 1967, as Congressman Mills refused to support one unless it was tied to reductions in federal spending. For his part Johnson would not eliminate Great Society programs or withdraw from Vietnam, so the budget deficit for fiscal 1967 came to $8.7 billion, and it was evident that the next year's deficit would be staggering. The dollar weakened; the total gold loss for the year would come to $307 million. Yet through all of this, the bulls remained in firm control on Wall Street. In the face of declining sales and earnings for leading automobile, steel, and housing-related companies, stocks continued to advance. Clearly, said Gerald Loeb, "the market has discounted the current economic slowdown."

But it was not that simple. The Dow stocks and other blue chips were lagging far behind the broader market. The focus now was on new, small firms whose shares were listed on the Amex or traded over-the-counter. Walter Mintz of Shearson, Hammill noted that there was "more uninformed buying than we'd like to see, including some based on tips and gossip." For example, Kalvar, a speculative favorite of the early 1960s, which had slipped back after the company failed to meet objectives, went from 35 to 250 in 5 months. National Semiconductor, a minor factor in the electronics industry, hired some executives from Fairchild Camera, and when the news broke, the stock jumped from 17 to 31 in a matter of hours, after which it declined to 24. EG&G, Dynalectron, and Computing & Software doubled and redoubled. Alphanumerical, another OTC item, sold for 36 in November of 1966; a half year later the stock was over 200, on rumors of a tie-up with IBM.

These so-called performance stocks did not attract institutional money. Nor did they wind up in portfolios of large mutual funds. For one thing, they often were thinly capitalized, which meant a major fund could not accumulate a significant block of the shares, and for another, they were selling for what seemed outlandish prices. "Even if business does turn around, how much further can performance stocks go?" asked one banker of a *Business Week* reporter, while the manager of a mutual fund added, "I happen to believe some performance stocks are too high to put new money into." The *New York Times* quoted an analyst as being troubled about the generic term afforded such stocks. They are supposed to perform, he noted, and so they did. "Often, however, they have nothing else—no history, no earnings, and not even halfway decent rumors." They were capable of wide swings. Anna Merjos, an analyst who followed these stocks, told clients that those "with a predilection for low-priced stocks over the blue-chips should have steady nerves—or an ample supply of tranquilizers." Clients who could stick it out, however, could have excellent profits. Even Abelson, who scoffed at those who played the performance stock game, started to recommend some of them; by April he was especially high on Tektronix.

By late April the Dow had managed to approach the 900 level, but the low-priced speculative issues were soaring, and these attracted most of the interest. Alarmed, the SEC announced that there would be an investigation of the phenomenon, but this did little to halt the fever. At the Amex, President Ralph Saul initiated a study of activity in several stocks, such as Alloys Unlimited, Pentron Electronics, Duraloy, Savoy Industries, and Rowland Products, all of which had impressive runups based on little but rumors. Even Federal Reserve Board Chairman Martin spoke out against "rampant speculation" and in particular leveled his attack against managers of performance-oriented mutual funds, which he said "contain poisonous qualities reminiscent of some aspects of the old pool operations of the 1920s."

Shortly thereafter indictments were handed down for six former executives and insiders at Pentron, who were charged with "conspiracy, manipulation, and fraud." But not even this could put a damper on the bull market in speculative issues. In June the blue chips sold off on news of a war between Israel and her Arab neighbors, but the performance stocks stood firm and in fact some of them moved up sharply. "I think the Middle East crisis would do wonders for the offshore drilling stocks," said one market letter, and such OTC items as Global Marine, Reading & Bates, Tidewater Marine, and Zapata Off-Shore went to premium prices.

By then speculators had pushed forward a new group of heroes, leaders to be followed, who appeared to have the golden touch with stocks. The go-go managers of the previous year retained many of their followers; Dave Meid, Fred Alger, and Fred Carr in particular performed well in this new phase. Gerald Tsai, on the other hand, fell from grace. His Manhattan Fund concentrated on old-line growth issues, the kind that performed sluggishly in 1967. In addition, Tsai himself was in a slump, having bought and sold issues at the wrong time. "I wonder whether he's really a swinger after all," said one mutual fund manager. By mid-1967 the leading *Wunderkind* of 1965–66 had been pushed aside.

This new group was composed of men who initiated and ran variations on the mutual fund theme. Some of them had leveraged operations, which meant they borrowed money for their funds and used it to invest in stocks. This was not a new idea, however, but in the bull phase of 1967 it did attract interest. More intriguing, however, was the hedge fund concept. These funds had the right to sell stock short, a classic technique used by investors who believed the issue was due for the decline. They then would borrow shares, sell them at market, await the decline, at which point they would purchase the same shares at a far lower price to return them to the lender. After the market collapse of 1966, hedge funds seemed a good idea—they could go both ways with the market, buying on the rise, selling on the way down. One analyst, who noted Tsai's fall from grace, observed that Tsai had opened Manhattan Fund at the wrong time, just prior to the decline. "If Gerry had put that half a billion in the bank and earned 5 percent he'd look like a genius now." If 5 percent from the bank was good, how much better Tsai might have done if he had shorted leading stocks? Manhattan Fund's charter forbade the practice, even if Tsai were of a mind to do so. There was no reason, however, why new mutual funds should reject the approach. In fact, several such operations already existed, the first and most famous headed by Alfred W. Jones of A. W. Jones & Co., who started one in 1949. But these were essentially private deals, even though several managed tens of millions of dollars.

The new hedge funds of 1967 began as private operations, but some went public later on. Hawthorne Associates, owned by Lawrence Blum and Harold Newman, had a hedge fund with a portfolio of close to $10 million, and Richard Paul, the research director for Gartman, Rose & Feuer, ran a hedge fund in his spare time. Charles Hurwitz, a former broker and analyst for a variety of Wall Street firms, organized Summit Management and in late 1967 planned the debut of a publicly owned organization, to be known as Hedge Fund of America. Within a year the 28-year-old Hurwitz was managing over $100 million and telling observers, "We think we'll be a dominant firm in money management. We think we're good." So he was. Hurwitz and others of his breed concentrated on the performance stocks, playing them both ways, and in the process turned in results far better than those of the older, more conventional funds.

The leveraged and hedge funds proved only a transition to the next stage, however, and after a while they faded. That new phase would be dominated by Fred Mates. A former elementary-school teacher with a passing interest in acting, Mates entered the securities industry in the early 1960s by clerking at Bache & Co. At the same time he dabbled in a variety of other businesses; at one point he put all his assets into a dealership for the Isetta, a novel automobile with three doors and one cylinder, which he felt might challenge the Volkswagen. It didn't. Close to bankruptcy, Mates sold his business and tried to recoup by investing his remaining money in stocks, especially the hot new issues. In order to get a salary and also to have a base of operations, Mates took a job as a broker at Newburger, Loeb. Shortly thereafter he began writing the market letter for the company, and since his selections often panned out, he developed a wide following. Mates would recommend those stocks he purchased for his own account, they rose, and so he made money not only for himself but also for those readers who accepted his advice.

Convinced he had found his niche, Mates started to skip from one brokerage to another, always at a higher salary, and for each he put out a market letter. As expected, his readers followed him to each new home. Clearly Mates had become a "hot broker," but this was not his ambition. Why work for others, he thought, when, by appealing to his readers, he might start a mutual fund bearing his stamp? The Mates Fund was organized in July 1967.

The Dow was rising at the time, as was trading volume. The prices of stocks of small glamour companies advanced smartly that summer and autumn, and the Mates Fund portfolio contained many of these. Thus, Mates enjoyed a good fortune concerning timing that had eluded Gerry Tsai the previous year.

In late September, however, the news turned bad. The North Vietnamese rejected still another Johnson peace plan, new outbreaks of fighting between Arabs and Israelis were reported, and the president's tax program remained stalled in Congress. Keith Funston had left the N.Y.S.E. by then, and his successor, Robert Haack, told reporters quite frankly that there was too much speculation on the Street.

The Dow peaked at 943 on September 25, and in the next two months lost slightly less than 100 points. The blue chips were in disarray, but the performance stocks held firm, and many of them actually advanced. In late October, when the results for mutual funds were released, it was learned that the top performer over the past twelve months had been Fred Carr's Enterprise Fund, while Winfield Growth, managed by David Meid, was in second place. T. Rowe Price New Horizons and Value Line Special Situations, both of which had portfolios loaded with performance stocks, were next. Investors were rushing to purchase their shares, and the press of business became so intense that New Horizons discontinued further sales—so it wouldn't grow too big.

As a new operation the Mates Fund was unranked, but, later on, statistics indicated it had done better in its first two months than almost all the others. Mates became a market star in November and December, when stocks bounced back from their lows to stage an impressive year-end rally. By January 1968, he had more than $1.7 million under management, with investors literally tying up his switchboard trying to buy his shares. Five months later Mates Fund had $17 million in assets, and at that point it announced a temporary halt to the issuance of new shares. Undaunted, eager investors and speculators went to the open market and tried to purchase shares there. This was unprecedented. Owners of Mates Fund found they might get premiums of more than 10 percent over net asset value for their holdings. Few took the offers, however, for Mates appeared to have discovered a new, foolproof formula for making huge amounts of money, and they wanted to stay aboard and share in his fortunes.

That the fund possessed an uncanny knack for finding bright situations was obvious, but so did other mutuals, and its use of leverage hardly was unique. Mates was different, however, in the way he employed letter stock to obtain instant paper profits.

Simply stated, letter stock was shares unregistered with the SEC for a limited or unlimited period, which could not be resold until they had gone through such a registration. Investors learned of letter stock in the early 1960s, when some conglomerates used it to acquire small companies. The conglomerate would obtain the firm's assets and earnings and in return issue letter stock to the old owners, who also would go to work for their new bosses. This stock would not be included in the conglomerate's capitalization, and it would not receive dividends. Thus, net earnings would increase while the total number of shares outstanding appeared to remain the same. The letter stock would become registered at some future date, of course, at which time the conglomerate's capitalization would be adjusted to reflect the change. Meanwhile the former owners would have a stake in the fortunes of the conglomerate and so would stay on to help make it a success, knowing that on registration day they could sell their stock and hoping it would be selling at a high price at that time.

This was a perfectly legal device, as was the next stage in the use of letter stock. Why couldn't a company issue such paper to a buyer—say, a mutual fund—and in this way obtain additional money with no immediate increase in capitalization? It was a simple, relatively inexpensive method of raising money that appealed to both parties. A small but promising outfit whose stock currently sold for $10 a share would sell letter stock to a mutual fund at $7, with the proviso that the shares would not be registered for three years. This was the kind of deal Mates liked, for it enabled him to "dress up" his portfolio.

The Mates Fund would purchase 10,000 shares of a letter stock at $7 and immediately value it at the current quote of $10 for the purpose of computing net asset value per share. Thus the fund would be able to show an instant profit of $3 per share, or a total of $30,000. Even should the stock fall a point or so, the Mates Fund still would have its paper gain.

The operation had some risks. Suppose the owners of Mates Fund shares wanted to liquidate their positions? Under normal conditions a fund manager might have to sell off part of the portfolio in order to have money for such redemptions. But the letter stock couldn't be sold, so Mates might become illiquid, and perhaps even close down. But Mates didn't trouble himself about redemptions in early 1968, not when would-be investors were trying to bribe his clerks to sell them shares, and the fund had to return $50 million worth of orders that came in after the sales window had closed. He did have some passing troubles with the SEC, which wanted more information regarding the way Mates used letter stock. "I've played it perfectly straight," he claimed. "I sleep nights."

The high rollers were in great demand in this period. Fred Alger was managing over $300 million in client money, and David Meid had to weed out his list so as to make way for some new accounts. Now these money managers were joined by a new generation of underwriters, adept at putting together flashy deals. A. J. Butler & Co. was the vehicle for Abbey Butler, who had underwritten Cameo Parkway Records at 2 and then maneuvered it to the point where it went over 50. His company was established on the basis of this performance. Butler used some of his profits—and borrowed money—to purchase seats on the major exchanges and then announced his willingness and availability to put together major deals for companies frustrated by the slow pace at old-line underwriters. At the time Butler was 30 years old.

Graham Loving, Jr., considered a veteran at 42, was a graduate of the Myron Lomasney organization, who set up Gralov Associates, a small unit that specialized in arranging deals with letter stock and hedge funds. "The idea of being a broker doesn't suit me," said Loving. "If I sold a million shares of stock, so what?" Instead he placed blocks of letter stock in private and fund hands. For example, he arranged the private sale of $1.7 million of convertible debentures for Elpac, Inc., 110,000 shares of Burns & Towne at $3 a share, and the complete private financing of Compusize. Loving also operated a magazine for teenagers and a $5.5 million hedge fund of his own. "A person can become a millionaire on Wall Street in a couple of years," said Loving. "This is an extremely difficult thing to do in most other businesses," he conceded. "The trouble is that most people lack guts."

And you had to be young. "Brains become sterile after a while," said Fred Alger. "We're no new breed," added Sanford Bernstein, of "Bernstein, Period," but his young mavericks would reject potential money managers of 35 or so as being over the hill.

The antics of these new bulls provided spice for investors, many of whom overlooked the fact that there was little else to cheer about. In November the Federal Reserve raised the discount rate to 4½ percent, and Martin once again warned against inflation, calling Johnson's policies "irresponsible." But on Wall Street the feeling was that this was the limit. To up the rate further would be to invite "disintermediation," when holders of term deposits withdrew their funds from savings institutions so as to invest in high-yielding government debt instruments and similar private paper. If this happened, the housing industry and others dependent upon credit would be shattered. "We are not going to bring on a money panic," said one Federal Reserve official, hoping to reassure Wall Streeters who thought they saw one coming. But the prime rate went to 6 percent, and some disintermediation began. Still, in late 1967 the Street felt that Martin had emptied his bag of tricks. All he could do now was talk. The Fed had gone as far as it could go, and if the financial district understood this, so did Lyndon Johnson.

From the Treasury came news of continued gold sales. The pound sterling was devalued and the dollar weaker than at any time since the end of World War II. Yet the market rallied from a November low of 850 to end the year a fraction above 905, for a gain in 1967 of close to 120 points on the Dow. This occurred in the face of declining corporate profits and dividends and increasing inflation. The only bullish news in December was a report that Congress would reconsider the tax measure early the following year.

The war in Vietnam continued.

Eleven

TIME, GENTLEMEN

THE YEAR OPENED with the usual spate of peace rumors, which quickly were dispelled. Still, there was a lull in the fighting, as though both sides were exhausted and weary of conflict. Perhaps it might be transformed into a *de facto* ceasefire, thought the *New York Times*. Peace in Vietnam might come by unspoken, mutual consent, and not the formalities of a signed truce. In late January, however, American troops crossed over into Cambodia, a signal the war would be expanded. And a few days later the North Koreans seized the U.S.S. *Pueblo* in the Sea of Japan and placed its 83 man crew in captivity. The president's reaction was immediate; the following day he called up 15,000 reservists, sent two squadrons of fighter planes to South Korea, and ordered the carrier U.S.S. *Enterprise* to cruise off Wonsan. Now there was talk of a second war on the Asian mainland.

The fighting in South Vietnam remained at a low level in early 1968, as both sides prepared to celebrate their country's new year. Taking advantage of the situation, the Viet Cong slipped troops into Saigon and on the morning of January 31 initiated what came to be known as the Tet offensive. This daring assault failed in its objective of capturing the city, and the Viet Cong losses were heavy. But North Vietnam had won a major propaganda victory. Americans sat in front of their television sets and saw films of enemy attacks on their embassy and on the same news programs learned of a further erosion of the situation in Korea. The hopes for peace melted. General William Westmoreland, who headed U.S. forces, said the war would continue for months, perhaps years to come. He asked for 206,000 additional troops and more air squadrons.

That month the president imposed mandatory curbs on investments abroad and continued to press for a new tax bill. He presented Congress with a record $186 billion budget. Without a tax increase, he said, spending would far outrun income, resulting in a major deficit, greater inflation, much higher interest rates, and further difficulties with the balance of international payments. Influential House Ways and Means Committee Chairman Wilbur Mills agreed with the diagnosis but offered a somewhat different cure. Johnson might have a tax increase but would have to slash spending as well. In Mill's view, the Great Society programs were a major cause of the deficit, and these would have to be brought under better fiscal control. Johnson continued to call for higher taxes, but he could do nothing without the support of Mills and his followers. An impasse had been reached.

The Europeans and the Japanese welcomed Johnson's strong tax messages. For years they had seen a rising tide of dollars engulf their economies. Once the world's most prized currency, the American dollar had become a glut on the market, contributing not only to world-wide inflation but also threatening international trade and their own domestic economies.

Foreigners used some of their surplus dollars to buy American securities, especially shares in major corporations. This flight from the dollar into shares indicated that the purchasers had far more faith in the ability of Standard Oil of New Jersey and IBM to turn a profit than in the will of the government to slow down the monetary printing presses. But there was another reason for increased stock purchases. Several nations, France in particular, experienced political unrest, and the foreigners sought American stocks as a safe haven for their funds.

Gold was preferable to paper, however, and the rush to the metal increased in intensity that January. "They have the peasant mentality," said one European coin dealer who reported a brisk business. "They still want to bite the coins." Financial experts noted a sharp pickup in the gold trade, both legal and illegal. In Hong Kong, South Vietnamese officials and generals were hoarding gold as a hedge against a military defeat. There was talk of Americans buying gold overseas and keeping it there in safe deposit boxes, thus skirting the law that forbade them from owning the metal. In January the Treasury's gold reserve fell below $12 billion, just $1.3 billion above the reserve required to back the dollar. House Banking Committee Chairman Wright Patman announced his intention to hold hearings on a measure that would remove the gold cover for the dollar, thus permitting the paper to be cast adrift, perhaps without any restraints.

Acting swiftly to shore up confidence in the dollar, Federal Reserve Board Chairman Martin called in reporters and told them he would do all in his power to defend the dollar. This meant tighter money and higher interest rates and continued pressure for a tax increase. Attempting to dispel rumors, Martin went on to say that as far as he was concerned, the price of gold would remain at $35 an ounce. Could this continue, however, if the Treasury sales accelerated without Congress having acted on the gold cover? Speculators appeared convinced a major change was in the works, that the dollar could collapse or at the very least play a diminished role in world finance. "General confidence no longer exists," said one European banking official. "No one believes the gold price will remain fixed." And in the midst of all this, South Africa, the world's leading producer of the metal, slowed its sales, indicating that country's belief it would get a better price for the metal within a few months.

Yet, the American mergermania continued, and investors appeared blithely ignorant of the ominous portents.

In January 1968, within a period of three weeks, Charles Bluhdorn of Gulf + Western announced three major acquisitions. His conglomerate would absorb machinery manufacturers Universal American (which had sales in 1967 of $200 million) and E. W. Bliss (1967 sales of $160 million) as well as Consolidated Cigar Corporation (1967 sales: $175 million). G + W's 1967 sales had been $649 million; as a result of these and other acquisitions, the conglomerate would post revenues of $1.3 billion in 1968.

Meanwhile James Ling of LTV was readying an even more spectacular deal, the takeover of another conglomerate, Greatamerica, at a cost of over $500 million in new bonds. Then, without waiting to digest this, he made a tender offer for the common stock of Jones & Laughlin, one of the nation's major steel firms, and within a few months he had over 60 percent of the shares at a cost of another $500 million. In 1967 LTV had sales of $1.8 billion; the following year's sales would come in at $2.8 billion.

That this would be a year of frantic activity was signaled in January by Bluhdorn and Ling. In 1967 firms with assets of $8.2 billion had been acquired through tender offers and related devices.

The figure would go to $12.6 billion in 1968. Mergers accounted for an increasing share of business activity. By way of comparison, a decade earlier assets of acquired companies as a percentage of new investment in American business came to less than 9 percent. The figure for 1968 would come to over 44 percent.

The rise of the conglomerates and their technique of growth by acquisition rather than expansion was one of the striking aspects of American business development in the late 1960s. As recently as 1963 only one firm thus classified had been ranked among the nation's 100 largest industrial corporations, and that one, ITT, had a long prewar history. Five years later, the top 100 list contained nine conglomerates; in addition to ITT there were LTV, Litton, Textron, and Gulf + Western. Tenneco (gas pipelines, land, and shipbuilding), Signal Companies (oil and gas, trucks, and aerospace), AVCO (aviation, farm equipment, abrasives, motion pictures, savings and loan associations, broadcasting, and insurance among other things), and Ogden (scrap metal, shipbuilding, and food services) rounded out the conglomerate representation. In different ways all of them claimed conglomeratization brought many blessings; in addition to diversification and a more efficient use of managerial talents, it enabled different kinds of businesses to relate better with one another. Sperry Rand, which insisted it was not a conglomerate, though it produced such items as computers, electric shavers, farm equipment, and hydraulic systems, preferred to be called "synergistic," saying it was proving that two and two could equal five. In other words, the gathering of diverse enterprises under one corporate roof really enhanced growth, creating additional goods and services as well as jobs.

Whether or not those who said such things actually believed it cannot be determined. On Wall Street, however, the dashing conglomerateurs were watched carefully, and their stocks—and those of companies they wanted—were featured performers in the last stage of the bull market. Some of their moves truly were dazzling, and none more so than one by James Ling.

In October Ling created a package of securities consisting of paper received in the Greatamerica takeover. Each unit contained 0.6 of a share of National Car Rental, one share of National Car Rental class A stock, a share of Braniff Airways special A stock, and 0.33 of a share of Computer Technology, to which he added 1.1 LTV

warrants. Then he offered varying amounts of units for each share of
LTV common stock or any of the firm's several classes of bonds ten-
dered him. For example, owners of 100 shares of LTV might receive
in exchange 110 of the new units, and then keep or sell its compo-
nent parts. He would give 10 units for $1,000 face value of the com-
pany's 6.75 percent debentures, 9.5 units for a like amount of the
5.75 percent debentures, and so forth. Owners of LTV paper called
their brokers for advice and found the experts couldn't make head or
tail of the offer. In time, the analysts sorted it all out, and tenders
were made, but the entire episode was bizarre and might be said to
have marked the high water point of the paper economy.

Shortly thereafter the Justice Department indicated it soon
would initiate a study of conglomerate mergers, and in addition was
weighing several antitrust actions.

A decade later novelist and critic John Hersey would write,
"There had been no other year in our history with such multiple
seismic tremors as '68 was to bring." Each surprise was followed by
another in rapid-fire order. "No single one of its shocks was to turn
the country around, but the shocks were to keep coming, and coming." The Tet offensive and the seizure of the *Pueblo* were considered of enormous importance in January, but these were to be
eclipsed by what followed—President Johnson's decision not to seek
re-election, the assassinations of Martin Luther King and Robert
Kennedy, the riots at the Democratic National Convention in Chicago, and in Europe the Soviet invasion of Czechoslovakia, to which
was added a bitter presidential election and a growing feeling of national uncertainty and insecurity. Surveying the decade as a whole
two years later, *New York Times* columnist James Reston wrote that
the 1960s began as realism, slipped into surrealism along the way,
and ended as abstract expressionism.

What publisher Henry Luce had called "The American Century" ended sometime in the 1960s, and this became apparent to
many in 1968. Foreign policy difficulties and an endless war cast
doubt on the ability of the nation's leaders to lead, while domestic
problems in the areas of race and "life styles" threatened the social
fabric. Certain basic, shared truths that had gone unquestioned
since the end of World War II now came under attack, and one of
these was a belief that a variant of capitalism best served the nation.
To some critics the system represented much that was wrong with

society and the people. To antiwar activists, businessmen had fina-
gled to get America into the Vietnam War in order to obtain profits.
Ecology-minded reformers drew attention to the destruction of the
landscape by businesses. Ralph Nader and other critics condemned
capitalism for the creation of a shabby, sensate civilization. In the
jargon of the time, many were "turned off" by the profit motive.

Yet Wall Street remained comparatively insulated from much
of this. Doubtless most of the brokers, analysts, managers, and
bankers who worked in the financial district were troubled by the
way the war had been fought as well as a variety of domestic problems, and since 1968 was a presidential election year, the feelings
were intensified. Probably more than the usual number of them became social activists and worked for candidates. Occasionally there
would be demonstrations at Wall and Broad, and even clashes between pro- and anti-war demonstrators. Young people tended to be
antiwar, pro–civil rights, and involved with ecological concerns,
while older men often supported the war and thought social changes
were taking place too rapidly. Of course, not all young people were
even mildly rebellious—not on Wall Streeet at least—while some of
the older generation became so, and their actions were featured in
the daily press and on television.

There also was a division between culture and counterculture.
The most obvious sign of this could be seen around noon. One
group of Wall Streeters went to clubs, restaurants, or saloons for
lunch and a few drinks, while others ate rapidly and then walked to
Trinity Churchyard or the Battery to smoke a joint.

An increasing number of Wall Streeters gave up drinks and
smokes at noon, however. Instead they would rush out and grab a
hot dog and diet soda from a street vendor or order a sandwich to be
sent to their desks or post on the floor. Volume was high and trading
often feverish. In 1968, while much of the nation became engaged
in major political and social debates and violence in the streets appeared more intense than at any time in the century, Wall Streeters
worked overtime and weekends to keep up with the pace of trading.

Early in the year, as was its custom, *Barron's* gathered a panel
of analysts and money managers to discuss prospects for the next 12
months. Most of them were troubled about the decline of the pound
sterling; several thought that currency would be devalued again.
But little consideration was afforded the difficulties facing the dol-

lar. With the exception of Fred Carr, they were cautious, even a trifle bearish regarding the future. Carr was "wildly enthusiastic" about Kentucky Fried Chicken and also liked Volt Technology. Belmont Towbin, of C. E. Unterberg, Towbin, conceded that some of the emerging growth stocks had done well in the past. Somewhat sadly he noted, "Unfortunately sometimes they emerge too fast, and too far, and then you have to go looking for others." John Dreyfoos of Dreyfoos, Ellis & Kluger recommended the purchase of several gold stocks as a hedge. Archie MacAllaster, manager for the Pilgrim Fund, thought it was too early to start playing that kind of game. "At some point I presume we'll see a rise in the price of gold, but I don't expect it in the near future." MacAllaster thought the pound would remain weak and that the Canadian dollar would be devalued.

All were concerned about the war. Walter Gutman, an analyst at Gruntel & Co. known for his eccentric views, looked upon the conflict as the last in a long line of American wars of expansion, each of which benefited the nation. "This war is part of basic U.S. policy to become even more powerful in that part of the world, and it's something that no President or Congress could or would stop." All the others disagreed. Palmer Weber of Troster, Singer responded that "the real problem isn't gold or the balance of payments or any inherent weaknesses in the American economy. The real problem is a horrible, miserable war that's costing us $36 billion a year." To this, investment counselor Gilbert Haas added his view that "at some point between now and the end of 1968, I think we will see a worldwide collapse in credit as a period of liquidation that will affect all equities." Like Dreyfoos, he favored the golds as a safeguard against the disaster. But Haas didn't believe the impending disaster had been caused by Vietnam spending. Would an end to the war lead him to alter his view? "Only to the extent that it would precipitate the decline more rapidly than I anticipate it will come anyway," he responded.

As for the others, they either were cautiously optimistic or optimistically cautious. One was "firmly convinced" the war would end in 1968, and so recommended the sale of military-industrial stocks. Another looked for a boom in the new-issues market but little by way of action elsewhere. Sander Lanfield, a partner in the odd-lot house of Carlisle & Jacquelin, took a "positive approach." "It's pretty hard at this point, of course, to tell exactly which areas are likely to do best. But if we have a reasonably good economic picture, and if profits begin to show signs of improving, I have a hunch that somewhere along the line prudence will return to the marketplace."

The operational words were "if," "prudence," and "hunch." The arts of hedging remained strong on Wall Street. Somewhere along the line Landfield would find an end to the bull market and not a revival of bullishness.

The market declined early in the year, and after a brief recovery fell below 900 on January 11. Bad news from Asia and the European money capitals, a growing realization that the fight against inflation would mean lower profits and higher interest rates, and challenges to Johnson's leadership from within his own party, all proved bearish for investment. In mid-February, with the Dow under 840, William McChesney Martin said we "are in a wartime economy" and that the government policies were insufficient for the task of holding down prices. Martin denied that wage and price controls were needed, but the Street thought otherwise, and prices fell to new lows.

It was then that the various political, economic, financial, and emotional forces that would end the bull market started to come together. There was a veritable gold rush against the Treasury in late February and early March—on March 8 alone some $180 million of the metal was purchased by foreigners. Chairman Martin flew to Europe to warn his counterparts there that unless these purchases ended, an international monetary collapse would soon take place, one greater in scope than that of the early 1930s.

This had a momentary effect, but then the purchases started up again, and on March 14 they topped $400 million, and panic set in. That day the Bank of England decided to close its gold window "temporarily." In New York the gold stocks—American South African, Anglo-American, Dome, and others—soared while the Dow gave up 12 points to close at 831. Words of assurance from Washington and the major New York banks did nothing to lessen the fears. "The bankers' declaration has not impressed people," said London gold dealer A. F. Hodgson, referring to around-the-clock meetings in Switzerland between Martin and his colleagues. "They want deeds, not words. The feel of the market suggests that demand will continue heavy, with a growing number of small buyers coming in."

On March 16 the international and central bankers agreed on a "two-tier system." Insofar as transactions between central banks were concerned, the $35-an-ounce price would be retained, but all other gold would be permitted to float freely and seek its own level. Shortly thereafter the Federal Reserve Bank upped the discount rate to 5 percent, as though to support this move. A brief rally followed, enabling the Dow to end the month above 840.

What did this mean? The open market gold price quickly rose above $35, and now the world had a new measure of confidence in all currencies. Gold clearly would have a growing international role, in large part because its quantity remained relatively fixed, while many nations—most notably the United States—had printed huge amounts of paper money during the past decade. The premium above $35 an ounce would be interpreted on Wall Street as a measure of the dollar's strength, and as it rose beyond $40 in early April, gold bug James Dines told his subscribers, "The gold crisis has only begun. You're going to see $100 gold—before Christmas."

Other analysts, many of them academicians, were far more troubled about the implications of the two-tier system for international liquidity. The structure that had its origins at Bretton Woods after World War II was being dismantled, and they weren't certain what would take its place.

While this debate began, the old one regarding the tax increase was ending. It seemed Johnson would get his 10 percent surcharge after all, and on Wall Street this was regarded as bullish. Then, on March 31, Johnson switched attention from gold and taxes to more dramatic fare. First he told the nation there would be a halt to the bombing of North Vietnam and then, toward the close of his address, he said he would not be a candidate for office in 1968.

This set off the "whipsaw market" of April, a month in which each day seemed to bring a new shock. The market's response to the Johnson speech was to jump by 21 points, the biggest gain in 5 years. Leading analysts now said a major bull move had been signaled and that the Index could be well over 1,000 by summer's end.

Four days later, on April 4, Martin Luther King was assassinated, and riots erupted in cities throughout much of the nation. On Wall Street euphoria was displaced by fears of social revolution, and the rally was aborted. Then the North Vietnamese agreed to attend peace talks, and word of this reached the trading floor on April 8.

Now a new rally began. But the Fed raised the discount rate on April 18, this time to 5½ percent. The New York banks promptly went to a 6½ percent prime. Not since 1921 had loan money rates been so high. Perhaps hoping to frighten Congress into accepting the tax surcharge, Martin warned that the nation was in the "worst financial shape since 1931." The market dipped, recovered, and then steadied toward the end of the mouth, apparently having discounted Hanoi's rejection of all American suggestions as to sites for a peace conference.

Wall Street was shaken by the sudden turnabouts and uncertainties regarding the international situation and the dollar, but analysts had experienced similar situations during the past two decades. What differentiated this market from its predecessors was volume. The trading floors had been hectic places in late 1967, with 10-million-shares days the norm. The pace intensified in January, when the 11 million mark was bested in more than half the sessions. In the back offices of brokerages throughout the district, at the exchanges and clearing houses, clerks worked overtime and weekends to clear up the enormous amount of paper generated by all this activity. Trading was somewhat quieter in February and March, and so the situation eased. Then, in April, came the busiest month in N.Y.S.E. history. At no session was less than 12 million shares traded, and on April 10 the Exchange experienced its first 20-million-share day.

The hopes for peace, fears concerning the nation's balance of payments, speculation regarding the prices of gold and silver, and the machinations of conglomerates all played parts in the churning at the N.Y.S.E. A growing belief that the prices of goods and services would rise sharply in 1968 didn't deter the speculators and investors; in fact it spurred them on, since for a generation they had been led to believe that common stocks were good hedges against inflation.

The truly wild action, however, was at the Amex and the OTC market. The go-go funds continued to boost stocks in small, often esoteric companies traded there, as well as the new issues. Interest was turning from the established glamours and military-industrial issues to peace-related stocks, especially new ones, that might catch the eye of Alger, Mates, Carr, or another of that crew—but not Gerry Tsai; his operation was merged into CNA Financial, and so he left the ranks of the new breed. Alger's faith in Kentucky Fried Chicken had proved justified; by late April the stock was selling for close to 100 times 1967's earnings. Imitators followed, among them Honey Fried Chicken, Minnie Pearl Chicken System, and Chicken Delight. It was a time when many cartoon characters and celebrities were being considered as fronts for chicken stores. Joe Namath, whose football and off-the-field exploits had gained him much newspaper and television space, was dickering with the idea, as were the Gabor sisters (for Hungarian Fried Chicken).

At the Amex such speculative stocks as Trans-Lux, Milgo Electronics, Marshall Industries, and Cavitron doubled in less than three months, while OTC items like Baird Atomic, Lear Jet, and Kalvar performed even better. Led by the chicken franchisers, the new issue market boomed. Minnie Pearl was offered at 20, and within three days the stock went over 40. Boothe Computer, a minor factor in the fast-growing computer-leasing industry, came out at 18 and instantly went to 46. Four Seasons Nursing Centers of America did as well. During the late winter and early spring, dozens of computer-related and health firms sold their new issues to a public eager to take almost anything that came along. It was 1961 and 1966 all over again, as Advanced Computer went from 7½ to 22 in two months and in the same period American Medicorp rose from 20 to 44. Similar gains in so short a period were posted by Life Sciences, National Data, and Superior Surgical. One broker told a *Business Week* reporter, "There are a lot fewer issues so far [in comparison to 1961 and 1966], and the companies aren't as junky." But Aaron Netburn of the New York Hanseatic Corp., a leading OTC house, warned, "Psychology can turn overnight like a key in a lock. Click—the party's over."

Peace talks opened in Paris in early May but bogged down almost immediately. In London the price of gold rose to $42 an ounce. There were reports of turmoil in France and Czechoslovakia. Yet prices held steady in the face of this bearish news, and volume on the N.Y.S.E. established a new record that month, when close to a third of a billion shares changed hands. Analysts were puzzled by this unusual combination of high volume and firm prices; it wasn't supposed to happen that way, especially when the new-issues market was so profitable and the Amex and OTC market were jumping. "The outlook is very good from the technical point of view, but rot-ten from the fundamental point of view," said Alan Shaw of Harris, Upham. Something would have to give, one way or the other. Without better economic and military news, prices surely would fall. "The technicians can hold up the market just so long," he thought.

N.Y.S.E President Haack was more concerned about volume. He was no stranger to the markets, having previously served as president of the National Association of Securities dealers. "Bob Haack is ideal for this kind of environment," said one member on learning of his selection. "He grew up in this business, and he knows it inside out. For the problems we've got now, there couldn't be a better man." Still, he was unprepared for the avalanche of trading, and moved in to curb it. In March he asked member firms with back office problems to "take steps to limit the growth of business or to reduce business," warning that unless this was done, "restraints may be imposed by the Exchange." Little was accomplished, however; brokers who for a generation had scratched around for new business and understood how to translate it into quick commissions hardly could be expected to cut back voluntarily. Besides, in this period most of them entertained visions of becoming a wheeler-dealer, with a suite of offices, a couple of secretaries, short vacations in Switzerland or the Bahamas, and all that went with that role. Small mutual funds were becoming major forces in the industry in a matter of months after having been founded. Young brokers with good records had lines of potential clients waiting patiently for audiences. Companies with hot prospects but little in the way of sales were being taken public and their stocks doubled and tripled. In America and overseas, change was in the air, and if some of it seemed dangerous, it was also exciting.

There was a stampede on Wall Street caused by new investors; in mid-1968 the N.Y.S.E. said there were 25 million shareholders, 15 percent more than in 1966. Each appeared to be looking for heat—a hot broker with a hot stock in a hot industry. Tantalized by stories of fortunes made in buying shares in companies involved with chickens and computers, they went to savings and loans, film-makers, mobile home manufacturers, and vendors of rock and roll items. "There's something for everybody at a banquet," said one fund manager. These people weren't going to follow Haack's advice and suddenly become "prudent."

In early June, with the somewhat reluctant support of the exchange community, Haack announced that the N.Y.S.E. would close down on Wednesdays so as to catch up with paperwork. The Amex and OTC markets did the same, along with the regional exchanges. Simultaneously the Federal Reserve Board hiked the margin requirement on listed shares from 70 percent to 80 percent, and the Senate Banking Committee reported out a bill that would give the Fed power to set margin requirements on over-the-counter stocks.

While grumbling to reporters about such interference, several firms with back office messes asked stronger ones for help. Unless this was done, they warned, a collapse of sorts might occur, which would be translated into panic. Already the number of "fails" (a term used to refer to a firm's inability to deliver certificates or complete transactions within the required time) was half again as much as at the same period in 1967. Billions of dollars in certificates could not be accounted for; there was talk of all sorts of conspiracies, from infiltration by Cubans to a Mafia plot to steal the district blind. None of this was ever proven true, but the small firm of Pickard & Co. had closed down, reportedly due to an inability to keep up with the volume of trading. No investor had lost a cent as a result of this, because the Exchange's Special Trust Fund had covered all shortages. But the fund hadn't the resources to do the same if several companies shut down, or if a major brokerage came up short. Thus, the Wednesday closings were part of a major rescue operation, which took shape as trading intensified and additional speculators rushed to get aboard and make quick killings.

Stocks at the Amex and the OTC market gyrated with little reference to what was happening in the nation and world; it was one of those periods when speculation truly does resemble action at gambling casinos, when external events are of lesser importance than hunches and tips. While activity at the N.Y.S.E. was more reflective of economic, military, and political events, there too the gaming instinct was taking hold. Stocks traded in a narrow range in May, June, and July, 20 points either side of Dow 910. The assassination of Robert Kennedy on June 5 had little effect on prices; nor did the advent of the 4-day week, news that the East Germans were cracking down on travel into Berlin, or U.N. Secretary General U Thant's warning that the Paris peace talks "will be deadlocked for a long time."

On June 28 President Johnson finally signed into law a new tax measure that not only boosted income and corporate rates by 10 percent but also provided for a $6 billion cutback in federal spending. After close to a year of debate and delay, the nation had a major anti-inflation program. There was no significant reaction on Wall Street, however. Even supporters of the measure conceded it had come too late to do much good that year. In 1968 the Consumer Price Index would rise by 4.7 percent, the steepest advance since 1951.

The big N.Y.S.E. stocks responded to all of this by see-sawing in what traders called "backing and filling." They did not react significantly to the news of rioting at the Democratic National Convention, to the nominations of Hubert Humphrey or the G.O.P.'s selection of Richard Nixon. But at the Amex and OTC market, aquaculture was the rage, with International Proteins, Wakefield Sea Foods, and Pan-Alaska Fisheries doubling. There was a vogue for geophysics (Chesapeake Instruments, EDO, and Seismic Computing) and desalination (Ionics and Aqua-Chem). Czechoslovakia was invaded by Soviet forces; speculators took little note of this. Now the off-shore drilling stocks had their turn. Zapata, Reading & Bates, and Offshore each rose by handfuls of points. "The ocean stocks right now are exceedingly speculative," warned Fuhrman Nattles of Kohlmeyer & Co. "This reminds me of the 1961 period and the electronics boom." O. Quintin Di Maria, publisher of the *Oceanographic Newsletter*, took a different point of view. "So what if ocean stocks carry high price/earnings multiples? So did IBM and Xerox when they started out. This is the biggest thing to hit the world." The mutual fund industry responded with the creation of Ocean Technology Fund and the Oceanographic Fund, both of which had favorable receptions. At a time when Southeast Asia was at war, parts of Europe faced rebellion, and many felt the United States was coming apart, speculators turned their attention to investment opportunities on the high seas and beneath them.

By late summer most economists were predicting a business slowdown. The impact of the new tax measure, high interest rates, and the Fed's tight money policy would result in a leveling off of the economy later in the year. At the time it appeared Nixon would win the presidency in November, and analysts believed he would accept a recession in order to control inflation. If this were so, stock prices should have fallen.

Still, there also were indications that the news might improve. For one thing, the world's bankers were erecting a system under which international accounts could be settled through the use of new "special drawing rights," which promptly were given the name of "paper gold." Both Nixon and Humphrey promised to end the war if elected, and the pledges were credible considering the country's mood, the opening of peace talks, and the military situation in Vietnam. By the summer of 1968, no single piece of news would have been more bullish than an end to the war. Finally, there were signs that interest rates had peaked, that Martin and his colleagues were pleased with the new tax measure and so were prepared to lower the discount rate.

The Dow rose from the low 880s in late July to just below 900 on August 30; the market was prepared to move up on good news and a change in psychology. That day the Fed lowered the discount rate to 5¼ percent, and while the leading New York banks held to their 6½ percent prime, it appeared likely that this too would be cut. Then the August figures for department store and automobile sales were released, and these showed that consumer confidence was high in spite of the events of the past summer. The balance of payments situation was improving, and on September 6 the First Pennsylvania Banking & Trust Co. cut its prime to 6¼ percent, thus putting pressure on the New York banks to follow suit.

Meanwhile Wall Street was solving its paperwork difficulties. The Wednesday closings helped, but in addition volume fell from its spring peak. The total fails for August came to little more than $3 billion, against $3.7 billion in July. More important, the "aged fails"—those more than 30 days old—declined from $837 million to $724 million in the same period. Then too there were persistent rumors that Johnson would pull some American troops out of Vietnam prior to Election Day, even though the peace talks were stalemated, so as to help the sagging Humphrey candidacy. Once the momentum toward withdrawal started, so the argument went, it would be difficult for any new president to halt.

The Dow crossed over the 900 level on September 3 and then rose steadily on heavy volume. On September 25 some New York banks went to a 6¼ percent prime, while others cut the rate even more, to 6 percent. Now stocks took off on extremely heavy volume, and by early October the Dow was above 950. Once again paperwork accumulated in back offices and the fails mounted. To further complicate matters, candidate Nixon told an industry group that if elected he would relax market regulation. Why he said this at such a time wasn't clear, since Nixon already could count on the votes of those who might welcome such a statement, and given the paperwork crisis, it seemed rather reckless. But his comments were interpreted as being bullish and so helped boost prices and expand trading.

This advance troubled analysts, in that it didn't seem warranted or substantial. For one thing, the market lacked strong leadership, and for another, trading appeared random, with no group in the vanguard. There was little glamour in the market, or joy either for that matter. Rather, the in-and-out trading had taken on a grim quality. Also, the business news was mixed. The third-quarter corporate earnings were high, but most analysts thought they would turn down in the fourth quarter or in early 1968. *Business Week* said there was a "mysterious quality" about the rally. "Faced with customers' queries about why the market has been soaring, a surprising number of brokers this week were answering with rare candor, "I just don't know." "I know of no market that hasn't tumbled when profits were trending down," wrote S. Jay Levy, author of a popular Wall Street letter. Levy concluded that "something unusual may be going on."

Where was the economy headed? Would there truly be peace in Vietnam in 1968 or 1969? Would the dollar be more secure in the months ahead? But more specifically, what was happening to interest rates? This was the key question on Wall Street. The district understood that higher rates would mean a declining market. The refusal of many banks to go along with the 6 percent prime was troublesome, as were persistent rumors the Federal Reserve was having second thoughts about easing up further on the discount rate. By then it had become evident that the 1968 budget deficit would be enormous, and some analysts said the red ink would continue into 1969, especially if the anticipated recession was deep and long-lasting. What might be done by way of fiscal and monetary policy in such an eventuality could not be determined, especially when an untried new president occupied the White House.

Stocks continued to advance in the face of all of this, while trading volume expanded beyond what most veterans had thought would be the breaking point. Speculators clearly were taking little heed of the monetary and economic warning signs, while investors were betting the Treasury and the Federal Reserve would take all necessary steps to prevent or at least mitigate the effects of a recession. FundScope, which monitored the mutuals, ranked Mates at the top of its list of best performing funds, which was dominated by the go-gos. The SEC noted that some 300 companies had registered stock for public offerings over the next few months, and the new-issues market was rolling along.

The bulls were gambling the indicators soon would turn around and that interest rates would do the same. Failing that, they anticipated a short, rather shallow recession, after which the market would pick up again.

What if the economy went into a decline comparable in scope to that of 1960–61? The bulls thought the current level of stock prices had discounted that possibility. The Dow Industrials was selling at 16 times anticipated 1968 earnings; in contrast, the Index had carried a P/E ratio of 19 as recently as 1964. At the very worst the new-issues market would dry up, and secondary and tertiary stocks on the Amex and OTC market would suffer sharp selloffs. But the leading blue chips—issues such as General Motors, IBM, General Electric, and Texaco—hadn't participated in this phase of the bull market or at the most had shown only minor gains. Surely they would not suffer unduly from any correction that might occur. In any event, the government hardly would permit a major recession, no matter who was elected, and it possessed the tools to make certain that any decline would be minor.

In late October it appeared the bulls had won their wager. The National Bureau of Economic Research reported many key indicators were pointing upward. The Fed acted to increase the money supply, which the Street interpreted as meaning it soon would mount an effort to hold down interest rates and permit the economy to expand, even at the cost of additional inflation. The Commerce Department not only refuted claims there would be a budget deficit in 1969 but suggested a surplus might develop as a result of the new tax bill.

For the moment, however, the financial community was more concerned with the presidential election. No matter who won, said the bulls, the nation would get out of Vietnam in 1969. According to them, the new president would blame the war on Johnson, claim a victory, and then stage as orderly a withdrawal as possible. Eisenhower had done it in 1953, they said, and Nixon or Humphrey would imitate him in 1969. Peace would bring a higher market; there had been major bull moves after every war in this century, despite declines in business and earnings.

For their part the bears noted that new presidents often demonstrated a tendency to take unpleasant corrective measures as soon as they came to office, so as to clear the way for improvements when they ran for re-election. As Ralph Rotnem of Harris, Upham observed, "Corrections—that is, market declines—during the first two years of a Presidential term have averaged 80 percent greater than declines in the last two years." Besides, Nixon had promised an all-out campaign against inflation, and that would mean lower corporate earnings, more unemployment, and perhaps a major recession. But Rotnem, turning around in his analysis, observed that investors might interpret strong anti-inflation programs as being bullish, and indeed such seemed the case in October, when analysts were predicting a GOP victory and stocks moved higher in what was called the Nixon market. "If we knew exactly what earnings would be a year in advance and assumed the market would go in the same direction," wrote Rotnem, "we would be wrong 42 percent of the time."

The market closed at 952 on October 31. That evening the president announced a bombing halt in Vietnam. The following day Shearson Hamill ran a half-page advertisement in the *Wall Street Journal* in which the brokerage stated, "For the stock market peace is strongly bullish—except for a tiny group of armament issues which have already suffered severely in price." The company went on to say that the arrival of peace would bring boom times to companies in the consumer goods and housing fields in particular. "To the extent that any stabilization in interest rates occurs, peace should be favorable to utilities of all types." Most analysts agreed. "Vietnam peace prospects are expected to remain the overriding determinant of market trends over the next few weeks," wrote Woodward Norton in the *Journal*. John Westergaard of Equity Research Associates said, "The key question is what will happen in Vietnam. Everything ties to it—inflation, taxes, spending. Nixon's talk of lowering taxes next year doesn't mean a damn thing unless the war ends."

Johnson's move did not set off a rally. Instead stocks drifted downward, and the Dow was at 946 on November 4, on a volume of less than 11 million shares, considered slow trading given the pace set during the past few months.

Nixon was elected the following day. On Wednesday, November 6, the market opened mixed but then moved upward, going above 954 by noon. A correction followed, but the Dow managed to end the day a fraction below 950. John Smith of Fahnestock & Co. said, "Nixon's victory had been pretty much discounted by the market in its rise earlier this fall," and Walter Mintz of the still optimistic Shearson Hamill observed that the Democrats still controlled Congress, which should be counted as a bullish factor. In the opinion of Monte Gordon of Bache, it was "sort of a post-election letdown," and most others let it go at that. The general view was that prices soon would pick up and the Dow was in good position for a rally to beyond the 1,000 mark sometime prior to Nixon's inauguration.

The rally began on November 8, when the Index jumped ahead more than 8 points and brokers hailed the return of the Nixon market. The impetus came from an unexpected source. In Europe there were rumors the franc soon would be devalued, and this sent a scare through money markets that reverberated in New York, as foreigners rushed in to purchase American blue chips. Both *Business Week* and the *New York Times* credited demand from overseas for the rise, the former adding that confidence in Nixon had something to do with it, too, while the *Times* observed the rally took place in spite of growing belief that the peace negotiations were going badly. Volume was high, and brokers and their clients were optimistic.

Despite the Wednesday closings, however, the paperwork crunch continued. The *Times* suggested the district close between Christmas and New Year's to clear up the mess. At the N.Y.S.E. Robert Haack thought it an idea worth considering, but the brokerages would have nothing to do with it. The personnel there were planning lavish holiday parties. Bonuses would be excellent that year, the result of record earnings.

That November the paper gold system appeared workable; perhaps the dollar would strengthen after all. The budget deficit clearly would establish a peacetime record (when the final figures were in, it came to $25.2 billion), but increasingly it appeared the administration's prediction of a surplus for 1969 made sense. With the com-

ing of a new administration, there was increased hope the war
would end. During the campaign, Nixon had said he had a secret
plan to do just that. Perhaps it would be revealed in January, and if
it worked, the market surely would explode. The consensus was that
peace could add over 200 points to the Dow.

Alan Corey III, a 25-year-old securities firm trainee, must have
thought so, and perhaps he also liked to tempt fate. On October 29,
the anniversary of the Great Crash of '29, he purchased a N.Y.S.E.
seat for half a million dollars, a price that matched the high established that year.

The market advanced in November, and volume was high;
Corey's investment seemed sound. Most groups participated, but
the leadership was poor. Attention was focused on such stocks as
Lionel, LTV, Glen Alden, and other speculative issues. Things
were hopping at the Amex, where Solitron, Kalvex, and a score of
speculative oil companies were doing well. The OTC market was
hot, as Graphic Sciences, Redcor, and Strategic Systems all rose by
more than 30 percent in a week.

Veteran analysts were troubled about the highly speculative
nature of the markets. Kenneth Safian of Smilen & Safian was telling
his clients to get out of thinly capitalized stocks and go to cash.
Stanley Nabi of Schweickart & Co. didn't like the look of the new issues. "There are a lot of fringe underwriters in now—ones I've
never heard of. And in the last few weeks the quality of the issues
themselves has deteriorated badly." "My thinking has changed in
the last week," said Walter Stern of Burnham & Co. "There seems
to be a weakening of the technical underpinning of the market," and
late in the month he predicted a recession and a decline of from 10
to 15 percent in the Dow, to which Nabi added, "This is getting to
look more and more like 1961."

It was a curious time. Many Americans were reading *The
Money Game* by "Adam Smith," the pen name for George Goodman
of the *Institutional Investor*, a book that both illuminated the way
the Street functioned and mocked the public's methods of investing.
"The real object of the Game . . . is the playing of the Game itself,"
wrote Goodman. "For the true players, you could take all the tro-
phies away and substitute plastic beads or whale's teeth; as long as
there is a way to keep score, they will play."

There was much to this, and, in the department stores, games based on the stock market were among the favorite adult gifts. "Transaction," "Broker," "Stocks & Bonds," "The Stock Market," and "Buy or Sell" were going well, according to *Business Week*. Evelyn Miller, a 67-year-old businesswoman from Cedar Rapids, Iowa, who said her investments had turned out quite well, was able to place her brainchild, "Walstrete," with Feature Games. "It's terrific," she said. "It's based on spinning a dial that changes stock prices. It's as close as you can come to playing the real market."

Twelve

NOT A BANG OR
A WHIMPER

THE FUNNY-MONEY GAME on Wall Street was being played
with its accustomed blend of deadly seriousness and fantasy in
late November 1968. New issues with little in the way of
assets but much in hope were being marketed at a hectic pace;
American Computer Leasing, Hillhaven, Convenient Industries of
America, and Data Architects were oversubscribed and immediately went to premium prices. Gulf + Western (1968 sales: $1.3
billion) was making a tender offer for the common stock of Sinclair
Oil (1968 sales: $1.5 billion), and the directors of that company were
fighting back. In a full-page advertisement in the *Times* and the
Journal, they asked, "Would you willingly exchange your stock in
Sinclair and turn its management over to a company that is not in
the oil business and could end up with $4 billion in debt?" Ap-
parently many of Sinclair's stockholders would; Charles Bluhdorn
told reporters he had "every reason to be confident of success."

The tender offer startled some old-timers. After all, G + W still
was considered an upstart, and here it was, trying to capture an old,
established firm even larger than itself. But why not? At the same
time, General Host (1968 sales: $201 million) was wooing Armour &
Co. (1968 sales: $2.4 billion), and a freshly minted conglomerate,
Data Processing Financial & General (1968 sales: $17.4 million),
was exploring the possibilities of obtaining a major interest in the
Great Atlantic & Pacific Tea Co., the nation's second largest super-
market chain (1968 sales: $5.4 billion).

Mergermania was at its peak. Continental Can not only won
out over North American Rockwell and Walter Kidde in its bid to

take over printing press manufacturer Miehle-Goss-Dexter, but also was eyeing Nekoosa Edwards Paper and on its way to becoming a conglomerate. As for Kidde, that firm already had turned its attention to U.S. Lines, the nation's biggest ocean shipping operation.

And so it went. Susquehanna tried to absorb Pan American Sulphur, against the wishes of management at that firm. Bangor Punta wanted Harley Davidson. Northwest Industries was making a play for the Chicago, Milwaukee, St. Paul, and Pacific Railroad. Eltra purchased the spark plug business of General Battery. Leasco Data was completing its acquisition of Werner Associates. Teledyne announced a drive to capture Ryan Aeronautical. At Investors Diversified Services, a financial-mutual fund operation, President Stuart Silloway said his firm was "aggressively" seeking merger candidates. "We feel we ought to add other strings to our bow." L'Aiglon, a small manufacturer of women's wear, reported lower earnings, but the company said it had plans to purchase companies in related and nonrelated fields. Its stock rose. ITT was putting the finishing touches on its takeover of Grinnell, and Harold Geneen already had turned his attention to the two or three dozen other large, medium-sized, and small operations he was considering gobbling up over the next year.

Houdaille Industries (1968 sales: $203 million) ran an ad proclaiming its intention to rise to the top of the conglomerate heap, and in it managed to use most of the trigger words in what came out as a paean to the mania:

> Bavooom
> Blast rock loose
> Construction boom
> Profit for Houdaille
> Big in construction
> Construction materials
> Big in machine tools
> Very sophisticated
> Computer controlled
> Big in industrial products
> Many kinds
> Very diversified
> Big in automobile products

Shiny bumpers
Big in processing industries
Reliable pumps
That's Who-dye
The multi-company company
Nineteen companies in all
1968 sales up again
Forecast over $200 million
Bavooom
Another sound of Houdaille
Bavooom
Another sound of growth

Prior to 1955, Houdaille had been a minor factor in the automobile supply industry, its major product being bumpers and bumper guards. For the past 7 years its common stock generally sold for below 10 times earnings and traded within a narrow range. Then the takeover campaign began, with the company issuing new stock and bonds to exchange for the assets, sales, and earnings of acquired entities. Houdaille now emerged as a glamour company, and the valuation afforded its stock demonstrated this. From 1963 to 1968, sales, earnings per share, and dividends doubled for Houdaille, but the price of the common stock rose fivefold.

In November ITT, G + W, LTV, and other conglomerates were preparing to print additional shares and offer new bonds so as to absorb more firms. Much depended upon the maintenance of high stock prices and low interest rates on bonds. These were the kinds of things that enabled Houdaille and the others to go bavooom.

It also helped pump up volume at the N.Y.S.E, Amex, and OTC market, and this swelled brokerages' earnings and attracted new people to the industry. In late November a N.Y.S.E. seat changed hands at $515,000, while one at the Amex went for $315,000. Each was a new record.

The mutual fund industry also was going bavooom. New funds were starting up at the rate of one a week in 1968, and most of them—such as Neuwirth, Doll, Franklyn Dyna-Tech, and Gibraltar—were "performance oriented." According to statistics released in early November, at the end of the third quarter the funds were managing more than $51 billion in assets, for a gain of over $8 billion in half a year. Sales were down slightly, but so were redemptions. Most of the new money seemed to be going to those funds that turned in outstanding records thus far in the year. Neuwirth, Gibraltar, and Mates led the list, each with advances of more than 80 percent. Franklyn Dyna-Tech and Doll were among the top 25.

These were some salient and obvious aspects of the investment picture in late November. The conglomerates were active, the mutual fund scene was intense, and trading volume was high. In Paris, President de Gaulle was resisting suggestions he accept a devaluation of the franc, and this was upsetting the European money markets. The outflow of funds to Wall Street continued, and in New York analysts wondered how far foreign buying would push the Dow. As had been the case in early 1966, the 1,000 mark seemed within easy grasp.

In Paris too, the Vietnam peace talks continued, but no one expected much to happen until Nixon took office. From Washington came word that the president-elect had chosen Henry Kissinger to be his chief adviser for national security affairs, and the Harvard professor was expected to have something to do with the negotiations in Paris. As for Vietnam itself, there was a lull in the fighting resulting from the traditional Christmas ceasefire.

The Dow closed at 985 on Friday, November 29, up 9 points on the day and 18 for the week. Volume remained strong, and there was little sign of selling pressures. Despite a weakening economy, higher interest rates, fears of inflation and recession, and the ongoing Vietnam War, the big stocks that comprised the Index remained strong, as did the conglomerates, their takeover candidates, and the new issues.

Where was all this buying coming from? John Schulz, a partner in the small firm of Wolfe & Co., thought he had the answer. In the first 8 months of the year foreigners had accumulated some $1.3 billion worth of American stocks on balance, and since most of the money went into the blue chips, the increased demand caused prices to rise.

Andreas Woudhuysen, partner in charge of foreign business at Burham & Co., agreed, and predicted the purchases would continue. "The greater the uncertainty in Western Europe, the greater the eagerness of investors there to put their money into the U.S.

market." What might happen if for one reason or another the foreigners stopped their buying? Woudhuysen didn't say, but the clear implication was that the market would decline, perhaps badly.

There were 199 new highs on November 29 against only 3 new lows, but Newton Zinder of E. F. Hutton was uneasy about the tone of the advance. "From a technical point of view the market continues to be in overbought territory, suggesting that a period of some consolidation may not be far away." Zinder did not anticipate there would be a serious decline, however; the correction "should be followed by further upside progress," with the Dow ending the year on a strong note.

In late November the Federal Reserve tightened up on the money supply, a signal that the discount rate might be boosted back to the 5½ percent level, after which the prime rate would follow. This was the conventional pattern: first the Fed would act, and then the major New York banks would react. But on Monday, December 2, the major banks took the lead away from the Fed. Led by the Chase Manhattan, they boosted the prime to 6½ percent. News of this unexpected move reached Wall Street in the morning, at which time the bond sector was strong and the Dow over 994, up by more than 9 points from Friday's close. Now bonds sold off; several new underwritings could not be marketed, while others were postponed.

At the N.Y.S.E. the Dow plunged 20 points in two hours and then recovered somewhat in the afternoon to close at 983, down by less than 2 points on the day. This was unusual behavior, even for that period, but there were no signs of panic, or even that investors were seriously troubled. IBM fell 4¾ points, Burroughs 3½, and Honeywell 3⅛; other high-multiple glamours followed them down. The gainers and losers that day were equally balanced, however, and there were 177 new highs. It did not seem to be a major top.

Stocks opened lower on Tuesday, and by late morning the Dow had given up close to 10 points. There followed an afternoon rally of some power but on diminished volume, as the Index added more than 17 points in two hours, peaking at 991 before falling back to close the session at 985, up by almost 2 points over the previous day's close. Brokers said this was typical of consolidation phases. "We don't think the stock market's upward momentum has been stopped," one of them told the *Journal*'s Charles Elia, "but investors are finding it sobering to see there is something of a counterbalance in the money markets to the inflationary spiral." Technicians are troubled by continued weakness in the utilities. This Index had topped out in mid-November and now was clearly on a downward path, due in large part to higher interest rates. If this continued, they warned, the Rails and Industrials surely would follow.

The markets were closed on Wednesday, as supervisors, clerks, and some executives labored to clear up the paperwork, while in the front offices and board rooms, analysts continued to ponder the meaning of the rise in the prime rate. The general feeling was that interest rates would continue to climb, that the Fed would increase the discount rate, and that the nation was in for a bout of tight money, which many believed a necessary antidote for inflation. If this were so, stocks were bound to decline. The foreigners would withdraw funds once the French crisis ended, while Americans would put their's into bonds and high-yielding commercial paper. There was agreement that much depended upon signals thrown out by the Nixon camp. The incoming president was believed a fiscal conservative; he probably would support a tight money policy in 1969. But he also had promised to end the Vietnam War, and if he carried through on this, the market surely would rise.

The analysts didn't know what to expect on Thursday, but instincts and training pointed the way to a down market over the near term. Most of them said as much.

Prices opened lower and after a brief rally fell sharply. Over 19.3 million shares were traded that day, making this the busiest session in a month and a half. The Dow gave up more than 7 points, its sharpest setback in more than 4 months. But there was a correction the following day, after which prices settled down, trading in a narrow range for the next week. No one spoke seriously of Dow 1,000; in mid-December the Street would have been happy to settle for stability until Nixon took over in Washington.

On December 18 the Fed, as expected, raised the discount rate to 5½ percent. Bankers responded by predicting a "credit crunch" was on the way, and they upped the prime to 6¾ percent as though to help fulfill the prophecy. "Everywhere on Wall Street, there was a new mood of wariness," wrote *Business Week*, while the *Times* editorialized on the need for "prudence" and the *Journal* wrote about "indecision."

Months later, everyone understood that the market had posted a major top in early December and that the decline had begun. In fact the great bull market that had originated in the midst of economic and social despair in 1949 finally had come to its conclusion—in a period of new malaise. Adjusting for inflation—a necessary exercise given the experience of the next decade—the Dow never has topped the interday high of 991 posted on December 3, 1968.

Those investors and speculators who failed to get out of the market later in the month or in early January 1969 hardly could claim they hadn't been warned of what might happen. The district's analysts had racked up spotty records over the past two decades, but in December they were almost uniformly bearish. "Scratch a portfolio manager these days and you'll find a fellow who's running scared," wrote Alan Abelson in *Barron's,* who went on to note that investors were "sitting up and taking nervous notice." Ralph Creasman of Lionel D. Edie told his readers, "We're cautious, particularly near term," and he added that should the European currencies stabilize while the Fed tightened the monetary screws, there could be a flight from the American markets. "If you let yourself go, you can build up quite a worry list." Monte Gordon of Bache stated the obvious: "If money gets tight, conglomerates can't get money to make a merger; housing growth slows down; investors can't borrow to buy securities." He expected all of this to happen in 1969. "I've been a roaring bull for a long time—to the point that I've begun to suspect my motives," wrote William Jiler of Standard & Poor's. "For the first time since 1961, my crowd behavior indicators are close to bearish. They're not there yet, but they're close." Kenneth Safian was nervous, too. "I've never been a long term bear. But now. . . ." Joseph Granville, editor of his own colorful market letter, stated his opinion blunty: "The year 1969 may replace 1929 as the grand example of historic economic collapse."

Certainly there were no signs of a similar collapse in early December. In an odd footnote to that period, a small promotional firm, "Day of the Bear, Inc." advertised "the perfect Christmas gift" for anyone interested in stocks. For $25 it would send purchasers a mounted tape of the N.Y.S.E. ticker for October 29, 1929—"Black Tuesday." "See the opening minutes of the crash that happened 40 years ago, a real conversation piece!"

Whether or not the company did well with its product is unknown. In retrospect, however, Black Tuesday had become the symbol for the crash that followed. Market historians may differ as to when the decline actually began, but that symbol has remained intact for a half century, along with images of brokers and clients jumping from windows, banks closing, and panic rampant on Wall Street.

There would be no similar symbol for the end of the bull market in 1968. No mounted tapes of transactions on December 3 or 4. No images of disaster. Some of the proposed conglomerate mergers fell through, many young companies never did float their stock, and most of the go-go funds either closed down during the next few years or were merged out of existence. The young lions of the late 1960s didn't jump from windows or put bullets through their temples. Instead they got jobs for other organizations or left the district to work elsewhere. Still, there can be little doubt that the longest and in many respects most powerful upward surge in the history of Wall Street ended sometime during the post-election season and before New Year's Day.

It came to an end not with a bang or a whimper or the long anticipated "another 1929." The market caved in amid feelings of numbness, uncertainty, and despair.

Bull markets often begin in much the same ways they end. At their start can be seen higher volume and small price advances. These are interpreted as rallies in a bear market, or simply a minor burst of trading fever after which stocks will settle back in their old grooves. So they do, but then there is another advance, slightly more hectic in feeling and broader in scope. The momentum intensifies, additional people enter the market, and speculation begins in earnest. Years later, after the market has demonstrated its stamina, one might be justified in claiming that the bull move had its origins in that first, faint stirring.

The same is true at the climax. Even in 1929, after one of the most dramatic selloffs in market history, most analysts found it difficult to believe that they were in the initial stage of a major bear market. In January 1930, the *New York Times* singled out as the most important news story of 1929 the Antarctic expedition of Admiral Richard Byrd; business leaders voiced confidence in the future; respected stock market analyst Roger Babson—who had warned against speculative excesses prior to the crash—thought the decline had run its course and that the market was due for a rally. Alexander

Dana Noyes, the most perceptive financial journalist of the period, wasn't at all certain as to the future course of market actions. "We do not yet know whether this present episode is or is not an old-time 'major crisis,' " he wrote more than two months after Black Tuesday. But two years later, Noyes, Babson, and the *Times* all understood that the Great Crash had brought the bull market of the 1920s to its knees.

While many on the Street predicted lower prices for 1969, no one of any importance there thought the bull market of the 1950s and 1960s was over. Customers' men with only a few years of experience were earning over $100,000 a year, wearing $300 suits, and taking weekend jaunts to Bermuda and Gstaad. They dined at the best Manhattan restaurants and knew the beautiful people. Not since the late 1920s had such people been so well paid, and the brokers and analysts of early 1969 enjoyed a higher status than had their counterparts 40 years earlier. The market declined in January and February, but this was not taken too seriously. There would be another rally. There always had been. And one did develop in March and April, as expected. But then the market fell once again. Still, most on the Street thought the long-term outlook was bullish.

Fred Mates suffered a blow in this period; he finally put some bad letter stock in his portfolio—a conglomerate called Omega Equities—and was investigated by the SEC. Mates Fund was hit by a flood of redemptions and was unable to make payouts for half a year. But there always was another bright young man to take the place of fallen stars. In early 1969 the spotlight fell on Cortes Randell, the founder of a conglomerate called National Student Marketing, which became a hot stock in late 1968 and catapulted onto the financial pages early in 1969, when it went from 82 to 120 in three months. Bernard Cornfeld went public with another mutual fund, this one called Great American Management and Research, or Gramco, and selected for its management team a handful for former Kennedy Administration officials, including Pierre Salinger, Kennedy's one-time press secretary and then senator from California. Gramco was an instant success and within a few months had over $100 million in investment money.

There still was glamour in investments, and there still were those who sought it out. But it was fading, speculators were becoming skittish, and the investors were troubled, though of course all this could not have been known at the time.

Today we know that a massive saw-toothed pattern would be traced by the Dow over the next decade. There had never been anything like it, and even now Wall Streeters haven't a name for this behavior (perhaps it could be termed the kangaroo market). There would be three major and one minor declines, during which the investment scene resembled that of the 1930s. These were interspersed with powerful and sustained bull moves, when part of the old euphoria returned. The switches were confusing and sudden and left analysts and brokers exhausted. Clients were whipsawed, and millions of them left the arena, most never to return.

At first it seemed the declines were caused by the usual factors—excess speculation, weak brokerages, shaky businesses, tight money, recession, political leaders who had lost public trust, and several other developments. All these were familiar to old-timers and students of the market. But above all was that ingrained fear of inflation. The Consumer Price Index rose by 6.1 percent in 1961, its worst showing since the early post–World War II period. Still, the new economists felt certain the rate could be cut by an administration and central bank willing to pay the price of deflation and recession. In other words, there could be a trade-off of steadier prices for unemployment. In 1969, American economists still felt they could regulate the economy in this fashion. So did Wall Streeters, and they were prepared for another recession, after which a recovery would be made and higher prices reached at the exchanges.

There was a recession in 1969–70, but as Walter Heller later wrote, "it failed to bag the inflationary cat." A new phenomenon had been discovered—"stagflation"—and it has bedeviled economists ever since. Attempts to deal with it generally were unsuccessful. Increasingly the American people lost confidence in their leaders. The Vietnam War and the Watergate scandal had much to do with this, but by the mid-1970s they had passed. Stagflation remained, the centerpiece of a myriad of economic problems that all the polls indicate are the chief concerns of the American people. Presidents Gerald Ford and Jimmy Carter managed to restore a measure of trust in the integrity of the presidency, but neither has been able to do the same for confidence in government to deal with inflation. At the same time, the status of economic forecasters and soothsayers fell to a level not seen since the early 1930s.

Some people came to view the 1970s as a replay of the 1930s; a half-century ago, the nation suffered through the Great Depression, which as late as 1938 seemed beyond the abilities of those in power to resolve. But in the 1930s Franklin Roosevelt had provided firm and credible leadership, while the Keynesians had solutions for economic ailments, even though they weren't taken too seriously by the New Dealers. There was no FDR on the scene in the 1970s, and no school of economists (outside of those who would readically alter the national fabric) to offer plausible and politically acceptable means of bringing stagflation to its conclusion.

These were some of the factors that troubled investors in the aftermath of the 1968 highs. Again, they were not evident at the time, but rather developed over several years. Disillusionment with investments grew slowly, as had been the case in the post-1929 period, and not even the sustained rallies in 1970–71, 1971–72, and 1975–76 could change this. In 1973 and 1976 the Dow topped the 1,000 mark, but there were few celebrations on the Street or people to claim that a new investment era had opened. Some analysts tried to adjust the Dow to take inflation into account. In 1979, when that Index was at 850, one statistician calculated that in terms of the 1959 dollar, it was below 500.

Just as depression had been a primary reason for the death of the 1920s bull market, so inflation brought an end to its counterpart in the 1950s and 1960s. The depression ended with the arrival of World War II, which led to huge budgetary deficits and put large amounts of money into circulation. Stock prices rose, but the depression psychology remained and had to be overcome before the great postwar bull market could truly begin. Some economists now believe the Great Inflation can be ended only by some similar development. They talk of what might transpire if peace (that is, an end to the cold war) breaks out, or if government in some other way cut back sharply on expenditures, while at the same time taking money out of circulation. Such a development would result in a major reorientation of the nation's economy, dislocations, and a period of bitter debate, confusion, and uncertainty. Most people would see their standards of living decline. Unemployment would rise, and demagoguery would be rampant. This is what it would take, they say, to put a cap on the Great Inflation.

It may be that inflation will be brought under control in this or some other way. When and if it happens, Wall Street surely will experience a change in direction, one that will come gradually. As interest rates decline, investors would return to stocks. Analysts may see a rally developing out of buying pressures, but they would not expect it to last. Years later, however, this small advance may be seen as the first stage in the next bull market.

SOURCES

My INITIAL RESEARCHES into Wall Street history began in 1958, and from that time to the present I have spent considerable time in the financial district, going through papers at the exchanges and commission houses and speaking with brokers, analysts, and exchange personnel. Some of the material gathered in this way went into the preparation of earlier books in the general area of financial history, but most of it has been reserved for this work.

In addition I have had access to the papers of Leslie Gould, one of the most distinguished journalists of the 1950s, which are on deposit at the Hofstra University Library. Gould wrote a financial column for the *New York Journal-American,* and in the 1950s he was at the peak of his power and prestige. Not only did he have an extensive clipping file, but Gould also wrote down his thoughts of many key figures of the period.

Public documents, market advisories, newspaper and magazine reports and articles, and related evidence also went into the making of this book. Every issue of the *Wall Street Journal, Barron's, Forbes,* and *Fortune* for the 1949–69 period has been studied, along with related material from the *New York Times,* the *New York Herald-Tribune, Time, Newsweek, Business Week,* and *U.S. News & World Report.* I benefited greatly from reportage in the *Institutional Investor* and other "inside" publications read primarily by people in the financial district. Several commission houses have permitted me to go through their back lists of market advisories. Market letters put out by services have been harder to come by. Understandably most of them refused to open them to a researcher who might point out their mistakes. But I have perused *United Business Services, Moody's, Standard & Poor's, Value Line,* and several others for at least parts of the period explored.

Books of the period have been less useful—except for the spate of tipster works that appeared in the mid-1960s, and few of these had the kind of readership afforded the financial press. Works by John Brooks, Chris Welles, and Martin Mayer are the exceptions to the general rule. "Adam Smith's" *The Money Game* appeared toward the end of this last bull market and provides a fine summary of this final phase of money madness.

The following is a selected bibliography of works consulted in the course of research.

BOOKS

Abbott, Charles. *Financing Business During the Transition*. New York, 1946.

Ahearn, Daniel. *Federal Reserve Policy Reappraised, 1951–1959.*. New York, 1963.

Almond, Clapper, Jr. *The American Economy to 1975*. New York, 1966.

Armour, Lawrence, and the staff of *Barron's*, eds. *How to Survive a Bear Market*. Princeton, 1970.

Baruch, Hurd. *Wall Street: Security Risk*. Washington, 1971.

Baum, Daniel and Ned Stiles. *The Silent Partners*. Syracuse, 1965.

Bernstein, Peter. *Economist on Wall Street*. New York, 1970.

Black, Hillel. *The Watchdogs of Wall Street*. New York, 1962.

Blyth, C. A. *American Business Cycles, 1945–1950*. New York, 1969.

Boorstin, Daniel. *The Americans: The Democratic Experience*. New York, 1963.

Brooks, John. *Business Adventures*. New York, 1969.

———. *The Fate of the Edsel and Other Business Adventures*. New York, 1963.

———. *The Go-Go Years*. New York, 1973.

———. *The Seven Fat Years*. New York, 1958.

Bullock, Hugh. *The Story of Investment Companies*. New York, 1959.

Bunting, John. *The Hidden Face of Free Enterprise*. New York, 1964.

Burns, Arthur. *The Management of Prosperity*. New York, 1966.

———. *Prosperity Without Inflation*. New York, 1957.

Cagan, Phillip *et al. Economic Policy and Inflation in the Sixties*. Washington, 1972.

Canterbery, E. Roy. *Economics on a New Frontier*. Belmont, Calif., 1968.

Cantor, Bert. *The Bernie Cornfeld Story*. New York, 1970.

Center for Strategic Studies. *Economic Impact of the Vietnam War*. New York, 1967.

Coe, James. *Common Stocks for Investors and Traders*. New York, 1961.

Crane, Burton. *The Sophisticated Investor*. New York, 1959.

Director, Aaron. *Defense, Controls, and Inflation*. Chicago, 1951.

Donovan, Robert. *Eisenhower: The Inside Story*. New York, 1956.

Drucker, Peter. *America's Next Twenty Years*. New York, 1957.

Elias, Christopher. *Fleecing the Lambs*. Chicago, 1971.

Ellis, Charles. *Institutional Investing*. Homewood, Ill., 1971.

Freeman, Roger. *The Growth of American Government*. Stamford, Conn., 1975.

Friend, Irving *et al. Investment Banking and the New Issues Market*. Philadelphia, 1965.

Fuller, John. *The Money Game*. New York, 1962.

Funston, G. Keith. *Wanted: More Owners of American Business*. Boston, 1954.

Goldsmith, Raymond, ed. *Institutional Investors and Corporate Stock—A Background Study*. New York, 1973.

Graham, Benjamin. *The Intelligent Investor*. New York, 1973.

———, David Dodd, and Sidney Cottie. *Security Analysis*. 4th ed. New York, 1962.

Gutman, Walter. *The Gutman Letter*. New York, 1969.

Hamby, Alonzo. *Beyond the New Deal: Harry S Truman and American Liberalism*. New York, 1973.

Hansen, Alvin. *Economic Issues of the 1960s*. New York, 1960.

Harris, Seymour, ed. *Saving American Capitalism*. New York, 1948.

Haveman, Robert. *The Economics of the Public Sector*. New York, 1970.

Hazard, John. *Success with Your Money*. New York, 1964.
———— and Milton Christie. *The Investment Business: A Condensation of the S.E.C. Report*. New York, 1964.
Heller, Walter. *New Dimensions of Political Economy*. Cambridge, 1966.
————. *Perspectives on Economic Growth*. New York, 1968.
Hickman, Bert. *Growth and Stability of the Postwar Economy*. Washington, 1960.
Holmans, A. E. *United States Fiscal Policy, 1945–59*. New York, 1961.
Hughes, John Emmet. *Ordeal of Power*. New York, 1963.
Javits, Jacob, Charles Hitch, and Arthur Burns. *The Defense Sector and the American Economy*. New York, 1968.
Johnson, Lyndon. *The Vantage Point*. New York, 1971.
Kaplan, Gilbert and Chris Welles, eds. *The Money Managers*. New York, 1969.
Katona, George. *The Mass Consumption Society*. New York, 1964.
Kent, William. *The Smart Money*. New York, 1972.
Kirkendall, Richard. *The Truman Period as a Research Field: A Reappraisal, 1972*. Columbia, Mo., 1974.
Knowlton, Winthrop. *Growth Opportunities in Common Stocks*. New York, 1965.
Krefetz, Gerald and Ruth Marossi. *Money Makes Money, and the Money Money Makes Makes More Money*. New York, 1970.
Krooss, Herman and Martin Blyn. *A History of Financial Intermediaries*. New York, 1971.
Loll, Leo and Julian Buckley. *The Over-the-Counter Securities Markets*. Englewood Cliffs, N.J., 1973.
Lynes, Russell. *A Surfeit of Honey*. New York, 1957.
————. *The Tastemakers*. New York, 1955.
Magee, John. *The General Semantics of Wall Street*. Springfield, Mass., 1958.
Mayer, Martin. *The New Breed on Wall Street*. New York, 1969.
————. *Wall Street: Men and Money*. New York, 1959.
Melman, Seymour. *Pentagon Capitalism*. New York, 1970.
————, ed. *The War Economy of the United States*. New York, 1971.
Miller, Norman. *The Great Salad Oil Swindle*. New York, 1965.
Nadler, Marcus, Sipa Heller, and Samuel Shipman. *The Money Market and Its Institutions*. New York, 1955.
Ney, Richard. *The Wall Street Jungle*. New York, 1970.
Nixon, Richard. *RN: The Memoirs of Richard Nixon*. New York, 1978.
Parmet, Herbert. *Eisenhower and the American Crusades*. New York, 1972.
Passell, Peter and Leonard Ross. *The Retreat from Riches*. New York, 1971.
Phillips, Cabell. *The Truman Presidency*. New York, 1966.
Plum, Lester. *Investing in American Industries*. New York, 1960.
Raw, Charles, Bruce Page, and Godfrey Hodgson. *"Do You Sincerely Want to be Rich?": The Full Story of Bernard Cornfeld and the IOS*. New York, 1971.
Regan, Donald. *A View from the Street*. New York, 1972.
Robbins, Sidney. *The Securities Markets: Operations and Issues*. New York, 1966.
Rolfe, Sidney and James Burtle. *The Great Wheel: The World Monetary System*. New York, 1973.
Rowen, Hobart. *The Free Enterprisers: Kennedy, Johnson, and the Business Establishment*. New York, 1964.

Scammell, W. M. *International Monetary Policy.* New York, 1975.

Schlesinger, Arthur. *A Thousand Days: Kennedy in the White House.* Boston, 1965.

Sederberg, Arelo. *The Stock Market Investment Club Handbook.* Los Angeles, 1971.

Silk, Leonard. *The Research Revolution.* New York, 1960.

Slichter, Sumner. *Potential of the American Economy.* Boston, 1961.

――――. *What's Ahead for American Business.* Boston, 1951.

"Smith, Adam." *The Money Game.* New York, 1967.

Smith, Gene. *The Life and Death of Serge Rubinstein.* New York, 1962.

Smith, Ralph. *The Grim Truth About Mutual Funds.* New York, 1963.

Sobel, Robert. *Amex: A History of the American Stock Exchange.* New York, 1973.

――――. *The Big Board: A History of the New York Stock Market.* New York, 1965.

――――. *The Great Bull Market.* New York, 1968.

――――. *N.Y.S.E.* New York, 1975.

――――. *Panic on Wall Street.* New York, 1968.

Solomon, Robert. *The International Monetary System, 1945–1976.* New York, 1977.

Stein, Herbert. *The Fiscal Revolution in America.* Chicago, 1969.

Stuart, Lyle. *The Secret Life of Walter Winchell.* New York, 1953.

Theobald, Robert. *The Challenge of Abundance.* New York, 1961.

Twentieth Century Fund. *Financing American Prosperity.* New York, 1945.

Tyler, Poyntz, ed. *Securities, Exchanges, and the SEC.* New York, 1965.

Vatter, Harold. *The U.S. Economy in the 1950s.* New York, 1963.

Weil, Gordon and Ian Davidson. *The Gold War.* New York, 1970.

West, Richard and Seha Tinic. *The Economics of the Stock Market.* New York, 1971.

Weston, J. Fred, ed. *Financial Management in the 1960s.* New York, 1966.

Wilkins, B. Hugel and Charles Friday, eds. *The Economists of the New Frontier.* New York, 1963.

Williamson, John. *The Failure of World Monetary Reform, 1971–1974.* New York, 1977.

Wise, T. A. and the editors of *Fortune. The Insiders.* New York, 1962.

United States. 84th Cong. 1st Sess. Senate. Committee on Banking and Currency. *Factors Affecting the Stock Market.* Washington, 1955.

――――. 84th Cong. 1st Sess. Joint Economic Committee. *Institutional Investors and the Stock Market.* Washington, 1956.

――――. 87th Cong. 1st Sess. Joint Economic Committee. *Variability of Private Investment in Plant and Equipment.* Washington, 1962.

――――. 87th Cong. 2d Sess. Joint Economic Committee. *1962 Supplement to Economic Indicators.* Washington, 1962.

――――. 87th Cong. 2d Sess. House of Reps. Committee on Interstate and Foreign Commerce. *A Study of Mutual Funds.* Washington, 1962.

――――. 88th Cong. 1st Sess. House of Reps. *Report of the Special Study of the Securities Market of the Securities and Exchange Commission.* Washington, 1965.

――――. 93rd Cong. 2d Sess. Senate. Committee on Banking, Housing and Urban Affairs. Subcommittee on Securities. *Securities Industry Study.* 4 vols. Washington, 1972.

――――. Securities and Exchange Commission, *Institutional Investor Study.* (H. R. Doc. 92–64) 3 vols. Washington, 1971.

INDEX